The Dying Terrorism

Ballot Defeated Bullet in Jammu & Kashmir

The Dying Terrorism

Ballot Defeated Bullet in Jammu & Kashmir

Jalil Ahmad Khan, IAS
Govt. of Jammu & Kashmir

and

Sudhir S. Bloeria, IAS
Chief Secretary
Govt. of Jammu & Kashmir

Manas Publications
New Delhi-110 002 (India)

Manas Publications
(Publishers, Distributors, Importers & Exporters)
4858, Prahlad Street,
24, Ansari Road, Darya Ganj,
New Delhi - 110 002 (INDIA)
Ph.: 23260783, 23265523
Fax: 011-23272766
E-mail: manaspublications@vsnl.com

First Published 2003

ISBN 81-7049-167-3

Typeset at
Manas Publications

Printed in India at
Nice Printing Press,
and Published by Mrs Suman Lata for
Manas Publications, 4858, Prahlad Street,
24, Ansari Road, Darya Ganj,
New Delhi - 110 002 (INDIA)

Dedicated to

All those who made the elections in Jammu & Kashmir possible

Preface

Historical mistakes are easily forgotten but hardly ever forgiven. Borrowing the idea from an Urdu couplet, it can be said that such blunders committed over moments are fated to be punished for centuries. The price of the historical mistakes is paid, more often than not, by the people who were not guilty of providing the slightest provocation or a cause for actions of those committing such monumental mistakes. When on a cold January morning in 1990, barely a week before the Republic Day, the Governor of J&K, having imposed the Governor's Rule in the State only hours before on receiving the resignation of the then Chief Minister to protest against the appointment of the new Governor, decided to dissolve the Legislative Assembly as a simplistic solution to the violent agitation against a government allegedly brought into existence through rigged elections, all were stunned by the swift chain of events and not many felt alarmed by the disastrous consequences the State was going to face on account of this act of the Governor who thought that the promise and the prospects of a fresh election would spontaneously make the atmosphere quiet and all would be well again very soon. Contrary to this naïve expectation, the consequential chain-reaction unfolded so dramatically that there was hardly any time left to understand its nature and dimensions with the requisite speed and to offer a quick and effective response. By the time an adequate and appropriate response was evolved and consolidated, the State had witnessed replacement of two Governors and a host of their advisers and had missed even on holding of general elections to the nation's Parliament held in 1991.For this the laws had to be amended by the Parliament to exclude the state of J&K- also the state of Punjab from the purview of the general elections. Holding of fresh general elections to the State Legislative Assembly was and did remain a remote possibility. Thousands had died in the meanwhile as a result of spurt of militancy. A widespread and general sense of insecurity prevailed. The future of the democracy in the state remained hung in a balance. The regulatory authority of the administration had almost totally collapsed.

Indian democracy is or at least was till the 80's at its adolescent stage. However, it has had the benefit of nursing by the British democratic model which had also provided the much needed environment and a value system for working out required constitutional framework. The same cannot be easily said of the erstwhile princely States, much so of a state like Jammu & Kashmir which had remained insulated from the influences of outside democratic movements and systems. Though it had seen its own version of a movement against the autocratic rule of the maharaja, seeking devolution of power to the people, no evidence of any democratic ethos having crept into its new polity in making and in the style of its subsequent governance is evident except what its democratic leaders sought to imbibe instinctively. This was particularly so because the change over from autocracy to democracy was neither planned nor smooth. It came rather suddenly and abruptly when the ruler was faced by threat of losing his kingdom to the raiders who were knocking at the doorsteps of his summer capital of Srinagar. The maharaja decided to sign the instrument of accession with India on October 26,1947 enabling the latter to send its troops the very next day to Srinagar to push back the aggression and to regain as much of the territory occupied by the raiders as was possible within a short span of time until the ceasefire was announced by the fighting forces under a UN resolution.

Two major consequences inevitably followed. One- the State got physically divided into two parts which have been influenced and motivated by two different sets of political ideologies ever since. Two, the people have not been in a position, though more distinctly in PoK, to cultivate, imbibe and affirm their faith in the democratic values and democratic institutions in a manner which would have strengthened the values of democracy with the passage of time. A direct perilous corollary to the second factor is that though the state of Jammu and Kashmir was quick enough to evolve a legal and institutional election mechanism of its own and which was later merged into the Election Commission of India and has also gone through numerous elections to its various democratic institutions including panchayats, urban local bodies as also the Legislative Assembly and also participated in the national parliamentary elections umpteen number of times, its people barring the winning parties and candidates had till recently yet to give credence to this most important democratic activity, and not for wholly unjustified reasons.

The years preceding 1990 were not only volatile in the Indian politics but also full of crises of dangerous dimensions. The declaration of national emergency by the Centre, defeat of Indira Gandhi and her subsequent comeback, operation Blue Star, assassination of prime minister Indira Gandhi, relative political instability involving frequent change of government at the Centre had cast their serious fallout on the political scene of the state of Jammu and Kashmir which had already suffered a political hiatus caused due to demise of political patriarch of the state, Sher-e-Kashmir, Sheikh Mohammad Abdullah in September 1982. It is not difficult to collect the evidence from the events of sorts which followed the death of Sheikh Sahib to come to a definite conclusion that a serious political drift had set in about this time. The drift was neither arrested nor controlled. The golden advice of nipping the evil in the bud was forgotten. Those responsible for conducting the affairs of the nation and the State were either inexperienced in politics or too busy with their political games of survival to respond adequately and properly to the ominous developments taking place quietly and inconspicuously inside the boundaries of Kashmir Valley. When the sporadic violent incidents started taking place in 1987 and

1988, they were not considered important enough to be responded by deploying more security forces, and taking other corrective measures. The drift continued. Rather, the Centre responded by sending a Governor whom the Chief Minister Dr Farooq Abdullah had earlier declined to accept. Dr Abdullah opted to resign.

The violence which followed the dissolution of the State Legislative Assembly in January 1990, not connected with or caused by the act of dissolution itself but possibly accentuated by the absence of a democratically elected government and a total absence of elected and other representatives of the people from the scene was of such a magnitude that it was bound to attract national, and more importantly wide international attention. Holding of a fresh poll in a credible and transparent manner became an issue of international significance. The vested interests working across the international borders saw a golden opportunity in drawing the world attention only if they could ensure that the elections were never held again in the State and failing that the people should not participate in any such exercise. The last option was that if the elections were held at all, the world should come to a categorical conclusion that the people of J&K were not a willing partner in the exercise and the failure of the election process would be taken by the international community as a referendum against India. This thinking had upped the stakes so heavily that the opponents of the elections were willing to go to any extent to thwart the democratic exercise by all undemocratic means. Holding out widely publicized open threats to the political leaders and workers including their killings in a significantly large number, holding out similar threats against the large number of employees who would provide the workforce for the election machinery, propaganda against the election process, and detailed plan of action to disrupt the electioneering and the poll process through disruptive activities and attacks on the polling stations, polling parties, election meetings and processions, security forces, candidates, political workers were part of this plan.

The complexities of the task of organizing general elections in the State have to be understood and appreciated in this background. Unlike the local body elections which can be handled independently in respect of each such body without affecting the mechanics of all other similar bodies, the general elections to the State Assembly have to be organized and conducted simultaneously, at best in quick successive stages and results announced simultaneously so that the House is constituted immediately after concluding the exercise. The process has a constitutional sanctity and even the Courts are forbidden from interfering in the proceedings on any grounds whatsoever. This further enhances the responsibilities of the election machinery to perform its task judiciously. In order to ensure that the task remains fully judicious, the entire election machinery including security forces are given to the control of the Election Commission and it's authority to give directions to any wing of the Executive in any manner for attaining the objective of conducting free and fair elections is generally not questioned and if questioned, hardly ever entertained by any forum.

The extraordinary factors faced in respect of J&K elections were numerous and complicated. It was a battle which had to be won at all costs. The task was to be performed despite heavy odds and many weaknesses and handicaps not faced in a normal situation. The administrative machinary which had loosened quite a bit even in simpler matters like collection of tax and non-tax revenue, prevention of routine crime, regulation of building activities in the urban areas, punctuality of attendance in the government offices was now faced with the challenge of shaking off all accumulated inertia and to work with clockwork precision, move in unison, anticipate all hurdles and overcome all of them to keep its date with the people against persistent violent bids from disruptive forces which had done their own planning and were determined to act at every step of the election process. These elements were not to respect any code of ethics or law. On the other hand the election machinery would only resort to due process of law even where it came to deal with the disruptive forces and all acts of disruption.

The result of all the planning and thinking by the government and the election machinery produced the outline of a most novel, unique and unprecedented exercise of a massive level which had to be implemented in a precise manner. A new law and procedure had to be created in order to meet the extraordinary situation. A comprehensive scheme of voting by a large number of Kashmiri Pandits who had migrated out of the Kashmir Valley had to be worked out to enable them to cast their votes in their respective constituencies without physically moving them to the Valley. The key election personnel had to be handpicked and kept to a bare minimum number. The logistics which were worked out involved massive movement and deployment of manpower for polling, mostly from other States and movement and deployment of security personnel in such a large number that the exercise would provide lessons to the posterity in arranging logistics in similar situations in future.

This book provides the historical background of formation of the State of J&K as a princely State of British India and its accession as a democratic State with the Union of India after it attained freedom which was preceded by the partition of the Country. It goes on to deal with the political developments upto 1990, leading to surfacing of militancy and collapse of democratic institutions thereafter. More importantly, it documents, for the first time, in great details the preparations made, the plans conceived and executed and reveals the nuts and bolts of the logistics worked out to achieve the given objective of restoration of democracy in the State and evaluates the colossal time and effort which had to be devoted to achieve this objective.

The authors wish to record their gratitude to all those who helped and supported this endeavour and are particularly thankful to Mr. Ashok K. Magotra an accomplished stenographer and expert in computer applications who worked tirelessly and diligently on the typing and formatting of this book.

J. A. Khan

Sudhir S. Bloeria

Contents

1 Introduction

Jammu and Kashmir, the crown of India, is situated in the north of the Union. It comprises three regions viz. Jammu, Kashmir and Ladakh with each having a distinct geo-climatic, ethnic and cultural identity. The State occupies a pivotal position on the political map of Central Asia and is strategically vital to the security of India. It is India's window to Central Asian Republics [of the Commonwealth of Independent States], sharing borders with Pakistan, Afghanistan, China and Tibet. Jammu and Kashmir as a single entity came into existence only in 1846, and prior to that, except for short periods in the history of Kashmir Valley, none of the three regions ever remained a single entity and were ruled in parts by different feudatory chieftains mostly at war amongst themselves.

In the modern times, Kashmir came under the rule of Sikhs in 1819, during the period when the Sikh kingdom under the dynamic leadership of Maharaja Ranjit Singh, was at its zenith. Though a shade better than the preceding Pathan regime, the Sikh rule too persecuted the people, fleeced the Kashmiris, and the practice of *begar* continued more harshly. Till 1846, Kashmir was administered by 10 Governors who were deputed from Lahore. The most famous among them was Mian Singh who came to Kashmir as the Governor in 1833. He has been considered as the ablest administrator amongst the Sikh Governors sent to Kashmir and is remembered for importing grains from Punjab to tide over the unprecedented famine which took place during his rule. Also during this period tax on marriages was remitted, agricultural loans were advanced free of interest, proper weights and measures were introduced and cases were decided quickly and justly.

In the Jammu region, which was ruled by scores of small principalities and fiefdoms, the most important principality was that of Jammu which had been ruled by a long line of Dogra Rajas till it was annexed by Sikhs in 1808. After the amalgamation of Jammu in the Sikh kingdom of Lahore many of the Dogras took service with the Sikh Darbar. The most famous and intrepid of them was Gulab Singh, eldest of the three brothers, the other two being Dhian Singh and Suchet Singh. All the three rose to great eminence in the service of Maharaja Ranjit Singh. In 1822, Ranjit Singh granted the province of Jammu to Raja Gulab Singh as a *jagir* in perpetual possession. Within a short period he subdued the territories and chieftains strung along the borders of his new kingdom and extended his possession to the entire Jammu region, including the important principalities of Kishtwar, Bhaderwah, Rajouri and Poonch.

In the summer of 1834, Gulab Singh sent General Zorawar Singh, one of his ablest military commanders, with a small force of Dogra soldiers to invade Ladakh through the newly acquired territories of Kishtwar along the hazardous Kishtwar-Paddar-Zanskar route. This was the beginning of a series of one of the most dazzling military conquests in the history of Indian sub-continent and resulted in the amalgamation of Ladakh, Baltistan and Western Tibet into the expanding kingdom of Gulab Singh. After seven years of continuous combat and conquests on the Himalayan tableland, Gen. Zorawar Singh died fighting the Tibetans on December 10, 1841, at Toyo, leaving behind a trail of glory. His achievements include not only the military conquests but also display of great administrative acumen resulting in pacification of the conquered territories. In the words of K.M. Panikkar, "To have marched an army not once or twice but six times over the snow clad ranges of Ladakh and Baltistan–15000 ft. above the sea level where the air is so rarified, people from the plains can hardly live with comfort, is a windfall achievement. To have conquered that country after successive campaigns and reduced it to a peaceful province is an exploit for which there is no parallel in the Indian history."[1]

Maharaja Ranjit Singh died in 1839, and immediately thereafter his son and heir apparent, Kharak Singh, also expired in an accident. In the aftermath of these two deaths a bitter struggle for succession broke out in the Sikh kingdom. The British involvement in the Sikh politics intensified as the disintegration sank deeper into the Sikh empire. Lack of a strong ruler, palace intrigues and internecine struggle amongst Sikh nobles and military commanders ate into the vitals of the kingdom.

In November 1845, war broke out between the Sikhs and the British at Sobraon, a small village on the banks of Satluj river. The Sikh nobles asked Gulab Singh to help and lead them but he didn't oblige them, probably with the objective of earning gratitude of the British. Sobraon was lost and with that the Sikhs lost their realm of freedom.The Victorious British armies entered Lahore on February 20, 1846. After the victory at Sobraon, the East India Company demanded the entire territory of Jalandhar region lying between Satluj and Beas Rivers, control of two rivers, demobilization of the Sikh army and a war indemnity of Rs. 1.5 crores. The Sikhs agreed to part with the territory but expressed inability to pay the huge indemnity, and as a substitute offered Jammu and Kashmir along with Hazara and Chamba principalities to the British. At the end of prolonged and often acrimonious negotiation, a treaty was concluded at Lahore between the British and the Sikh King Duleep Singh on March 9, 1846, in which it was provided that as equivalent to one crore rupees, Sikhs would cede all the territories and forts situated between rivers Beas and Indus including the provinces of Kashmir and Hazara. Almost simultaneously the British started negotiations with Maharaja Gulab Singh and the two parties reached an agreement on March 16, 1846.

The text of this Treaty of Amritsar is as follows:

"TREATY BETWEEN THE BRITISH GOVERNMENT on the one part and MAHARAJAH GULAB SINGH OF JAMMU on the other concluded on the part of the BRITISH GOVERNMENT by FREDERICK CURRIE, Esquire, and BREVET-MAJOR HENRY MONTGOMERY LAWRENCE, acting under the order of the RIGHT HONOURABLE SIR HENRY HARDINGE, G.C.B., one of HER BRITANNIC MAJESTY'S MOST HONOURABLE PRIVY COUNCIL, GOVERNOR GENERAL of the possessions of the EAST INDIA COMPANY, to direct and control all their affairs in the EAST INDIES and by MAHARAJAH GULAB SINGH in person – 1846.

Article I

The British Government transfers and makes over for ever in independent possession to Maharajah Gulab Singh and the heirs male of his body all the hilly or mountainous country with its dependencies situated to the eastward of the River Indus and the westward of the River Ravi including Chamba and excluding Lahul, being part of the territories ceded to the British Government by the Lahore State according to the provisions of Article IV of the Treaty of Lahore, dated 9th March, 1846.

Article 2

The eastern boundary of the tract transferred by the foregoing article to Mahrajah Gulab Singh shall be laid down by the Commissioners appointed by the British Government and Maharajah Gulab Singh respectively for that purpose and shall be defined in a separate engagement after survey.

Article 3

In consideration of the transfer made to him and his heirs by the provisions of the foregoing article Maharajah Gulab Singh will pay to the British Government the sum of seventy-five lakhs of Rupees (Nanukshahee), fifty lakhs to be paid on ratification of this Treaty and twenty-five lakhs on or before the Ist October of the current year, A.D. 1846.

Article 4

The limits of the territories of Maharajah Gulab Singh shall not be at any time changed without concurrence of the British Government.

Article 5

Maharajah Gulab Singh will refer to the arbitration of the British Government any disputes or questions that may arise between himself and the Government of Lahore or any other neighbouring State, and will abide by the decision of the British Government.

Article 6

Maharajah Gulab Singh engages for himself and heirs to join, with the whole of his Military Forces, the British troops, when employed within the hills or in the territories adjoining his possessions.

Article 7

Maharajah Gulab Singh engages never to take or retain in his service any British subject nor the subject of any European or American State without the consent of the British Government.

Article 8

Maharajah Gulab Singh engages to respect in regard to the territory transferred to him, the provisions of Articles V., VI., and VII., of the separate Engagement between the British Government and the Lahore Durbar, dated 11th March, 1846.

Article 9

The British Government will give its aid to Maharajah Gulab Singh in protecting his territories from external enemies.

Article 10

Maharajah Gulab Singh acknowledges the supremacy of the British Government and will in token of such supremacy present annually to the British Government one horse, twelve shawl goats of approved breed (six male and six female) and three pairs of Cashmere shawls.

This Treaty of ten articles has been this day settled by Frederick Currie, Esquire, and Brevet-Major Henry Montgomery Lawrence, acting under directions of The Right Honourable Sir Henry Hardinge, G.C.B., Governor-General, on the part of the British Government and by Maharajah Gulab Singh in person, and the said Treaty has been this day ratified by the seal of the Right Honourable Sir Henry Hardinge, G.C.B., Governor-General.

(Done at Amritsar the sixteenth day of March, in the year of our Lord one thousand eight hundred and forty-six, corresponding with the seventeenth day of Rubee-ul-Awal 1262 Hijree).

(Signed) H.Hardinge (Seal).

(Signed) F.Currie.

(Signed) H.M. Lawrence.

By Order of the Right Honourable the Governor-General of India.

(Signed) F. Currie,

Secretary to the Government of India,

With the Governor-General.

The Treaty of Amritsar is at times politically but improperly referred to as the "Sale Deed of Kashmir". The British did not create their Indian Empire by making money out of selling territories. The expansion of the British influence in the sub-continent and the colonization of this huge land mass doesn't indicate any tendency on the part of the British policy makers to make money out of the sale of their physical possessions. The Treaty of Amritsar has to be seen and interpreted in the light of the geo-strategic considerations existing at that point of time to the British rulers in India and in the backdrop of disastrous and humiliating Anglo-Afghan War a decade earlier. In fact, the whole philosophy and compulsions of the British in arriving at the formulation of the Treaty of Amritsar was succinctly explained by the then Governor General in his letter to the Secretariat Committee dated March 14, 1846, excerpts of which read as:

> "It will be seen by the draft of Treaty now forwarded that, in consequence of the inability of the Lahore Government to pay the sum stipulated as indemnification for the expenses of the war, or to give sufficient security for its eventual disbursement, the Hill territories, from the Beas River to the Indus, including the provinces of Kashmir and Hazara, have been ceded to the British Government.

> It is not my intention to take possession of the whole of this territory. Its occupation by us would be, on many accounts, disadvantageous. It would bring us in collision with many powerful chiefs, for whose coercion a large military establishment at a great distance from our provinces and military resources would be necessary. It would more than double the extent of our present frontier in countries assailable at every point, and most difficult to defend without any corresponding advantage for such large additions of territory. Now, distant and conflicting interests would be created and races of people, with whom we have hitherto had no intercourse, would be brought under our rule, while the territories, excepting Kashmir, are comparatively unproductive, and would scarcely pay the expenses of occupation and management.
>
> On the other hand, the tract now ceded includes the whole of the Hill possessions of Rajah Gulab Singh and the Jammu family. Its possession by us enables us at once to mark our sense of Rajah Gulab Singh's conduct during the late operations, by rewarding him in the mode most in accordance with his desires, to show forth as an example to the other chiefs of Asia the benefits which accrue from an adherence to British interests, and to meet the expenses of the campaign, which we declared our determination to exact, and which, excepting by the cession of territory, the Lahore Government is not in a condition to afford."

In this way, the State of Jammu and Kashmir came into existence in 1846. Gulab Singh got the possession of province of Kashmir on November 9, 1846, after defeating the last Governor of Sikh empire, Sheikh Imamudin. Gulab Singh faced considerable difficulty in forging an integrated political structure as the territories transferred to him were extremely heterogeneous and suffered from disparities in ethnic and cultural patterns, languages, etc. The three regions did not share a common history nor a mutually interacting culture. The province of Jammu, to which Dogras belonged, presented few problems. However, situation in Kashmir was worse due to blackmailing, oppression, 'begar' or forced labour and the hilly areas were infested with robbers. Within a decade he managed to bring peace and order in his kingdom.

Gulab Singh tried to rule the State justly and entrusted its civil administration to a council of ministers called as Dewans. Maharaja had, however, retained with himself the important departments of foreign relations, finance, revenue collection and taxation. He had vested in him the power to hear cases in the first instance as well as in appeal against a *nazrana* of rupee one presented with the petition. Gulab Singh died in 1858. His son Ranbir Singh succeeded to the throne two years before his father's death. During his time, the British Government wanted to appoint a Resident in Kashmir, but he did not allow them to interfere in the internal administration of the State.

Within a few years of creation of the State some territorial adjustments were made between the British and Maharaja Gulab Singh. Subsequently, more territory was added during the reign of Maharaja Ranbir Singh, with the conquest of Gilgit, Chitral, Hunza and Nagar in the Northern Region. After the territorial adjustments, the State of Jammu and Kashmir comprised an area of 2,22,870 sq.kms. by the end of 19th century, the largest of the Indian princely states in the pre-independence era.

Maharaja Ranbir Singh died in 1885. His throne was inherited by his son Partap Singh who died in 1925 intestate and was succeeded by his nephew Hari Singh. Maharaja Hari Singh was one of the enlightened rulers amongst the Indian princes of the time, and introduced far reaching reforms for the benefit of his subjects, most notable being the institution of the concept of State Subjects, prohibition of untouchability and larger representation of Muslims in the State services. However, with the freedom struggle gaining momentum and the concept of self-rule sweeping across the country, some educated Kashmiri Muslims organized themselves in 1931, and raised their voice against the ruler of the State. This resulted in proclamation of Constitution Act on April 22, 1934, providing for establishment of Legislative Assembly and the Maharaja laying down his own legislative, executive and judicial powers.

In November 1932, the Muslim leadership called a general convention at Srinagar in which delegates were invited from all over the State. The Jammu and Kashmir Muslim Conference was founded, with Sheikh Mohammad Abdullah elected as its president. The history of the Muslim Conference is the record of the struggle of the middle and upper class of Muslims during the period (1932-38) for the achievement of their rights, especially in the matter of distribution of State services.

On 28th June, 1938, a meeting of the working committee of the Muslim Conference was held in which Sheikh Mohammad Abdullah moved a resolution suggesting to change the name of the party to National Conference and to amend the constitution so as to throw its doors open to non-Muslims.

Another promulgation of J&K Constitution Act on September 7, 1939, by Maharaja was an important event. It further rationalized executive, legislative and judicial powers. It provided for uni-cameral Praja Sabha. Though the Praja Sabha's powers were limited and circumscribed by the princely prerogative, yet it passed many important Bills, which received the assent of His Highness. Though constitutional reforms in Kashmir gave the people some opportunity to associate themselves with the administration of the State, yet this was not what they were striving for. National Conference regarded the Constitution Act inadequate. It wanted a representative Government and an elected legislature.

In 1941, the National Conference became a formal member of the All India States' People's Conference with affiliation in most princely states. Sheikh Mohammad Abdullah was elected the president of the All India States' People's Conference in 1946. During this period, he came closer to Congress Party especially Pandit Jawaharlal Nehru. In 1944, the National Conference adopted 'Naya Kashmir' as the manifesto of the party. It envisaged a scheme of constitutional reforms for the State, a bill of rights and a frame of representative political institutions besides a plan for economic, cultural and educational development. It pledged to secure the people of the State the right to equality, right to self-determination, emancipation from oppression, poverty, ignorance and superstition, and "to secure their participation in the historic resurgence of the people of the East and the working masses of the world."

On July 19, 1946, the National Conference launched the famous 'Quit Kashmir Movement' against the Maharaja who reacted swiftly and suppressed the movement, which caused nationwide repercussions. Sheikh Mohammad Abdullah and other prominent leaders of National Conference were arrested and charged with sedition. Pandit Nehru who was at that time one of the top leaders of Congress and would be Prime Minister of free India tried to come to Kashmir on June 18, 1947. At Kohala, he was told by a magistrate of the Maharaja's Government, that his entry in Kashmir had been banned by the Government of Jammu and Kashmir. The Magistrate advised Nehru to go back to British India but Nehru refused and at Domel, he was arrested and kept in detention for two days.

This incident further cemented an already existing friendship and feeling of brotherhood between Jawaharlal Nehru and Sheikh Mohammad Abdullah as also increased animosity between these two and Maharaja Hari Singh. This inter-personnel relationship between the three most important personalities, in relation to the State of Jammu and Kashmir, was to have a crucial impact on the future course of events adversely affecting not only this region but the entire nation.

Raiders in Kashmir

With the end of Second World War and its consequential impact on the stability and continued existence of British Empire, the culmination of India's struggle for independence became inevitable. The date for India's independence and creation of Pakistan as a separate state was announced on June 3, 1947, by Lord Mountbatten, the then Viceroy of India. With this the British paramountcy on Indian princely states, including Jammu and Kashmir, was to lapse with India becoming independent on August 15, 1947, and the creation of Pakistan a day earlier. While almost all the Indian rulers decided to merge their domains with either of the two dominions, Jammu and Kashmir, along with Hyderabad and Junagarh, was one of the three princely states which had not taken any decision either way by 15th August. Maharaja Hari Singh had probably entertained visions of keeping his State as an independent entity by maintaining equal distance from the dominions of India and Pakistan, in spite of the advice from Lord Mountbatten, Mahatma Gandhi and other political stalwarts of India to make up his mind about the accession to either of the dominions. Jammu and Kashmir was also one of those princely states which did not join the Constituent Assembly of India set up under the Cabinet Mission Plan that had commenced functioning since December 1946.

On the contrary, the State requested for a Standstill Agreement with both India and Pakistan on August 12, 1947. Whereas India did not take this offer, Pakistan executed the same and promised to continue the existing arrangements with Jammu and Kashmir State in providing Post and Telegraph facilities, foodgrains, essential commodities and military hardware as here-to-before. However, soon after Pakistan came into existence, her rulers put into operation well thoughtout plans to force the Maharaja to accede to Pakistan. A multi-pronged strategy was adopted to achieve the same which was based on economic blockade of the State, subversion of Muslim population, particularly the military personnel, and an armed invasion.

The economic strangulation of the State was carried out effectively and in a well planned manner resulting in shortage of essential commodities which adversely affected the efficacy of the State administration and created disaffection amongst the general public. Conditions became more difficult with the outbreak of large-scale disturbances in the two Punjabs after the announcement of partition which resulted in large influx of refugees into and from the south and southwest parts of the State. Muslim refugees moved through that area from east to west and the non-Muslims in the opposite direction. This put tremendous strain on the fabric of communal amity of Jammu region. Pakistan simultaneously launched a very effective propaganda campaign against the State and its rulers. The Muslims in the border areas and in the State army were exhorted to revolt against the Hindu Maharaja and also turn against their neighbours of the minority community. During the months of September and October, large-scale communal disturbances were engineered on the western borders of the State, particularly in the Muzaffarabad-Poonch-Mirpur belt. The stage was now set for Pakistan to put into motion the final phase of forced occupation of the State by an armed intervention.

The invasion of Kashmir by the tribals was meticulously planned, carefully timed and competently executed. By the middle of October, the economic blockade had choked the State's economy and paralyzed its administration. Civil disturbances were effectively engineered by instigating the Muslim population inhabiting the border areas of Jammu division, and the armed raids on isolated State forces' garrisons had effectively neutralized the military capabilities of the State army. The main attack was planned by the Army Headquarters of Pakistan with the code name "Operation Gulmarg". The strike force consisted of ten groups of about one thousand men each called Lashkars under the command of their respective tribal chiefs with stiffners provided by the Pakistan army personnel. Each Lashkar was joined by one army major, a captain and ten JCOs. According to the plan the raiders crossed the border on the night of October 21/22 and attacked Muzaffarabad town. The Muslim troops of the state army manning the key posts of Lohargari and Ramkote joined the raiders forgetting their oath of loyalty to the ruler and betraying the confidence of their commander. After capturing Domail, an important communication center, the road to Uri lay almost undefended, with practically nothing between raiders and the Srinagar city.

Realizing the dangerous situation, Brigadier Rajinder Singh, Chief of Staff of the State Forces, rushed at the head of a force consisting of 150 men. He chose Uri as his main defensive position and made preparations to halt the enemy advance. The next day, on 23rd October, first clash between the raiders and a small group of the brave soldiers led by Brigadier Rajinder Singh took place, and due to overwhelming number of raiders the defenders were forced to fall back on another defensive position. For the next three days this pattern continued. The gallant Brigadier and almost the entire force of his brave soldiers died fighting the enemy but not before successfully delaying the advancing raiders by four very valuable days. The raiders managed to enter Baramulla town on the night of October 26, and the town was put to sword and fire, plunder and rapine. Brigadier Rajinder Singh's rearguard action and the raiders' lust for loot and plunder in Baramulla gave a critical breathing space to the Indian forces which started landing at the Srinagar airfield on the morning of October 27 to effectively meet the advance of raiders to Srinagar.

From August 12 onwards, the day when Maharaja had requested for Standstill Agreement with India, his repeated pleas to Government of India, first for material assistance and later for military help, did not evoke any positive response from New Delhi. It was only on October 24, that the Government of India realized the gravity of developing situation in the State and the imminent fall of Srinagar. In view of the seriousness of the situation V.P. Menon, Secretary, Ministry of States, was sent to Srinagar the next day to assess the situation. He returned on October 26, along with M.C. Mahajan, Prime Minister of Jammu and Kashmir, and apprised the Government of India of the critical condition prevailing in the Valley, stating that raiders might reach Srinagar in a day. The Defence Committee of the Cabinet chaired by Lord Mountbatten decided that the Indian troops would be sent to the State only after its formal accession to India. V.P. Menon flew back and returned the same day with Instrument of Accession, duly signed by the Maharaja, as well as a request for sending troops to meet the raiders' invasion of the Valley. With Maharaja signing the Instrument of Accession, the State of Jammu and Kashmir became an integral part of India on October 26, 1947.

The first batch of Indian troops consisting of 1 Sikh under the command of Lt.Col. Dewan Ranjit Rai started landing at Srinagar airport on October 27, from 0830 hours onward. The next day in a major clash with raiders at Pattan, about 20 kms. away from Srinagar, Col. Rai got killed and the raiders managed to move closer towards Srinagar threatening the city once again.

With the landing of additional troops and military hardware at a feverish pitch of almost brigade strength, effective defences were built around Srinagar city and the airport and the Indian forces became ready for a riposte.

A crucial battle took place at Shalteng, about eight kilometers north of Srinagar, in which the raiders were decisively defeated, suffered heavy casualties and were routed. They were forced to flee towards Baramulla leaving behind five hundred dead and a large quantity of ammunition and supplies. However, the raiders were pursued to Baramulla and beyond with the Indian troops recapturing Uri on November 13, and thus clearing the Valley of the raiders. The first clash between the Indian and Pakistan forces which started on October 27, 1947, lasted for over 14 months till the declaration of UN brokered ceasefire on January 1, 1949. During this period, the tribal raiders, trained, supplied and stiffened by Pakistani army as well as direct involvement of the Pakistan army, during the later stages managed to reach up to the outskirts of Srinagar city in the Valley, occupied the entire Rajouri and Poonch belt in Jammu division as well as the whole of Northern Areas and Ladakh region right up to the Zojila Pass. At one point of time even Gurez, Tangdhar, Handwara and Kupwara were also under the occupation of Pakistani forces. The Indian army fought some of the most gallant and outstanding battles and cleared most of the Valley, Ladakh region and Poonch and Rajouri towns with memorable actions taking place at Shalteng, as already described, the breakthrough at Zojila on November 1, 1948, and the linkup with Poonch on November 22, 1948. On the debit side Bhimber, Mirpur and Kotli in the Jammu region could not be wrested back from the Pakistani occupation. In Kashmir the very important objectives of Domail and Muzaffarabad eluded the grasp of the Indian army. Had the operations continued there was all the possibility of getting back the entire occupied territory in the foreseeable future.

The Government of India had made a formal request to the United Nations on January 1, 1948 about the invasion of the Jammu and Kashmir by the nationals and tribesmen of Pakistan under Art. 35 of the UN Charter. The Security Council was urged to take effective action against Pakistan for this misadventure. The tortuous course of proceedings proved that India's faith in the UN was misplaced. Pakistan successfully deflected the course of discussion from the main issue of its aggression against the Indian territory and was helped in this by the attitude of the Western Powers, utilizing this opportunity in their overall strategy of cold war scenario. The Security Council on January 17, 1948, asked both India and Pakistan to refrain from doing any act which might aggravate the situation. The United Nations Commission for India and Pakistan (UNCIP) visited the two countries in July 1948, and appealed to both the governments for not taking offensive action which might intensify the conflict. On August 13, the Commission adopted a resolution calling for a ceasefire. India accepted this resolution after obtaining certain clarifications from the Commission but Pakistan didn't agree to it. The UNCIP made a subsequent resolution on December 11, 1948, with a view to bringing Pakistan's acceptance of its earlier resolution of August 13. The Government of India accepted it on 23rd December, with Pakistan conveying its concurrence two days later. The acceptance of the resolution by the two countries led to cessation of hostilities on January 1, 1949, and the existing ground situation was demarcated as the Ceasefire Line.

According to Government of India's official account of operations in Jammu and Kashmir during 1947-48, the Indian army lost 76 officers, 31 JCOs and 996 other ranks, making a total of 1103. The wounded numbered 3152, including 81 officers and 107 JCOs. Apart from these casualties the State Forces lost about 1990 officers and men. In terms of territory, Pakistan was able to retain under its illegal occupation approximately 30 percent of the state's territory amounting to 83,294 sq kms[2].

Through a combination of bold military maneuvers, an artful use of guerilla tactics combined with conventional warfare, a highly skilled pursuit of foreign policy coupled with diplomatic finesse during the deliberations in the United Nations brought adequate rewards for Pakistan. Not only one-third of the territory of the Jammu and Kashmir State came into her possession and continues to be so till today, Pakistan also gained control over the strategically important Northern Areas including the province of Gilgit.

In contrast, India not only lost that much of territory, it also failed, more than once, to take advantage of its military strength in forcing a lasting solution of the problem during the conflict of 1947-48. As in the military field, India's position in the United Nations, as also before the world community, has continuously been defensive and reactive. Pakistan, on her part, also came to realize that it pays to be aggressive and belligerent, especially in respect of Jammu and Kashmir.

India's acceptance of cease-fire on January 1, 1949, has been adversely commented upon right from the beginning by military experts and political analysts. After a slow and cautious beginning, Indian armed forces had made considerable progress in regaining control over the territories lost to Pakistani invaders, especially during 1948. By the end of November, the link-up with Leh had been effected, the siege of Poonch broken and entire area between Nowshera and the Pir Panjal cleared of the enemy. In the Valley, the raiders had been thrown back from Jehlum Valley as well as across the Nastachun Pass to the other side of the Kishan Ganga, and Valleys of Gurez and Tilel Valleys were re-occupied. India had the capacity, if there was matching political will and strategic vision, to send additional requisite forces and war material to Jammu and Kashmir and launch the summer offensive in 1949 with a view to clearing the enemy's ingression in Skardu and Gilgit in the northern sector and recapturing Muzaffarabad, Kotli, Mirpur and Bhimber, in the west, thereby getting back all the lost territory of the Jammu and Kashmir State. No doubt this would have meant taking a calculated risk of possible escalation of conflict spilling over beyond the confines of the State resulting into a wider conflagration, but it was probably a chance worth taking. In any case, India had the moral as well as legal right to use all the means and resources at her command to clear the entire tract of her territory from the occupation of the enemy. That this right was not exercised, for whatever reasons, has cost the nation extremely heavily as we have witnessed during the past over half a century and the end of problem is yet not in sight.

The fact that Pakistan was placed in an adverse situation also gets corroborated by Pakistan's acceptance of the UNCIP Resolution of 13 August, 1948, in December same year, after having earlier rejected it. Even on the political scenario, with the death of its founder Mohammad Ali Jinnah in September 1948, Pakistan's political structure had been badly shaken and its leadership was struggling to come to grips with the situation created by the demise of their mentor. The hold of Pakistan's main political party, the Muslim League on North-West Frontier Province and Baluchistan - two of the four provinces of the then West Pakistan - was tenuous at best. Its economy too was not in a good shape having not yet recovered from the trauma and after effects of the partition. Till the creation of Pakistan, a significant chunk of the economic activity which had revolved around the two main centres of Lahore and Karachi was largely in the hands of the Hindu traders and businessmen. Their large-scale migration to India had seriously affected Pakistan's economy thereby undermining her capacity to sustain military adventure against India. After the successful Police Action in Hyderabad in September 1948, India could spare more troops to be deployed against Pakistan. On all these accounts the Indian position, from the military point of view, stability of its political institutions as well as its leadership and the economic and financial scenario was much stronger as compared to Pakistan. But these advantages were not pressed home.

Constitutional Development

Almost simultaneous to the signing of Instrument of Accession, Maharaja Hari Singh appointed Sheikh Mohammad Abdullah, President of National Conference and the most popular political leader in the State, as Emergency Administrator under the Jammu and Kashmir Constitution Act 1939, even though the Maharaja continued to be the Head of the State. In his proclamation of March 5, 1948, Maharaja Hari Singh promised the people of the State to give them the right to have a Constituent Assembly for the purpose of framing a Constitution. On October 17, 1949, the Indian Constituent Assembly adopted Article 370 of the Constitution incorporating a temporary and special provision for the State of Jammu and Kashmir. This Article also envisaged the convening of the Constituent Assembly in the State. These were first and definite steps towards the framing of a constitution and the institution of democratic and popular rule in the State. Maharaja Hari Singh left the State on the pretext of ill health in 1949, and by a proclamation installed his son Yuvraj Karan Singh as the ruler of the state. During the same year the Indian Constituent Assembly was coming to an end of its task of framing the Constitution for the country. A large number of Indian states had been represented in the Indian Constituent Assembly from the beginning but so far as Jammu and Kashmir was concerned, the Yuvraj on the advice of his Council of Ministers nominated four representatives to the Indian Constituent Assembly in June 1949.

Yuvraj Karan Singh issued a proclamation on May 1, 1951, directing the constitution of a Constituent Assembly consisting of representatives of the people elected on the basis of the adult franchise. It was envisaged that the State would be divided into a number of territorial constituencies each containing a population of about forty thousand for electing one member to the Constituent Assembly. A delimitation committee was to be set up to make recommendations as to the number of constituencies with the limit of each constituency. The elections to the Constituent Assembly were held on the basis of adult franchise by direct and secret ballot. These were completed by October 15, the same year. The National Conference won all the 75 seats out of which 73 members were elected unopposed. The first meeting of the Constituent Assembly was held in Srinagar on October 31.

Due to certain developments, Sheikh Mohammad Abdullah was removed from the post of Prime Minister of the State in August 1953. Till that time the Constituent Assembly had taken certain major decisions on the recommendations of the Land Compensation Committee. No compensation was to be paid for expropriation of the big landed estates to the tillers of the land.

The 'Basic Principles Committee' had recommended that basis of the political set up of the State should be fully democratic; let the hereditary rulership be abolished and instead there should be an elected Head of the State to be designated as Sadar-e-Riyasat and that the State should have its own flag. After Bakshi Ghulam Mohammad took over as Prime Minister of Jammu and Kashmir, succeeding Sheikh Mohammad Abdullah, the work of the Constituent Assembly picked up considerably.

An advisory Committee on Fundamental Rights and Citizenship and Basic Principles was set up on October 20, 1953. The Assembly met on February 6, 1954, and adopted the reports of the Basic Principles Committee on Fundamental Rights and Citizenship. The Drafting Committee presented its report on February 12, 1954, and the report was adopted on February 15, 1954. The adoption of this report embodied the ratification of the State's Accession to India.

The Customs barrier between the State and the rest of India was removed from April 13, the same year at the initiative of the State Government. Dr. Rajendra Prasad, the President of India, visited the State in April for the first time after the ratification of the accession, and in his statement in Jammu he said, "Any break in the relationship of the State with India was inconceivable."

The Jammu and Kashmir Constitution was adopted by the Constituent Assembly on November 17, 1956, and came into force on January 26, 1957. Under provisions of this Constitution elections to the State Legislative Assembly were held for the first time the same year.

The Constitution of Jammu and Kashmir includes unamenable provision regarding Jammu and Kashmir being an integral part of the Indian Union as also clearly defining its geographical boundaries to be those which existed before the Pakistani aggression. In this respect the following provisions of the Constitution need special mention:

"3. **Relationship of the State with the Union of India** – The State of Jammu and Kashmir is and shall be an integral part of the Union of India.

4. **Territory of the State**. –The territory of the State shall comprise all the territories which on the fifteenth day of August 1947, were under the sovereignty or suzerainty of the Ruler of the State.
5. **Extent of Executive and legislative power of the State.**- The executive and legislative power of the State extends to all matters except those with respect to which Parliament has power to make laws for the State under the provisions of the Constitution of India."

Section 147 of the Constitution deals with the procedure relating to amendment of the Constitution. The power of the State Legislature to amend the Constitution has been circumscribed and limited by the caveat, which lays down the following:

"Provided further that no Bill or amendment seeking to make any change in-

- **(a)** this section; or
- **(b)** the provisions of section 3 and 5; or
- **(c)** the provisions of the Constitution of India as applicable in relation to the State, shall be introduced or moved in either House of the Legislature."

Thus Sections 3, 5 and proviso to Section 147 of the Jammu and Kashmir Constitution lay down the fundamental principles and the basic parameters regarding finality of the accession of the State with the Indian Union as expressed through the popular will of the people.

In view of the provisions of Article 370 in the Indian Constitution and the fact that the Constituent Assembly in the State had been constituted and had started functioning, the President of India issued the Constitution (Application to Jammu and Kashmir) Order, 1950, specifying the matter with regard to which the Parliament would be competent to make laws for the State. The subject matter of the order related mainly to the elaboration of subjects already specified in the Instrument of Accession and certain additions were also made. Two Schedules were added. One of the important results of this order was that the residuary powers which in the case of other Indian States vested in the Centre, in the case of Jammu and Kashmir it was to belong to the State.

Subsequently, particularly during the beginning of 1960s, New Delhi considered speedier constitutional integration of the State. By December 1964, a series of Constitutional measures were undertaken in consultation with the State government making Articles. 356 and 357 of the Constitution of India applicable to the State by virtue of which the Centre could, under certain circumstances, assume the reigns of the State administration and exercise its legislative powers. The nomenclature of the heads of the State and the Government were changed from Sadar-e-Riyasat and Prime Minister to be Governor and Chief Minister respectively, so as to conform to the pattern in the rest of the country. The head of the State was to be nominated by the Centre instead of being elected by the State Legislature as was initially envisaged in the Constitution of Jammu and Kashmir. Thereafter application of certain central laws has been extended to the State of Jammu and Kashmir from time to time. At the political level, the issue of various presidential orders and application of central laws has been and remains a source of friction between the Centre and the State, particularly in relation to existence and interpretation of Art. 370 of the Indian Constitution. Art. 370 is and has been the basis of the Constitutional relationship of India with Jammu and Kashmir. It gave the State special status not available to any other member state of the Indian Union. This part of the Constitution reads as under:

Article 370. Temporary provisions with respect of the State of Jammu and Kashmir:

"(1) **Notwithstanding anything in this Constitution, —**

(a) the provisions of article 238 shall not apply in relation to the state of Jammu and Kashmir;

(b) the power of the Parliament to make laws for the said state shall be limited to:

i. those matters in the Union list and the Concurrent list which, in consultation with the Government of the State, are declared by the President to correspond to matters specified in the Instrument of Accession governing the accession of the State to the Dominion of India as the matters with respect to which the Dominion Legislature may make laws for that State; and

ii. such other matters in the said list as, with the concurrence of the Government of the State, the President may by order specify.

Explanation: For the purposes of this article, the Government of the State means the person for the time being recognized by the President as the Maharaja of Jammu and Kashmir acting on the advice of the Council of Ministers for the time being in office under the Maharaja's proclamation dated the fifth day of March 1948;

(c) the provsisions of article 1 and of this article shall apply in relation to that State;

(d) such of the other provisions of this constitution shall apply in relation to that State subject to exceptions and modifications as the President may by order specify;

Provided that no such order which relates to the matters specified in the Instrument of Accession of the State referred to in paragraph (i) of sub-clause (b) shall be issued except in consultation with the Government of the State.

Provided further that no such order which relates to matters other than those referred to in the last preceding proviso shall be issued except with the concurrence of that Government.

(2) If the concurrence of the Government of the State referred to in paragraph (ii) of sub-clause (b) of clause (1) or in the second proviso to sub-clause (d) of that clause be given before the Constituent Assembly for the purpose of framing the Constitution of the State is convened, it shall be placed before such Assembly for such decision as it may take thereon.

(3) Notwithstanding anything in the foregoing provisions of this article, the President may, by public notification, declare that this article shall cease to be operative or shall be operative only with such exceptions and modifications and from such date as he may specify:

Provided that the recommendation of the Constituent Assembly of the State referred to in clause (2) shall be necessary before the President issues such a notification.

Right from its inception Art. 370 has been an object of serious and continuous, often acrimonious, debate across the political spectrum of the country as well as amongst the local luminaries. The interpretation with respect to this Article ranges from the opinion of Ayyangar who opined, "The Constituent Assembly of the Jammu and Kashmir State has met and taken decision on the Constitution of the State, the range of federal jurisdiction over the State, the President may on the recommendation of that Constituent Assembly issue an order that Art. 370 shall either cease to be operative or shall be operative only subject to such expansion and modification as may be specified by him". On the other hand there are those who believe that as given in the heading of the Article itself these provisions were meant to be purely temporary and the State's constitutional relationship with the Union as well as its own democratic and political development having been established, there is no further need for this Article in the Constitution of India and it should, therefore, be abrogated. At the other end of the spectrum is the interpretation that any change in the provisions of Art. 370 or its absolute deletion from the Statute Book could only have been made by the Constituent Assembly of Jammu and Kashmir and that body being no more in existence, there is absolutely no scope or provision to either amend or abrogate Art. 370. The debate is endless and goes on unabated.

The Elections

As mentioned earlier, the first elections in the post- independence era were held in Jammu and Kashmir in 1951, for the constitution of the Constituent Assembly. The Constitution of Jammu and

Kashmir provided for a Legislative Assembly comprising 100 members, of these 25 seats had been earmarked for the people of the area under illegal occupation of Pakistan. The first general elections to the State Assembly under the newly adopted Constitution were held in 1957. The elections of 1951 and 1957 were held under the control and supervision of the State Election and Franchise Commission. Later elections were conducted under the supervision and control of the Election Commission of India. In 1976, the State Government constituted a Delimitation Commission headed by Justice J.L. Kapoor, a retired judge of the Supreme Court of India, with other members being T.V. Vasu, sitting judge of Calcutta High Court, and N. Swaminathan, Chief Election Commissioner of India. The Commission recommended 76 constituencies for the Legislative Assembly as against existing 75. The new segment added was that of Surankote in Poonch district. Overall strength of the Legislative Assembly was kept at 100 and the number of seats earmarked for the people of PoK was reduced to 24 by an amendment in the State Constitution. By another Constitutional amendment in 1988, eleven more Assembly segments were added thus raising the total strength of the Legislative Assembly to 111 and a Delimitation Commission was entrusted the task of carving out 11 new constituencies. In pursuance to Section 4 of the Jammu and Kashmir Representation of People Act 1957, the Commission by an order dated April 27, 1995, delimited 87 constituencies raising the strength from existing 76 members. Regionwise it meant 46 Assembly seats for Kashmir Valley as against the earlier 42; 37 for Jammu region as against earlier 32 and four for Ladakh region as against earlier two.

The 1957 elections to the State Assembly were swept by the National Conference winning 68 seats–out of which 43 were won uncontested (37 in the Valley and six in Jammu region), Praja Parishad won five seats, the others two[3]. Corresponding figures for 1962 general elections were 70 seats for National Conference (including 34 uncontested–33 in the Valley and one in Jammu region), three for Praja Parishad and two independents. The next general elections to the Assembly were held in 1967, when Ghulam Mohammad Sadiq was the Chief Minister (the designation of Prime Minister of the State had been changed to Chief Minister by then and the existing National Conference had been converted into the Indian National Congress). In this battle at the hustings, the Indian National Congress secured 61 seats (including 22 uncontested – 21 in the Valley and one in Jammu division); the National Conference, under the inspiration of Sheikh Mohammad Abdullah, who was then under detention, contested 38 seats and was declared successful in Eight of them. Almost similar pattern emerged in the 1972 elections with the Congress winning 58 seats out of which five were uncontested. The results of this election were significant because the number of independents was as high as nine, but more importantly, Jamat-e-Islami (JEI) for the first time contested elections fielding 22 candidates and won five seats in the Legislative Assembly. Some political analysts believe this to be the beginning of taking roots by this religious fundamentalist and perniciously separatist outfit which is seen to be the mother of secessionist elements in the State ever since.

The Indo-Pak war of 1971, and the emerging of Bangladesh into a sovereign nation had its emotional and political impact on the people as well as political establishment of the State. A process of reconciliation between Sheikh Mohammad Abdullah and the Centre was initiated. By February 1975, Syed Mir Qasim, the then Chief Minister of the State, was persuaded by the Central Government headed by Indira Gandhi to abdicate in favour of Sheikh Mohammad Abdullah, who under an agreement reached with the Central Government – commonly called as Indira-Sheikh Accord - became the Chief Minister of the State on February 22, 1975. He appointed his trusted and old associate, Mirza Afzal Beg, from Kashmir, Devi Dass Thakur, a sitting High Court judge of Jammu and Kashmir High Court, from Jammu and Sonam Narboo, a retired Chief Engineer from Ladakh, as his three Cabinet Ministers. After assuming the Chief Ministership Sheikh Mohammad Abdullah also revived the National Conference while simultaneously heading the Government in which Congress had more than 2/3 majority.

The understanding between Sheikh Sahib and the State unit of Congress did not last long after the Congress lost power at the Centre during the post emergency elections to the Lok Sabha in March 1977. The local Congress leadership made a bid to regain power in the State by announcing withdrawal of support to the government and staking claim to form the alternative government in the State on the basis of their strength in the Assembly. However, the Governor dissolved the House and called for fresh elections. In the ensuing electoral battle in July the same year the National conference romped home with sizeable majority of 47 seats with 15 going to the newly constituted Janata Dal and INC getting only 11 seats, all in Jammu region.

By this time, the Constitution of Jammu & Kashmir had been amended to provide for a six years term of the House following a similar amendment which had been brought in the Indian Constitution in respect of the life of the Lok Sabha . The life of the Lok Sabha was restored to five years after Janata Party came in power. However, the amended provision in the Constitution of Jammu & Kashmir was retained and continues to exist as such till date. Therefore, the next general elections to the State Assembly were due in 1983. Sheikh Sahib bade farewell to this world and to his long spread political career on September 8, 1982, and was succeeded by his son, Dr. Farooq Abdullah. The succession created a rift within the family. G. M. Shah, the elder son-in-law of Sheikh Sahib and an old political worker of National Conference, chose to float his own Awami National Conference (ANC) to contest elections against the ruling National Conference in 1983. National Conference won 46 seats while no seat went to ANC. The opposition, led by the Indian National Congress which had won only 25 seats, couldn't believe that after Sheikh Sahib had left the scene, the people of the Valley would reject the Indian National Congress which had directly and indirectly ruled the State for 22 long years between 1953 to 1975.

During the post election period, the opposition leadership took to streets in Jammu region asking for dismissal of the elected government. It is widely believed that the Centre took extraordinary interest in this agitation despite its preoccupation with the problems of extremism prevalent in the state of Punjab. However, immediately after operation Blue Star in June 1984, Governor B. K. Nehru was prematurely shifted to Gujarat and in his place Jagmohan was brought in. Soon afterwards, about a dozen dissident members of the Legislative Assembly grouped together under the leadership of G. M. Shah, who was not a member of either House of Legislature, supported by the opposition INC, and staked their claim to form the government. This happened on the 2nd July, 1984. The Congress Party provided support to the new Government from outside only to withdraw it in March 1986. This time Governor's Rule was imposed in the State as per provisions of J&K Constitution.

The next six months saw emergence of new political equations. The then Prime Minister of India, Rajiv Gandhi, who was also a close personal friend of Dr. Farooq Abdullah engineered the "Rajiv Farooq Accord" leading to reinstallation of Dr. Abdullah as Chief Minister with Congress support in November 1986, and subsequent sharing of seats in general elections held in March' 87. The jointly contested general elections were widely believed to have sowed the seeds of discord against the National Conference and the Centre in the Valley of Kashmir. This period also witnessed emergence of several political groups with their local pockets of influence, some of them having secessionist leanings. These groups came together to form an alliance under the name of Muslim United Front (MUF) and contested elections against the NC and INC. During and after the elections, National Conference was charged by MUF with rigging of the elections.

Terrorism in Kashmir raised its head in the post-1987 election scenario and was spearheaded by the young political activists who supported and worked for the MUF candidates. 'Ballot to be replaced by the bullet' was the slogan of these young men who drew moral support from the MUF and material support from across the border. Incidents of bomb-blasts in empty parked buses, empty public places etc., became more frequent. During the Parliamentary elections held in November 1989, the electorate was threatened not to participate in the polls. It was reported that at one of the polling stations, a coffin was kept by a terrorist organization with a warning that the first elector who came to the polling station for casting his vote, would be returned lying in the coffin - dead. Only a few dared to defy the diktat. Whether it was genuine fear or political disinterest which caused a very low polling turnout will continue to be analyzed forever by the political observers.

The country was simultaneously passing through a difficult political phase. In the absence of adequate support from the Centre, not much attention was given to control disturbed conditions of Jammu & Kashmir. Indian National Congress had lost 1989 general elections to the Parliament and the new coalition government at the Centre made Mufti Mohammad Sayeed, a senior politician from the Valley, as its Home Minister. It probably prompted the terrorist organizations to kidnap his daughter, Dr. Rubiya Sayeed. Her release was secured, at the behest of the Centre, in exchange of release of five terrorists who were then under detention. This was seen as a major success by the youth of Kashmir and the first big achievement of the gun which forced the mighty Governments of India and of Jammu & Kashmir to kneel down. The event caused a widespread euphoria, particularly in the downtown area of Srinagar which had to be immediately placed under a prolonged spell of un-declared curfew. The deteriorating law and order situation or may be the political considerations prompted the Government of India into appointing Jagmohan as Governor of Jammu & Kashmir a second time. Dr. Farooq Abdullah, who in the meanwhile had made it clear to the Central Government that he would not accept Jagmohan as Governor of Jammu & Kashmir, immediately rushed to Delhi and announced his decision to resign even before Jagmohan could take oath of office in the Raj Bhawan at Jammu in January 1990. Jagmohan assumed administration of the State, dissolved the House, working under a belief that the terrorism which had its origin in the alleged rigging of the 1987 Assembly Elections would die naturally as soon as the people were promised fresh elections to the State Assembly. The rest is history. The next Assembly elections were not held in Jammu & Kashmir till September 1996, involving the most prolonged spell of President's Rule in any state of the country and encompassing a massive security, administrative and logistic exercise at an unprecedented scale unheard of and unthinkable till then for restoration of an elected government in any part of the country.

Notes

1. K.M. Panikkar, Gulab Singh 1792-1858 Founder of Kashmir, Martin Hopkinson Ltd., London, 1930.
2. Presently out of the total area of 2,22,236 sq.kms. that comprises the State, 83,294 sq.kms. is under the occupation of Pakistan. Out of this it has seceded 5180 sq.kms to China. A large chunk in the Ladakh region of 37, 555 sq. kms. is under the occupation of China leaving an area of only 1,01,387 sq. kms with India.
3. Detailed partywise position in each of the Assembly segments is given in Annexure-I.

2 Pak Designs

The creation of Pakistan was not the result of only perceived apprehensions and ambitions of a group of Indian Muslim intellectuals and leaders. It was decidedly the outcome of a well-thoughtout and spiritedly executed policy of 'divide and rule' to suit the interests of British Empire in India, to start with and later to serve the interests of a declining status of Britain as a world power and emerging cold war scenario in the post-Second World War period. Right from the day of creation of Pakistan on August 14, 1947, the Pakistani rulers, encouraged by the British representatives and officers in India as well as its ruling establishment in London, had set their eyes on the absorption, control and in extreme eventuality forcible occupation of the State of Jammu and Kashmir. Their plans were put into operation right from August 12, 1947, when Pakistan signed Standstill Agreement with the Maharaja of Jammu and Kashmir. Over the next year and a half Pakistani establishment, actively assisted by the British officers commanding Gilgit Scouts, first successfully took control of Gilgit and areas north of it without even firing a single shot. The tribals which first created communal problems on the western borders of the State and then launched regular invasion of the Valley on October 21/22, 1947, were trained, equipped and encouraged by Pakistani army headed by senior British military officers and British Commissioner of the North-

West Frontier Province. That Pakistan was able to occupy and keep for itself almost 37 percent of the territory of the State is not only the testimony of the vicious design of her rulers right from her birth but also a sad reflection on the inadequate response, lack of focussed retaliation and irresolute determination to deal with the adversary on the part of the Indian establishment. The Indian government was not only dependent almost entirely on the senior British functionaries in India, including the military commanders, for planning and conduct of the operations against Pakistan but also it didn't listen to the advice and pleas of senior Indian military officers. The Indian government also didn't fully realize the strategic importance of the Northern Areas as is clear from the fact that during the entire fourteen months of conflict, no serious effort was made to remove the illegal Pakistani occupation from a vast stretch of Skardu-Gilgit area and tracts further north.

During the entire period of conflict, Pakistani attitude towards India was consistently of unconcealed hostility. On the contrary, the Indian Government always gave an impression that it was dealing with Pakistan at two different levels. At the worst, Pakistan was an adversary in the limited context of Jammu and Kashmir, and in other matters the dealings between the two countries continued at a normal pace. The transfer of substantial amounts of money to Pakistan as well as the flow of defence materials to that country continued even while the two armies were engaged in a combat in one part of the country. Indian attitude towards Pakistan, a belligerent state, was so magnanimous that when Pakistan approached the Joint Defence Council of India and Pakistan to raise a new regiment for East Pakistan, the permission was given to do so at the end of November 1947. If Pakistan mistook it as a signal that India regarded the conflict in Kashmir to be disconnected from the rest of Indo-Pak issues where business as usual would prevail, it could not be blamed for it.

Not even once, during the entire period of operations, the Government of India undertook any move whereby Pakistan could feel threatened for her mis-adventure in Jammu and Kashmir. On the contrary, it appears that efforts were made to re-assure the adversary that the entire conflict would remain localized and a *cordon sanitaire* would be put around Jammu and Kashmir. Not even a threat was held to strike at the vulnerable areas of Pakistan, outside Jammu and Kashmir. Even within the State, the air force, where India enjoyed complete superiority, was made to operate with practically hands tied behind its back.

India's acceptance of the cease-fire also is an indication of the inability of the leadership to take advantage of a favourable situation and turn it into a national advantage. Pakistan had all along, right from January 1948, refused to accept the Resolutions of UNCIP. Pakistan had also meanwhile enlarged its area of operations wherever she could, like Gurez, Ladakh, and attempts to overrun the Punch garrison, and so on. It only agreed to a cease-fire when both military as well as domestic circumstances turned unfavourable. One year of conflict had put a heavy strain on Pakistan's limited financial resources. Her industrial infrastructure and the economy were not capable of sustaining protracted operations. Jinnah had died in September 1948, thereby shaking the political stability of Pakistan. A series of important victories by the Indian troops had demoralized the Pakistani forces and more so the irregulars and raiders whose continued interest in operations could only be sustained by unbridled success. On the other hand, there was marked improvement in India's military position in Jammu and Kashmir during that period. The breakthrough at Zojila and subsequent linkup with Leh was closely followed by the breaking of the siege of Punch, during November 1948. Shortly before that, the successful police action in Hyderabad had removed a major irritant in the Indian polity. It had also released 19 battalions, which had been stationed for the Hyderabad area. These were now available for deployment in Jammu and Kashmir. It was from that relative position of strength that India agreed to accept the cease-fire, thus bailing Pakistan out of a difficult situation.

It was not the armed forces of the country which did not play their part effectively. Under the circumstances, and within the constraints imposed, the Indian army and the Indian Air Force acquitted themselves reasonably well. It was, in fact, the political and the military leadership at the highest level which can be said to have been found wanting.

An explanation of the course of action adopted by the Indian Government has been made in the official history of 1947-48 Operations as, "rightly or wrongly the Government did not decide to have a general war with Pakistan. Nehru, the apostle of peace, must have hoped that the Pakistan's aggression on Kashmir would prove temporary aberration, that all enemy forces would be peacefully withdrawn from the State under the impartial advice of the UN and that India and Pakistan would live ever afterwards as close and friendly neighbours. It was a vision worth pursuing, even though it finally proved a mere illusion."

Pakistan on her part also learnt some lessons, useful from that country's point of view. Pakistani rulers realized that in relation to India belligerence pays. The military commanders learnt a valuable lesson that a mix of covert operations and open aggression is both cost effective as well as gainful. At the tactical level, leaving initiative to the local commanders and using local resources brings rich dividends and pays handsome return. This was proved time and again, particularly in the initial advance of the raiders within a short period of seven days from Muzaffarabad right up to the outskirts of Srinagar city notwithstanding the four days of bravely fought rearguard action by Brig. Rajinder Singh and his small band of spirited defenders. These tactics also enabled a body of less than one thousand local tribals commanded by Pakistani officers to occupy the entire Nubra Valley, Kargil and Leh regions, with the exception of Leh town, till they were thrown back by the Indian breakthrough at Zojila. Pakistani establishment also realized that high pitched propaganda coupled with skillful management of UN systems and securing powerful friends is a formidable combination. The rulers of Pakistan, political as well as military and the civil services, also appeared to have reached the conclusion that taking a practical view of the concept of sovereignty and its selected circumspection is always useful to the ruling elite, particularly as long as the essential national security interests as perceived by them and their own continued control over the levers of power within that country remains intact. They also assumed right from the beginning of the conflict, a belief which seems to have strengthened over the decades, that the cost of mis-adventure against India would always be affordable and never be prohibitarily expensive. India, they perceived, would tackle the aggressor defensively and not undertake vigorous counter offensive. Indian inclination to localize areas of conflict was also seen as a point of advantage for the purpose of planning and execution of aggressive designs by the Pakistani military commanders.

While Pakistan had managed to gain substantial part of the territory of Jammu and Kashmir by her aggression and diplomatic manipulations, her efforts to build institutions necessary for a modern nation state did not prove successful. The political structure of the newly created State, in the wake of India's independence, had not been able to take shape. Instead of consolidating, a process of disintegration started, right from the beginning, in the political institutions of the nation. In stark contrast to the completion and adoption of the Indian Constitution, even the exercise of preparing the constitution in Pakistan had not been seriously started till after two decades of its coming into being. After Jinnah's death in September 1948, there was hardly a leader of similar political stature who could provide stability to the nation. In fact, the basic problem with the Pakistani leadership was the absence of leaders with mass following in any of the four provinces of the then West Pakistan which was the nerve centre of the political power and most of the eminent Pakistani leaders had belonged to the Indian provinces. The result was inevitable. In less than a decade, the Muslim League ceased to be a political power in both wings of Pakistan. Khwaja Nazimuddin succeeded Jinnah as the Governor General of Pakistan. After the assassination of Liaqat Ali Khan, he made the then Foreign Minister, Ghulam Mohammad, the Governor General and himself became the Prime Minister. In a polity beset with serious problems of corruption, intrigue and political instability, further accentuated by external influence and covert intervention in its internal affairs, the governments in Pakistan changed swiftly. Ghulam Mohammad, following his appointment as Governor General, shortly thereafter, dismissed Nazimuddin as the Prime Minister. He himself was followed by Iskander Mirza in less than two years. Mirza was a former Commander-in-Chief of the Pakistani Army. He also contributed to the political uncertainty of Pakistan by setting in motion a process of political intrigue and effectively blocking attempts at constitution making by sowing the seeds of distrust amongst various political elements. Mirza dismissed five Prime Ministers in less than three years. In 1958, Iskander Mirza's rule was brought to an end in a military coup spearheaded by Ayub Khan, another C-in-C of the Pakistan Army, who was then the Defence Minister. Thus, even a facade of civilian rule in Pakistan disappeared with the country coming under martial law and being ruled by a dictator with an iron fist.

However, in the field of foreign policy and defence the rulers of Pakistan, in spite of the political instability and absence of strong domestic institutions, did well for themselves and got for the country billions of dollars worth of military and economic aid. Lt. Gen. Akbar Khan (Retd), who had been put in command of all the tribals during 1947-48, has mentioned in his memoirs the attitude of the rulers of Pakistan as, "I heard the expression that 'Pakistan was like the beautiful woman who should sell herself to the highest bidder' and ultimately our relations with the US were not very far removed from such description. The more acceptable reason that gradually evolved that we needed strength to liberate Kashmir and for our defence against India." Pakistan's becoming a member of SEATO and CENTO, as well as functioning as one of the frontline states in the heightened era of cold war reflected this mind-set. The focal point of all foreign policy initiatives as well as defence build-up by Pakistan was unremitted and blatant hostility towards India. With Indo-Chinese relations taking a nosedive during the closing years of 1950s, Pakistan started making overtures towards China with the same intent. The rulers of Pakistan, to whichever political thought or ideology they belonged to, had convinced themselves that making Jammu and Kashmir as part of Pakistan was the singular aim of its ruling class. Arguments to justify this included stability of the nation, providing it strategic depth, vindication of the two nation theory which was the very basis of the formation of Pakistan and the addition of Jammu and Kashmir to West Pakistan would give edge to the western wing in terms of territory as well as population over the East Pakistan which would legitimize its policy of subjugation of the latter.

The adventurism of Ayub Khan was equally matched by his fiery and impulsive Foreign Minister Z.A. Bhutto. Both convinced themselves of their military superiority over India. The developments in the first few years of the decade of the 1960s, like humiliating fiasco with China, death of Nehru, serious political dissentions within the ruling Congress party, food shortage and poor performance of Indian economy, were interpreted by Pakistani rulers as signs of instability which were further reinforced by their perspective of India's Prime Minister Lal Bahadur Shastri as a weak and ineffective leader. It was thought to be the most opportune time by the Ayub-Bhutto duo to make a serious bid to annex Jammu and Kashmir by force. A plan was put into operation for this purpose in August 1965, to infiltrate a large body of well trained guerrillas into the Valley and Rajouri-Poonch area with full backing of the Pakistan Army, which in their opinion had always possessed the superior military manpower made even more formidable by the acquisition of Patton tanks, Star-fighter and Saber jets for which India had no equivalent in its armed forces. It was to be, in a way, a repeat performance of 1947-48 bid with, as the Pakistani rulers saw it, almost complete chances of success. The guerrilla infiltration into Jammu and Kashmir planned under the code name "Operation Gibraltar", came to be noticed when on August 5, 1965, a Gujjar, Mohammad Din, was approached in Gulmarg area by two Pakistani infiltrators for helping their party with rations, ponies as well as information regarding Indian forces and their dispositions. Mohammad Din managed to slip away and informed the local police station about the presence of armed guerrillas in the vicinity. He was not the only one to have acted in that manner to smash the Pakistani assessment that the Muslims of Jammu and Kashmir were smarting under the Hindu Indian regime and were eagerly waiting to be liberated by their Muslim brethren from Pakistan. A large number of locals informed the police and the military authorities of the presence of armed infiltrators in their vicinity. These timely disclosures enabled effective and vigorous counter action by the Indian army. A large number of infiltrators were eliminated and arrested. "Operation Gibraltar" had floundered on the bedrock of secular and nationalistic commitments of the people of the State, and failed.

The dismal end of "Operation Gibraltar" did not make Ayub Khan and Z.A. Bhutto to realize the futility of their efforts. This failure in fact had an opposite effect and they, along with Gen. Moosa, the Pakistan Commander in Chief, decided to launch a full scale invasion across the ceasefire line and began attacking a number of Indian positions all along accompanied by heavy shelling, while continuing the armed infiltration. In a spectacular response, the Indians attacked and occupied the tactically important and heavily defended Haji Pir Pass on 24th August. The loss of Haji Pir Pass was not only passing into Indian hands an important landmark, it also dealt a heavy blow to the Pakistani military prestige. On the morning of September 1, 1965, Pakistani forces launched a massive armour thrust, backed by large scale infantry and heavy shelling in Chhamb in Jammu Sector. "Operation Grand Slam" had been launched by Pakistan as a last and desperate gamble by its ruler.

In spite of the valiant fight put up by the Indian forces in this sector, the sheer volume of the attacking force, strength of their armour forced the Indians to withdraw and Pakistanis made substantial gains, capturing the Indian territory up to Munnawar Tawi, managed to cross it and seriously threatened Akhnoor thereby putting the Jammu-Rajouri-Poonch road, the only communication link for the Rajouri-Poonch sector, into serious jeopardy. In fact it was the Pakistani plan to cut off Jammu-Poonch road by capturing Akhnoor, as also cut off the Jammu-Pathankote road thereby 'bottling' the Indian forces in Jammu and Kashmir while simultaneously dealing a crumbling blow to the Indian war machine in the plains of Punjab and deserts of Rajasthan. The Indian Airforce also joined the battle and helped the infantry and armour to stop the Pakistani thrust. In the ensuing fierce clashes on the ground and in the air, the Pakistani advance was held around Jourian-Kalith area and they reached nowhere near their objective of Akhnoor nor was Pakistan Airforce able to cause damage to the vital bridge near Akhnoor.

Having realized the sinister intentions of the Pakistani invasion, India decided to give a befitting reply, crossed the international border and struck Pakistan in Lahore-Sialkot sector on 6th September. In the ensuing seventeen days, the Indian forces almost reached the outskirts of Lahore and were practically knocking at the doors of Sialkot. During this period, in a spectacular defensive action in Khemkaran sector in Punjab the myth of superiority and invincibility of Patton tanks of Pakistani armour were laid to rest with Khemkaran being practically converted into a 'graveyard' of Pattons. With the cease-fire declared on 23rd September, the 1965 confrontation between India and Pakistan came to an end, signaling the dismal failure of a very determined Pakistani attempt to annex Jammu and Kashmir by force, second time within a period of twenty years. But for timely rescue efforts made by America, the United Kingdom and the Soviet Union Pakistan was in imminent danger of losing both Lahore and Sialkot, while not being able to realize any of its military objectives or capturing of even a single important area in the India territory. However, the declaration of cease-fire itself, and subsequent events, were to prove that ignoble performance of Pakistan military machine was more than counter balanced by its impressive performance in the field of foreign relations and diplomacy.

Next armed conflict with Pakistan took place in 1971 in the aftermath of elections in Pakistan when Zulfiqar Ali Bhutto, leader of the largest political party in West Pakistan, was not prepared to allow Mujib-ur-Rehman, a Bengali, and having secured more number of seats due to larger population in the then East Pakistan, to form government at the centre. The story of Bhutto's intransigence and army's brutal repression and the civil war in

East Pakistan leading to the emergence of Bangladesh is only too well known. The two-nation theory founded in the genteel living rooms of Uttar Pradesh was finally laid to rest in the paddy fields of Bangladesh. During the 1971 war with Pakistan while most of the activity took place in the erstwhile East Pakistan, in Jammu and Kashmir major operations were conducted in Jammu sector where Pakistanis again took the initiative by attacking the Indian forces on 3rd December, and managed to occupy areas right up to the Munnawar Tawi. In Kargil sector the Indian troops succeeded in capturing some of the important enemy posts overlooking Kargil town thereby removing threat to Kargil and further securing the road to Leh.

In the aftermath of 1971 operations, Bhutto came to power on December 17, 1971, and was ousted by military coup headed by Gen Zia-ul-Haq on July 5, 1977. He was later executed on the charge of complicity in a political murder on April 5, 1979. With this Pakistan's brief attempt to establish a democratic polity came to an end and Zia-ul-Haq ruled the country with an iron hand of a military dictator till his death in an air crash in August 1988.

Even though Pakistan had lost the entire Eastern Wing and majority of its population in the emergence of a new nation, due to certain favourable circumstances its recovery in terms of economic parameters as well as national psyche was quick and smart. Certain international factors as well as internal developments accelerated this process. Bhutto firmly changed the national identity of Pakistan from its South Asian secular roots to a theocratic Islamic country almost completely identifying with West Asian group of Islamic nations. In the later part of his regime, he came under considerable pressure from the Sunni fundamentalist elements and introduced certain Islamic measures for appeasing them including putting restrictions on some religious sects. Gen Zia, on assuming power, picked up the thread of Bhutto's policy of Islamization and carried it still further. Through the mechanism of administering stronger doses of Islamization in the country he tightened his control over the population and the institutions of Pakistan and proclaimed Nizam-e-Mustaffa to be the law of the land on July 10, 1979.

Pakistan's changeover to a theocratic state and adoption of West Asian identity also coincided with amassing of huge petro dollors wealth in oil rich nations of this region. Pakistan received handsome assistance from these rich Muslim countries, particularly Saudi Arabia and Libya. Pakistan's efforts to match with the growing capability of India in the fields of nuclear technology, cleverly projected by Bhutto as pursuit in the acquisition of a nuclear 'Islamic Bomb' helped elevating the status of Pakistan even more, enabling her to get much more liberal financial aid from the West Asian countries.

The Soviet intervention in Afghanistan in December 1978, and the rise of Ayatullah Khomeini in Iran, a few months later, pushed Pakistan once again as a frontline state and the most favoured ally in the eyes of the United States and her global interests. The stability of Zia's regime and continuation of his rule became an important consideration in the policy formulations of the USA, which further helped Pakistan to consolidate her economy and build up military capabilities. The ISI's considerable and active involvement in organizing and sustaining anti-Soviet resistance by armed groups in Afghanistan provided Pakistan with enormous supplies of unaccounted arms and explosives, slush money and expertise to organize and spread armed insurgency. It learnt a lot from the CIA and learnt it well. The expertise that ISI acquired from its experience in Afghanistan as well as learning from the CIA was used first to create problems in Indian Punjab and then with improved techniques in the State of Jammu and Kashmir.

Another important factor which enhanced the capabilities of Pakistan to undertake covert operations, related to rise of fundamentalism and jehadi culture during the 1980s. This was the direct outcome of policies of Pakistani rulers for Islamization of the country's polity, in spite of the liberal outlook of the majority of its population, as well as the Wahabi influence which accompanied dollops of financial aid from Saudi Arabia. Coupled with armed insurgency rising in Afghanistan next door, the existence of a large number of warlike tribes in the North West Frontier and Baluchistan provinces of Pakistan and the burning desire of Pakistani rulers to create problems in Jammu and Kashmir, once again added external dimensions to the rise of Islamic fundamentalism and jehadi culture in Pakistan.

While Pakistan was recovering from the trauma of creation of Bangladesh and had acquired considerable capabilities in 1980s to create problems in India, her endeavours became more prone to success due to certain developments taking place in Jammu and Kashmir. The toppling of duly elected government of Dr. Farooq Abdullah and its replacement by his brother-in-law G.M. Shah with the help of defections from National Conference legislators in 1984 hurt Indian credibility grievously in the eyes of the people of the Valley. Two years later, Dr. Farooq Abdullah and Prime Minister Rajiv Gandhi entered into an accord paving the way for his return to power on November 7, 1986, following revocation of Governor's Rule in the State. Although the elections to the State Assembly were due in 1989, Dr. Abdullah decided to go in for the polls in March 1987, which were contested by the National Conference and the Congress with electoral understanding. Although the National Conference was able to form the government with considerable comfort and ease, its alliance with the Congress was not liked generally by the rank and file of the party and the public opinion in the Valley. It certainly removed an alternative channel earlier available to the secular political dissent, more so in the Kashmir region. Allegations and charges of manipulations in the elections also adversely affected the credibility of the National Conference leadership. Many political analysts consider the National Conference-Congress accord and electoral manipulations on some seats in the Valley as grave political mis-calculations, which became an important factor in the rise of terrorism in the State. Poor state of governance provided by the coalition further added to the disaffection amongst the people.

The rise of Jamat-e-Islami (JEI), which had acquired political legitimacy in 1972 elections, was particularly noteworthy during the communal disturbances, which took place in the Valley in March 1986, leading to the dismissal of G.M. Shah's government and imposition of Governor's Rule. It became focus and rallying point for the secessionist fundamentalist forces in the Valley and was used as a recruitment and training ground by Pakistan for building up a cadre of sympathizers, armed terrorists as well as a very strong channel for influencing and subverting important sections of government employees. The Jamat-e-Islami particularly targeted the police, education department and the judiciary for fulfillment of its nefarious designs and when the time came the internal subversion of loyalties to the State engineered by the JEI manipulations hit the State structure with telling effect.

The initial Indian response to the terrorism when it started smouldering and erupting was tentative, hesitant and less than effective. It took quite some time for New Delhi to realize the full implications and sinister designs of the developments that were taking place in the Valley in spite of an earlier painful experience of Pakistan backed insurgency in the state of Punjab. The Indian inability to comprehend the dimensions of the emerging threat to the peace and public order, its ramifications impinging upon the national security also indirectly helped the success of Pakistan's efforts to create problems in the State.

Pakistan's economic recovery, particularly during the 1980s, and her leading role in the spread of Islamic fundamentalism on a global scale as well as its catapulation as a frontline state for the American designs in Afghanistan equipped and encouraged her to make another try to foment trouble in Jammu and Kashmir. Though the end remained the same, the means adopted were different this time. Learning from the past mistakes a direct confrontation with India was avoided. Recourse was taken to initiate a proxy- war conceived and executed by Pakistan's Inter-Services Intelligence, supported by high profile media blitz working in tandem with foreign office. The Pak inspired, trained and backed terrorists started armed insurrection in 1989, which reached its peak during 1990-93 period. This turbulence was fueled by a potently dangerous mix of fundamentalism, class conflict and political adventurism leaving in its wake a trail of bloodshed and misery.

3

The Virus is Injected

The blueprint of activities prepared and set in motion by the ISI aimed at creating and spawning disturbances in the State by misleading the Muslim youth and exploiting the discontentment amongst the population against the actual and perceived failures of the State administration. The traditional political leadership was unable to channelise the growing discontentment. In the ensuing political vacuum and with the National Conference leadership and cadre failing to rise to the occasion, a new generation of youth trained by Pakistan and steeped into the teachings of Jamaat-e-Islami began to take advantage of the developing situation. The law and order situation in the State started deteriorating from the beginning of 1988 with pro-Pakistani elements becoming increasingly active accompanied by stray incidents of triggering of explosive devices, particularly, in the city of Srinagar.

The disturbances, bandhs and acts of violence continued during 1989 with increased regularity and intensity, marking a show of defiance during the Republic Day and observing death anniversary of JKLF founder Maqbool Bhat on 5th February, as well as violent demonstrations triggered on February 13, to protest against Salman Rushdie's book *The Satanic Verses*. During the later part of the year a more sinister pattern of terrorist violence emerged with the targeted killings of well-known members of the minority

Kashmir Pandit community. The fundamentalist elements started enforcing new codes of Islamization on a sullen population by acts of arson and violence. Cinema houses and bars were attacked and destroyed, wine shops closed, video parlours ransacked. Acid was thrown on some Muslim girls in Srinagar city for walking on the streets without burqa. The first political murder took place on August 21, 1989, when terrorists killed a National Conference worker Mohammad Yousuf Halwai. The selective killings and attacks on minority community and intimidation of J&K Police, its ineffective leadership at the middle and senior levels further reduced the effectiveness of the police force. The terrorists thereafter stepped up the activities targeting the officials of State government as well as Intelligence Bureau to demoralize and undermine the administrative apparatus. The terrorists had succeeded in creating fear and apprehensions in the mind of the people of the Valley to such an extent that in spite of the presence of popular government at the helm of affairs, with a strong cadre based political organization at the grassroot levels, the participation of the people in November 1989 Parliamentary elections was dismally low. In Baramulla constituency 38235 votes were polled by an electorate of 698284, the Srinagar seat went uncontested and in Anantnag constituency as against an electorate of 736495, only 37377 votes were polled. A significant incident affecting the growth and course of terrorism in the State took place in the month of December in the kidnapping of Rubia Sayeed, the daughter of the then Union Home Minister Mufti, Mohammad Sayeed.

With the terrorists succeeding in securing their demands for release of their associates from police custody, following the kidnapping of Rubia Sayeed, there was a sudden spurt in their morale and activities. Correspondingly, the State police perceived this as a set-back in its efforts to contain the disruptive activities. During 1989, a total of 2154 terrorist related incidents took place including 49 attacks on the security forces and 840 cases of arson and explosion resulting in the death of ninety-two persons. This last figure included thirteen members of the security forces, three government officials, three politicians and equal number of members of judiciary. Destruction by torching of government property also took place on a significant scale which affected 191 government buildings, including 172 educational institutions. Some 427 private houses and 16 bridges were also destroyed.

The activities of terrorists spread beyond the confines of Srinagar city and also picked up momentum from the beginning of 1990 onwards. Amidst administrative collapse and destabilization of political structure, the Government of India appointed Jagmohan as the new Governor of the State on January 18, 1990. In protest, Dr. Farooq Abdullah and his cabinet resigned the same day creating a political vacuum in the State and with this the Central Government became directly involved with the rising discontent and terrorism in the Valley. A series of huge processions chanting pro-independence slogans started taking place in Srinagar city, seriously affecting the civil administration, working of the courts as well as offices of the State and the Central Governments. In January the same year seven central government employees were killed which included four of the Indian Air Force and three of the IB. During the next month, four government officials were killed including Director of Doordarshan Srinagar, Lassa Koul, and one IB official. These figures rose to nine during the month of March and included Deputy Director, Food & Supplies, and Assistant Director Information, Srinagar. These killings and other acts of intimidation, looting and in certain cases outraging the modesty of the women folk- coupled with_processions, chanting of slogans from mosques of Srinagar after evening prayers as a chorus on recorded cassettes and otherwise, through high-pitched loud speakers, general feeling of tremendous insecurity, an uncertain future and total lack of confidence in the ability of the administration to rein in the unfolding events triggered migration of the Kashmiri Pandit community and other non-Muslim population from the Valley on a scale virtually amounting to ethnic cleansing as a part consequence of the well-thought of strategy of Pakistan for complete Islamization of the Valley drawing a wedge between communities in pursuance of her basic objective of gaining territorial control over this area.

Kashmiri Pandit Migration

The first quarter of 1990, particularly the month of March, saw an euphoria in favour of "Azadi" in support of which large processions were taken out in Srinagar and elsewhere in the Valley. Some members of the minority community (Kashmiri Pandits) could occasionally be seen participating in such processions reluctantly. It was around this period that mosques and shrines were used by terrorists and their supporters for raising anti-India and pro-Independence slogans.

Though some terrorist groups outwardly promised a conditional safety to non-Muslims in the Valley so long as they were not too close to the establishment, yet prominent Hindus began to be targeted. These included Tikka Lal Taploo (BJP), P.N. Handoo (Asstt. Director of Information) and N.K. Gunjoo (Retd. Session Judge). Similarly many others continued to fall to the bullets of terrorists and panic spread through the minority community resulting in an exodus from the embattled Valley, their only fault being that they opposed secession of the State from the Union of India. The strategy appeared to be "kill one and frighten one thousand" and simultaneously arouse religious frenzy and spread hatred against the Pandits by describing them "Informers and agents of Brahminical imperialism".

The first to leave the Valley were the urban Pandits. Terrorist outfits operating in the Valley started identifying and denouncing intellectuals of the community followed by intimidation and violence, gunning down, kidnapping, molesting, etc. Places of worship and houses of Kashmiri Pandits also became targets of the secessionists. The cumulative effect of all this was mass exodus of Kashmiri Pandits from the Valley to seek shelter in Jammu and other parts of the country, particularly during the months of January-March 1990. A large number still preferred to stay back hopeful of a letup in the persecution violence and the reassurances by their friends and neighbours of the majority community. However, continued threat to life and property gained momentum as also tauntings, ridicule, accusations as well as warnings issued to the Pandits forced them to leave.

During 1990-93, 126 temples, 2050 houses and 183 shops of the Kashmiri Pandits were set ablaze and the number of Pandits killed reached a figure of 116. Till middle of 1990, 29,529 Kashmiri Pandit families migrated from the Valley and by 1992 this number rose to over fifty- five thousand. The years of terrorism also witnessed use of their houses by terrorists and ultimate destruction. In spite of policy statements and efforts of the Central and State governments, the Kashmiri Pandits' return to the Valley remains a distant dream.

In the year 1992, due to increasing pressure of the security forces in the Valley, the terrorists started subversive activities in remote areas of Doda, Kishtwar, Bhaderwah and Ramban in district Doda, and Mahore, Gool Gulabgarh and Chenani in district Udhampur where they had created local cadres. The terrorists in these areas used Gujjar *kothas* for shelter forcing them to provide food, and they also extorted money. The terrorists now started targeting minority community by kidnapping youth and killing them as well as looting/setting ablaze the properties. This caused panic resulting in migration of Hindus from their native villages to towns within the district and outside. The minority community members started fleeing to the safer places from such areas where terrorists had established their strongholds and had targeted the Hindus. Two hundred and thirty three families of minority community migrated to Udhampur, Jammu and Kathua districts. All requisite steps were taken to bring back migrants by creating new security posts in remote and vulnerable areas and organizing Village Defence Committees (VDCs) in Doda and Udhampur districts.

Kidnappings and Killings

Apart from the ethnic cleansing forcing the migration of a large segment of non-Muslims from the Valley, the terrorists also resorted to selective kidnapping and killings of important Muslim personalities with a view to spread terror amongst the local population and to silence the voice of dissent as well as intimidate pro-India elements and people who did not support their activity.

As already mentioned, the kidnapping of Rubia Sayeed by JKLF activists on December 7, 1989, was a landmark in the development of terrorism after early indicators of 1988-89. She was set free by her kidnappers in exchange of five jailed terrorists after seven days. The incident marked ascendancy of terrorism and in the following years a number of killings/abductions of intellectuals, religious scholars and political leaders were carried out. Some of the more important incidents during 1990 to 1996 which demonstrated the designs of terrorists to systematically destroy the politico-religious fabric are as follows:

- Mir Mustaffa, was elected to the State Assembly in 1987, as an independent candidate from Chadoora Constituency. He was very popular among the people of his constituency. He was the member of the Hanfia sect of Muslims and opposed to the fundamentalist doctrines propagated by Jamait-e-Islami (JEI) and would often criticize its activists in public. He was kidnapped by the terrorists of Hizbul Mujahideen on March 23, 1990, while on way to his home. He was tortured for two days and killed brutally.
- Vice Chancellor of Kashmir University and a well- known scholar of Islamic literature, Prof. Mushir-ul-Haq, was kidnapped by terrorists of JKLF on April 21, 1990, near the outer gate of Kashmir University, when he alongwith his Private Secretary was leaving the University Campus for offering prayers in a local mosque. The dead body of the scholar was recovered later.
- A towering personality and Chairman of the Awami Action Committee, Moulvi Mohammad Farooq, a popular religious personality of Kashmiri Muslims, who was held in great esteem by the people, was killed by the terrorists of Hizbul Mujahideen(HM) on May 29, 1990. Three terrorists of this outfit entered his residence at Nageen, and shot at the Moulvi at point blank range injuring him critically. He had a firm faith in peaceful political activity and communal harmony which did not suit the designs of Pakistan and the terrorist outfits created by the ISI.

- A veteran freedom fighter and one of the very few living contemporaries of Sheikh Mohammad Abdullah, Moulana Syed Masoodi had retired from politics and was living at Ganderbal. Since he was considered a pro-India political leader during his early days, he was considered a threat to the ongoing terrorism and was especially an eyesore for pro-Pak terrorist outfits. On December 13, 1990, a group of armed terrorists of Hizbullah entered his house and opened fire killing him in front of his family members.
- H. N. Wanchoo, a well-known trade union leader and a Human Rights activist, was one of the first persons who pleaded the cases of the arrested/killed terrorists in courts of law. He had filed a number of petitions in the J&K High Court in this regard. On December 5, 1992, he was kidnapped by terrorists from his Jawahar Nagar residence at Srinagar and his dead body was recovered from Karan Nagar area. Ashiq Hussain Dar and Mohammad Qasim Faktoo, Publicity Chief of Jamat-ul-Mujahideen (JUM), a pro-Pak outfit, after arrest revealed that Wanchoo was killed on the orders of JUM Chief, Hilal Ahmed Mir, as he did not want association of any Hindu with the movement.
- A renowned surgeon, Dr. Abdul Ahad Guroo, was considered an over ground worker and sympathizer of JKLF. He became the victim of inter-group rivalry between JKLF and HM after appearance of reports of his being in favour of resolving the Kashmir problem through dialogue. He was kidnapped by the terrorists of HM on March 31, 1993, while he was leaving Soura Medical Institute. His dead body was found on the road next morning.
- Prof Abdul Ahad Wani, Head of Department of Law of Kashmir University, was a well-known intellectual of the Valley and close to the ranks of JKLF. Dr. Wani was opposed to the violent means to solve political problems. He was kidnapped from his office in Kashmir University Campus on 31 December, 1993, and later his dead body was found on the road in Hazratbal area adjacent to the campus.

- Dr. Qazi Nissar, an eminent Islamic scholar and Mirwaiz of South Kashmir, was abducted by the terrorists of HM during the night of June 19/20, 1994, from his house in Anantnag and was shot dead near Bona-Dialgam from where his dead body was recovered. He had earlier been threatened by JEI for not toeing their line. His killing sparked wide-spread anti-Pakistan and anti-terrorism demonstrations in Anantnag.

Contours of Terrorism

The terrorist outfits incrementally stepped up violence resulting in increased number of incidents as well as areas of operation starting from 1989 and reaching its peak in 1993. The contours of Pakistan strategy in fomenting and sustaining terrorism in Jammu and Kashmir had following connotations:

- Recruiting and training of Kashmiri youth as terrorists;
- Providing safe sanctuaries to senior leaders of terrorist groups kept in Pakistan/POK to control and guide the terrorists;
- Supply of weapons and communication equipment as well as funneling of funds;
- Subversive propaganda through electronic and print media as also sending secessionist leaders from Jammu and Kashmir as well as POK to various countries abroad for influencing international opinion;
- Liquidation of Indian support structure in the State, including elimination of important personalities and suppression of all political dissent and opposition by spreading fear and terror; and
- Communalisation of the society to destroy the secular fabrics of the State.

The terrorists in the initial stage of this turmoil were dedicated youth belonging to the middle class families as they were the ones who had perceived to have suffered the most due to pick and choose policies of the Government. They were indoctrinated to believe that the only way left to their sustenance and progress was through Azadi Independence. Thus they became ready to make sacrifices for the so-called Azadi. This influenced them to take up arms to achieve their goal. Soon, however, some elements from the lower strata of the society including lumpens and criminals joined terrorism in order to make easy money and evade arrest and punitive action by the police by becoming jehadis. Pakistan provided training and weapons to anyone who went across to that side and the youth were trained to create disturbances and anarchy in the State. With the passage of time, criminality in these terrorists took precedence over the ideals and "Azadi". They didn't hesitate to kill their own people on slightest suspicion or minor difference of opinion by dubbing them as informers. Though at the beginning some of the people willingly provided shelter and food but with the increase of criminals in the terrorist groups their attitude began to change as a result the terrorists started kidnapping and killing innocent people who refused to give them the money and shelter. Terrorists also committed heinous crimes against the women whom they had promised Azadi, respect and honour. As the initial euphoria wore out, atrocities by terrorists against different sections of the society progressively increased resulting in disenchantment of the masses with the "movement'.

The terrorists also spread the arc of their activities south of Pir Panchal to the districts of Poonch, Rajouri and Doda including the hilly tracts of Udhampur district in Gool-Gulabgarh belt. This enabled the terrorists to increase the number of their hideouts as well as establish some training camps to impart local level training to the new recruits. Spilling over of the activities over the Pir Panchal also provided the terrorists with the opportunities to slip across the ridge line whenever the pressure of the security forces became intense on either side of the Pir Panchal range.

However, by 1992, the security forces had started tightening their grip over the terrorist activities as also vigil along the Line of Control (LoC) increased. In the interior areas the security grid had started taking shape with the induction of additional units of army and para military forces. The intelligence gathering mechanism of all different organizations, particularly the IB, was made more effective and the information from the local population started flowing appreciably. All this reduced the effectiveness of the terrorist operations and resulted in the differences in the ranks of the local terrorists who were no longer willing to undertake confrontation with the security forces and were content in sneak actions of throwing hand grenades or detonating explosive devices or firing from distance. ISI responded by adopting twin strategy of marginalizing the local terrorists and inducting in large number of mercenaries of Pakistan and of foreign origin particularly from Afghanistan to effectively take control of the terrorist outfits. Only a very few local commanders remained on the scene. The JKLF, which had pioneered the terrorist movement with the slogan of Kashmiriat, was made redundant, and terrorist organizations motivated and funded by the Pakistan, including Hizb-ul-Mujahideen, Allah Tigers, Muslim Jaanwaz Force, Ikhwan ul Musalimeen, etc., came to the fore.

The JKLF was not only marginalized, but motivated intelligence was fed to the security forces resulting in the elimination and arrest of important commanders of this outfit, further facilitating the transfer of control of the terrorist movement from indigenous elements to the foreign mercenaries. The process of taking over the terrorist movement by the foreign mercenaries masterminded by the ISI was completed in 1993-94, and it co-incided with the coming into being of two very pernicious and extremely fundamentalist diehard outfits of Lashkar-e-Toiba and Harkat-ul-Ansar. By the end of 1994, there were about twelve hundred foreign terrorists operating in the State. The induction of foreign mercenaries also ensured greater control of the ISI over the terrorist organizations and their command and control structure. These could be effectively used for creating incidents like destruction of Charar-e-Sharief and abduction of foreign tourists which could not only create internal problems for India but also attract the world attention thereby highlighting the Kashmir issue internationally. However, taking over of levers of control of terrorist organizations by foreign mercenaries, unleashing of mindless violence on the local population coupled with harassment that they were subjected to, alienated the local Kashmiris from the so-called movement. From 1990 to the middle of 1996, four hundred and thirty foreign mercenaries had been killed by the security forces and 108 were arrested. Amongst the killed 141 belonged to Pakistan/POK and thirty-five came from Afghanistan.

The year 1993 witnessed two important developments of far reaching consequences on the terrorist activities in the State – one was the siege of Hazartbal shrine and the other creation of All Party Hurriyat Conference (APHC). On October 15, 1993, the terrorists entered Hazartbal, the most famous shrine in the Valley, and replaced the two locks on the outer door of the strong room where the Holy Relic is kept. To ensure the safety of the Holy Relic, shrine and the public, the area was cordoned off by the security forces. The terrorists who were armed to the teeth and had taken some civilians as hostage inside the shrine were asked to free the hostages, come out of the shrine and surrender with the promise of safe passage to them. After holding out for a few days and later in desperation they set fire to the barracks in the vicinity of the shrine. However, the pressure of the security forces and tight cordon that had been thrown around the Hazaratbal area led to the surrender of the terrorists before the security forces on 16th November. A potentially dangerous situation was tackled imaginatively and Pakistani design for engineering large-scale disturbances was thus foiled. This success was soon followed by a well planned and competently executed operation in Sopore, clearing the entire town and areas around it of the terrorist elements. This was a major success for the security forces as Sopore till then used to be mentioned by the local press as well as Pakistani media as a "liberated zone". The successful tackling of the terrorist presence in Hazaratbal and the clearing of the Sopore town were major successes for the security forces and adversely affected the morale of the terrorists. Some analysts see these two operations as a turning point in favour of the State apparatus in its long struggle since the rise of terrorism in J & K.

From time to time efforts had been made by different conglomerate groups/parties to come together in various formulations to achieve diverse goals and objectives. In April 1986, one such endeavour was made in the form of Muslim United Front (MUF) under the chairmanship of Moulvi Abbas Ansari, by coalescing Islamic groups, with Quran and Sunah as the guiding principles, to "work for the protection of Islami Tashuakhus, Milli and awakening about Islamic tenets". The main constituents of the front were Umat-I-Islami, Jamat-E-Islami, Indian Union Muslim National Conference & Muslim Welfare Tulba. Each of these groups had specific view point regarding status of J&K State and ideology regarding the conduct of public life. The front started on a promising note but soon realized that the infiltration of certain elements had prevented forging of unity among various Muslim groups and suggested that the body should be renamed as 'Rabita Milat-E-Islami'. However, in September 1986, its constitution was released with the overt aim of uniting Muslims so that they could lead an honourable life and follow Islamic tenets. The front contested the elections of 1987 but failed to make a significant headway excepting four seats but raised the issue of rigging in the post election period.

With the advent of active phase of terrorism in 1990, yet another effort was made to bring various groups/parties together in March 1990 under the banner of Tehreek-i-Huriyat-i-Kashmir, a thirteen-party alliance. These parties were Islamic Students League, Islami Jamiat-e-Tulba, Jamat-e-Islami J&K, Muslim Conference, Dukhtaran-e-Milat, Mahaz-e-Azadi, Tahreek-e-Nifaz-e-Shariat, Islami Study Circle, Jamiat-e-Ehli Hadees, Hilal-e-Ahmer Relief Committee, Peoples League, Bar Association and Operation Balakote. It again met the same fate as the MUF due to tussle within it over the issue of leadership and began losing its hold following the arrest of its convener, Mian Abdul Qayoom, who remained under detention for over two years.

In September 1991, the JK Liberation Council was constituted with Moulana Abbas Ansari of Itihad-ul-Muslimeen as its patron-in-chief. Excepting after issuing occasional press releases, it became redundant very soon.

Against this backdrop yet another effort was made to form a body to "agitate for the goal of self-determination". All the erstwhile constituents of Tehrik-i-Azadi of Dr. Inayat Ullah Indrabi, attempted to come under a common umbrella in encompassing different sections of society including government employees and workers. This came to be known as All Party Meet which held its first session in December 1992, in which all constituents met and decided to form a common political platform under the banner of All Party Hurriyat Conference (APHC). The Conference held its first session on March 7, 1993, and entrusted the assignment of drafting the constitution to the Human Rights activist and ex-Chief Justice of J&K High Court, Mufti Bahau-ud-Din Farooqi, besides forming a sixteen-member executive body of the APHC.

APHC, a loose grouping of twenty-three outfits, was formally introduced to the people on September 3, 1993, which incidentally was Friday following Id-e-Milad, at Hazratbal, in which over 2.5 lacs people had gathered for prayers. Notable absentee was Syed Ali Shah Geelani, who again was absent from the formal session of APHC which was held at Mirwaiz Manzil in Srinagar on September 15, 1993. However, Geelani, on behalf of APHC, addressed a gathering at Hazratbal on September 17, and stated that one of the important purposes of the APHC was to bring into focus the Kashmir problem before the international community.

APHC assumed significance during the law and order problem created at Hazratbal shrine in October 1993, when some terrorists entered there and put the safety of the Holy Relic in jeopardy. But peaceful solution of Hazratbal problem resulted in humiliation in public for APHC.

APHC initially seemed to be an impressively broad based platform but the diversity and heterogeneity showed inherent contradictions as became evident from the fact that in a significant development all the major terrorist organizations decided that thenceforth all the calls of hartals would come from APHC and no call from any individual or party would be implemented. But calls of hartal and protest continued to be given by the individuals and parties unabated. The dissensions within the ranks of APHC have constantly come to fore as each constituent, over the years, has tried to establish its hegemony.

Though top APHC leadership had not been able to present a unified front, the group had been equivocal in its opposition to any form of elections. They insist on the right of self-determination for the people of Kashmir and emphasize that the sufferings during 'Jehad' were not to get an elected government. The APHC had been indulging in door to door campaign as part of its anti-election propaganda. They gave a call for "Jamia Masjid Chalo" for April 15, 1996, on the eve of Parliamentary elections and a similar call was issued on September 20, 1996, on the eve of 3rd phase of polling in districts of Srinagar and Budgam in the Assembly elections. On the eve of Assembly elections, the APHC leaders tried to vitiate peace repeatedly but timely action by the administration prevented situation from taking an ugly shape. Also, APHC leaders like Ali Shah Geelani and Abdul Gani Lone had sought and were provided security by the State government. Over the years there have been serious allegations that top APHC leadership had misappropriated funds received to finance terrorism.

By the end of 1994, the security forces had unmistakably gained an upper hand over the terrorists and the life of public in general as well as the functioning of the State government had returned almost to normal. Even though the terrorists could undertake isolated incidents of killings and intimidation of the local population, particularly in hilly and far-flung areas, and also occasionally engage the security forces in isolated incidents of violence, their presence had been reduced to the level of nuisance. The terrorist apparatus so carefully and laboriously planned, raised and sustained by the Pakistani rulers and ISI with the aim of annexing control of the State of J&K had nowhere reached the intended objective. The entire effort had almost petered out. There were certain developments and factors which helped the security forces in turning the corner and gaining control over the situation. The establishment of Unified Headquarters in May 1993, resulted in a more focussed and better coordinated conduct of operations against the terrorists by pooling resources of different security agencies as well as intelligence organizations. The re-establishment of effective intelligence network, particularly in the Valley, also helped this process and resultantly flow of information as well as cooperation from the local population increased considerably, further enhancing the operational capabilities of the security forces.

Creation of a three-tier security grid was also an effective tool in meeting the terrorist problem effectively. The first line of deployment was along the LoC which was suitably strengthened and gaps closed to the extent possible. Further in the rear the deployment of security forces was tactically sited with a view to intercept the infiltration and exfiltration efforts. The third ring of deployment was made around major towns and urban centers as well as vital installations. This pattern of deployment and intelligence based offensive actions against the terrorists paid handsome dividends. The creation of two sectors of Rashtriya Rifles, one each in Valley and Jammu divisions, further enhanced the efforts of the security forces.

Important parameters of terrorist related activities and the success of the security forces during the period 1990-1995 are given below:

Year	1990	1991	1992	1993	1994	1995
Terrorist violence	4158	3765	4817	5247	5829	5938
Civilians killed	1012	947	1167	1136	1189	1355
Attacks on Security Forces	732	1358	1934	2288	2675	2570
Security Force Personnel killed	154	168	177	195	198	234
Terrorists killed	550	844	819	1310	1596	1332

By the beginning of 1995, the security situation in the State had been brought well under control and the State government felt so confident in its grip over the situation, that the Government of India began hinting about the conduct of elections to the State Legislative Assembly leading to installation of the popular government. Soon the plans for conducting the elections became unmistakably evident. Since for the peaceful conduct of elections further blunting of the capability of the terrorists was a pre-requisite, the counter insurgency efforts were intensified with the augmentation of forces in certain areas and concerted efforts were launched in this direction all over the State.

4 The Die Is Cast

The improvement in the overall security scenario and also taking into consideration the increased cooperation being received from the local population towards combating terrorism in the State as well as realizing the yearning and the need of the people for the return of democratic government, prompted the Government of India to initiate election process in 1995 with a view to install a duly elected government. The elections were proposed to be held in the month of June though no formal notification was issued for this purpose. However, before setting into motion various measures leading to election to the Legislative Assembly of the State, the Election Commission of India had initiated moves in this direction.

Electoral Preparations

The 1989 general elections to the Parliament did not produce a stable government at the Centre. Fresh general elections had to be held in 1991. The ground conditions of the Kashmir Valley were considered to be so bad that the Law had to be amended by the Parliament to exclude the State of Jammu & Kashmir (also Punjab) from the purview of the general elections to the Parliament. In the meanwhile, Governor Jagmohan was replaced by G. C. Saxena, after the assassination of Moulvi Mohammad Farooq, May 27, 1990. Unsuccessful attempts for restoration of an elected government in Jammu & Kashmir continued. Possibility of revival of the dissolved Assembly was also explored. After conducting 1991 general elections to the Parliament, excluding the State of Jammu & Kashmir, the Election Commission of India appeared to be in no hurry to prepare for the general elections to the State Assembly. No intensive revision of electoral rolls had been ordered by the Commission since 1983. The general elections to the State Assembly held in 1987 had been conducted after a pre-poll summary revision of the electoral rolls. Because of the dissolution of the Legislative Assembly in January 1990 and with no immediate prospect of the next general elections in sight, the Commission did not order even the annual summary revisions of electoral rolls. When the Commission introduced a compulsory Photo Identity Card Scheme for all electors, Jammu & Kashmir was kept outside the purview of this scheme.

Gen K V Krishna Rao (Retd) succeeded G C Saxena in the Raj Bhawan in March 1993. Efforts of the State government to hold elections to the State Assembly were intensified. The Commission ordered summary revision of the electoral rolls in September 1994, after a gap of many years. Under the election law, the electoral rolls are required to be prepared and maintained in such manner as the Commission decides from time to time. It is to be noted that the two Central Representation of the People Acts govern the conduct of Parliamentary and State Assembly/ Council elections in the entire country except elections to the J&K State Legislative Assembly/ Legislative Council. For the latter, the J&K Legislature has enacted another "Jammu & Kashmir Representation of the People Act" which though is modeled on the lines of the Central Acts. The State Act recognizes the authority of the Election Commission of India in the same manner as is done by the Central Act. Therefore, unlike in respect of other States, the Election Commission of India issues two different notifications simultaneously-one each under the Central Act and the State Act-to cover the preparation of electoral rolls for use in the Parliamentary elections as well as the State Assembly elections respectively. Ultimately only one set of electoral roll is prepared for both the elections except that in respect of the Parliamentary elections, the electoral rolls are also prepared in Hindi language in Devnagri script in addition to Urdu language which is the official language of the State of J&K. The electoral rolls of Parliamentary constituencies also have a supplementary list of electors who are ordinarily residing in the State but are not its Permanent Residents as defined in the J&K Constitution and hence, are not eligible to vote during general elections to the State Assembly.

As per the notification issued by the Election Commission of India in September 1994, the draft electoral rolls were required to be published by displaying copies in the offices of the District Election Officers, Returning Officers, Assistant Returning Officers, Tehsildars, Block Development Officers, Panchayats, Municipalities and Wards, etc. Soon afterwards a news item appeared in a section of the press that some youth appeared in the local office of the Srinagar Municipality and made a bonfire of the displayed set of electoral rolls in full public view after holding out threats to the concerned officers against resorting to any such action in future. The Commission asked for a detailed report from the Chief Electoral Officer who confirmed the incident. He added that he was not in a position to follow and implement the instructions of the Commission issued in this behalf. After receiving such a reply from the Chief Electoral Officer, the Commission took only forty-eight hours in replacing him in consultation with the State Government as required under law. The Governor gave a free choice to the Commission from out of all senior officers. After a new CEO was appointed by the Commission, a prominent newspapers published from Chandigarh came out with an editorial that the State Government had definitely become serious in holding the Assembly elections for the first time as it had posted a very senior, experienced and competent officer as CEO to take up and execute the plan. With this the preparations for a gigantic, unprecedented and hugely challenging exercise of restoration of democracy in Jammu and Kashmir had commenced.

The instructions given by the Commission for commencing summary revision of the electoral rolls (in reference to the first of January, 1995) had already fallen flat. This had created a serious violation of the rules, as the state election machinery has no powers to take any action in digression of the policy instructions of the Commission. The Representation of the People Act is a unique law which mainly deals with the procedural aspects and empowers the Commission to solely exercise 'superintendence, direction and control' over the elections. The very first directions of the Commission had evoked non-compliance. Therefore, the immediate task was to convince the Commission that instead of applying their model procedure of preparation of the electoral rolls, they should apply a modified version of their instructions in respect of Jammu and Kashmir, particularly in the Valley which had been already notified as a "disturbed area" under the Disturbed Areas Act. This suggestion was accepted by the Commission which issued the modified version of their instructions about display of rolls and also shortened the list of the Electoral Revision Officers (EROs) and Assistant Electoral Revision Officers (AEROs). The election machinery undertook the responsibility of ensuring wide publicity to the programme, involvement of the political parties and political activists and making available adequate number of different types of application forms for addition, correction and deletion of the names. The last date for submission of such application forms had to be extended on demand of various political parties as at this point of time, at least the main political parties and their activists were enthused with the prospect of forthcoming general elections to the State Assembly. The response in Kashmir Valley was comparatively much less as majority of political parties and groups did not consider the situation to be conducive for holding of elections in near future.

A very important feature of our electoral law is that the voting is not compulsory and the onus for securing right of voting for self and for members of one's family by making an application within the prescribed time limit to the Electoral Revision Officer squarely lies on the elector. However, the law does not restrict scope for any elector to seek inclusion/ correction/ deletion of names only to the time of an intensive or summary revision of electoral rolls. He can approach the Electoral Revision Officer of his area at any other time of his choice but before the last date of filing of nomination papers by the candidates in pursuance to any election notification until completion of that election.

The Commission had come out with some more instructions to bring about improvements in the electoral process including permanent numbering of ballot boxes assembly constituency-wise through a process of embossing the number both inside and outside so that a ballot box issued to a particular polling station could be easily identified. Simultaneously, the Commission had desired that the ballot papers received from different polling stations should be mixed before counting of votes for any constituency so as to ensure secrecy.

Despite the fact that majority of the political parties were not in favour of conduct of elections at that time, the election machinery was required to remain in a high state of preparedness for holding of elections at short notice. Therefore, apart from going through the process of amendment of rules and procurement of additional number of ballot boxes and their numbering, the election department also procured the requisite quantity of paper for printing of ballot papers as also all the requisite stationary and material for use at the polling stations at the time of polls. Those who are somewhat familiar with the poll process would have the idea that over seventy different items are used at every polling station. Verification and sorting of all these items requires a large number of hands to work day and night. Electronic Voting Machines had not entered the arena to save many of these laborious problems in preparing for the polls.

A piquant situation was created because of existence of a Delimitation Commission which had been created long ago with the mandate that total number of seats of the Legislative Assembly, inclusive of 24 seats reserved for the electors belonging to the part of the State under occupation of Pakistan, were to be increased from 100 to 111 thereby increasing the available seats for elections from 76 to 87. Despite the fact that the draft report had been published on the July 4, 1989, and several Presiding Officers of the Delimitation Commission had come and gone, the report had not been finalized. The Delimitation Commission had to be persuaded by the State Government to expedite its report which was finally submitted on April 27, 1995. The report received several adverse comments from various political segments. However, as a Delimitation Commission report cannot be challenged in any court of law nor the Government can alter or modify it, it had to form the basis of future Assembly elections.

The new delimitation of the assembly constituencies necessitated re-notification of the constituency-wise lists of polling stations, inviting and dealing with objections to the new list of polling stations, physical verification of each building to meet the guidelines of the Election Commission of India in reference to space, number of electors, entry and exit points, safety and security of the locations, accessibility, etc. There was a direct clash of interests in respect of many of the proposed polling stations between the Election Commission's guidelines oriented to the convenience of the electors and the security requirements. As such, a most feasible and balanced combination of the two needs had to be forged by the District Election Officers in consultation with the political parties on one hand and considerations of security requirements on the other. Some of the polling stations had to be re-located in more secure buildings/ areas. In respect of polling stations with smaller number of voters, clubbing of polling stations was also resorted to. The numbering schemes of polling stations changed thus and fresh sets of polling-stationwise_brass seals and presiding officers' seals had to be quickly prepared.

It was in May 1995, when T. N. Seshan, the Chief Election Commissioner, accompanied by the Union Home Secretary visited Srinagar with a view to having an on the spot assessment of the situation. After meeting the representatives of the political parties and holding discussions at length with the State administration, law and order authorities and political parties, the Chief Election

Commissioner decided to have further clarifications from the State and the Central Governments regarding security arrangements, provision of polling staff, in case the local employees in some pockets were prevented from performing the election duty, and participation of the political parties. Another important challenge of the polling arrangements was how to enable the large number of Kashmiri Pandit electors who had shifted from their homes located in various constituencies of the Valley and lived in and around Jammu city, in Delhi and in many other places scattered all over the country. A lot of time had to be spent in collecting this data. Special AEROs in Jammu region and Delhi were appointed for them during the summary revision of the electoral rolls. Special arrangements were made to collect their applications and to forward them to the respective EROs (Deputy Commissioners) so that they were not deprived of their fundamental right of franchise. Internet links were established with all the Deputy Commissioners/ Collectors throughout the country for this purpose. Based on the experience of the summary revision of the electoral rolls, a detailed scheme was prepared for establishing special polling booths for Kashmiri migrants in the migrants' camps based on the concept of postal ballot for which Special Assistant Returning Officers were nominated at Jammu & Delhi.

Initial Moves

The beginning of election process was put into high gear during the month of April 1995, with five high-powered meetings taking place within a span of three weeks starting from April 10, 1995. First meeting took place in Jammu, which was convened by the Chief Secretary in which the Chief Electoral Officer of the State, the Additional Chief Secretary (Home) and all the Deputy Commissioners of the Jammu region participated for a brainstorming session relating to the conduct of the elections and various measures that were required to be undertaken to complete this stupendous task successfully. Similar discussions were held five days later at Srinagar with the Deputy Commissioners and other functionaries of Kashmir division. The Governor also addressed this gathering emphasizing the importance of task at hand and absolute necessity to complete it successfully, underlining the fact that elections to the Assembly and the return of the popular government would be the most befitting reply to Pakistan and its henchmen.

Third meeting in this series was held in the Ministry of Home Affairs, New Delhi, and was chaired by the Special Secretary in charge of Jammu and Kashmir Affairs Department, in which, apart from senior officers of the State Government, representatives of army and central para military forces (CPMFs) also participated. It was an extended brainstorming session in which all aspects of the elections, the problems anticipated and the proposed measures to overcome the difficulties were discussed, assessed and important decisions arrived at. Four days later this meeting was followed by another discussion between the State law and order authorities and a Central team wherein details were worked out regarding the requirement of transport and other logistic arrangements- needed for large scale induction and deployment of CPMFs which would arrive in the State to manage and oversee the peaceful conduct of elections. Last conclave in this series of discussions and consultations was again held in the Ministry of Home Affairs on May 1, 1995, where the plans so far drawn were further fine tuned and final decisions regarding availability of additional forces, the requirement of funds and various issues pertaining to coordination amongst different agencies were tied up. These meetings helped in forging together a functional team of senior officers who would be responsible, individually for optimum functional efficiency of their respective organizations and also work as a cohesive and well-knit team to achieve the ultimate objective.

As an outcome of these discussions and brain storming sessions, a blueprint of electoral process started emerging keeping in view the availability of resources as well as related constraints their of and taking into consideration the imperatives of ground situation as also considering the fact that the terrorist activities, though in control, were not fully eliminated. The requirement of considerable additional forces was a pre-requisite for the smooth conduct of elections. The deployment of these troops was planned in three phases, viz, requirement of additional troops in the pre-poll phase, forces that would be needed for actual conduct of elections and the deployment needed to ensure maintenance of security of people after the electoral process was completed at least for a couple of months. Whereas, the requirement for pre and post poll phases was worked out to at least 150 companies of CMPFs, the level of additional forces needed for actual conduct of elections depended upon the number of phases in which it would be completed. As it had become evident that not more than 130 companies of additional forces would be available for pre as well as post poll duties and not more than 400 additional of CPMFs would be mobilized and provided for poll duties, the planning of elections was had to be based on these assumptions. It was, therefore, proposed to go in for a five-phase election spread over 19 days to elect representatives of the people to the 87 Assembly constituencies. The total number of polling stations worked out to 6500 in fourteen districts of the State, (six each in Jammu region and Kashmir Valley and two in Ladakh region). Jammu district had the largest number of 933 polling stations while Kargil had the least number of 167 polling stations. Depending upon the security situation and the threat perception in the particular area each polling station was categorized into normal, sensitive and hyper- sensitive groups and the security of the polling stations accordingly planned. For normal polling stations, deployment of one section was considered adequate whereas for sensitive ones, and hyper-sensitive polling stations, this was increased to two and three sections respectively. In addition, appropriate complement of the State police for normal regulatory duties was also taken into consideration.

The contingency of likelihood of the State government employees, particularly in the Valley, not performing the election duty due to terrorist threats was also taken into consideration and contingency plans were prepared to work out the requirement of the polling staff that would be required to be got from outside the State, including over a thousand Urdu knowing

Presiding Officers. It was envisaged to get these polling persons drafted from amongst employees of the Central as well as other State governments.

As the preparations for elections picked up additional CPMFs started arriving in the State which were deployed in different districts. The districts of Srinagar, Baramulla, Anantnag and Jammu got a lion's share in the deployment of the additional forces.

In the pre-poll phase it was envisaged to provide security to the candidates and also for facilitating their interaction with voters, including holding of public meetings; and this process had started right from April itself with the arrival of additional troops and their deployment in various sensitive areas. Important political personalities were also provided, to the extent possible, bulletproof vehicles and escort vehicles for their security. This was an area where large shortages were felt and efforts were made to acquire these as quickly as possible. The facilities of making bullet proof vehicles in the country being limited, the need and requirement of such vehicles was always more than its availability. Apart from the area security and deployment of road opening parties, in Valley and Doda district, each candidate was to be provided with one section of Para-Military Force as static guard, one section as escort and two PSOs. In other districts of Jammu province, Leh and Kargil districts of Ladakh every candidate of a recognized party was to get one section for static guard and escort duty. Similarly it was decided to make available one bullet proof vehicle, one escort gypsy to the candidates of the Valley and Doda and for those belonging to other districts only an escort vehicle was to be given by the State.

As the availability of forces was much below the required level the entire polling process had to be planned in a manner so as to ensure optimum utilization of the available manpower and its movement from one set of deployment to another to cover as little distance as possible and for this four to five days gap between each phase was accordingly built in the proposed election schedule.

Logistics, mobility and host of other administrative arrangements needed serious consideration and deliberate planning. This was particularly so in the matter of providing transport to such large number of troops that were expected to arrive in the State and move from place to place for couple of months. As most of the units and sub-units were to move posthaste, they were not expected to carry their permanent transport along, and vehicles for their mobility within the state, on arrival by air or by trains, were to be taken care of and provided by the local police administration. For this, thousands of vehicles of different capacities were to be requisitioned and put into operation. In addition, a number of helicopters were also needed for carrying troops and polling parties to far-flung areas, casualty evacuation as also supervision of the electoral process. All this had to be planned, coordinated and achieved within a period of two months and this was a tall order. However, everyone connected with the poll process was putting in his best both individually as well as at the organizational level to ensure success of this huge enterprise. The task of coordination, deployment of force and working out security forces' requirement was given to the Central Reserve Police Force (CRPF). This required coordinating with the State officers to work out requirement and deployment of forces for each phase, tying up accommodation and other logistics, to liaise with the Ministry of Home Affairs (MHA) for properly equipping the troops in order to make them self sufficient to deal with the disturbed situation as also to cater to three basic necessities of transport, water and accommodation, etc. The coordination was also required with PMFs to tie up the force requirement, movement and accommodation, etc. All this had to be planned and executed in the face of the continued threat of terrorists acts of violence and sabotage, which was expected to pick up during the electoral process. To ensure proper coordination at all levels and smooth induction and deployment of troops after properly clubbing them and also to put in place an effective command and control structure, the Ministry of Home Affairs appointed Addl. Director General of Police, Northwest Zone of CRPF, M.B. Kaushal, as the Chief Coordinator for the elections. He was to function as such in addition to his existing duties. However, at the ground level, a very competent and dedicated officer, A.S. Gill, was posted as IG CRPF, Jammu and Kashmir, as well as designated as the State Coordinator of all the CPMFs for the purpose of conduct of elections. He was to play an important and crucial role in the successful completion of this task.

The seat of the government was in the meanwhile shifted to Srinagar as part of annual exercise and government offices opened in the summer capital on May 8, 1995. In spite of a call of general strike, a good number of government employees reported on duty which was quite encouraging and an indication of the positive turn around in the mood of the employees and the people in general. However, the trouble was brewing at Charar-e-Sharief, not far away from Srinagar. Pakistan's machinations to sabotage the election process were fully at work. The focus of the ISI attention was the holy shrine of Charar-e-Sharief, a symbol of communal amity and religious beliefs of the people of Kashmir. Due to increasing pressure from the security forces, the terrorists had started taking shelter in different mosques and places of worship considering these to be secure and in the knowledge that security forces would use utmost restraint in such places. The presence of terrorists around Charar-e-Sharief was first noticed in January 1995, when encounter with the security forces had taken place around that area. By the first week of February, zzzzzzzzza good number of local and foreign terrorists headed by an Afghan war veteran Mast Gul had entered and taken control of the Charar-e-Sharief shrine. The security forces laid a cordon around that area and blocked all routes of exit. Since the shrine was in the middle of a built up area it required a large number of troops to fully seal the area and due to paucity of additional forces, some gaps did remain in the cordon thrown around by the security forces. The government announced amnesty for those who would surrender before the security forces to ensure safety and sanctity of the shrine and the lives of the innocent people living in the Charar town.

Various steps were taken by the administration to pursuade the terrorists to surrender, including sending local representations to establish contact with them as it was not intended to enter the shrine forcefully lest it get damaged in the process or may willfully be harmed by the terrorists. As the encounter between the terrorists and the security forces picked up, in and around the town, the local population started migrating to safer places. This stand off carried on for over two months with the government expecting repeat of the success achieved during the Hazaratbal episode in October/November 1993. But this time the terrorists had different intentions, obviously under instructions from across the border. In any case they had no respect or reverence for the Sufi shrines like the Charar-e-Sharief which are spread all across the State and represent the peculiar and particular aspect of the religious belief of the majority of people of the State. On 9th May, the town was put on fire by the terrorists to create pressure on the security forces and make good their escape. Over six hundred houses and one hundred shops were destroyed and damaged in the inferno that engulfed major portion of the town in spite of the best efforts by the fire brigade. All the terrorists withdrew from bunkers they had established in various parts of the town and regrouped in the shrine and mosque buildings and fortified it further. During the night of 10th and 11th May, in a desperate attempt to breakthrough the security forces cordon, the terrorists set the shrine on fire. A fierce encounter ensued between the terrorists and the security forces in which about twenty terrorists were killed and a top ranking terrorist of Harkat-ul-Ansar, Abu Jindal, was captured alive. However, the leader of this nefarious group Mast Gul succeeded in escaping.

Burning of shrine at Charar-e-Sharief sent a wave of anger and consternation amongst the people of the Valley as was expected. It was also a major setback to the overall law and order situation. The people came out in large numbers in urban centers, to give vent to their anger and frustration on this senseless destruction of one of their holiest shrines. For a couple of days, curfew had to be imposed in Srinagar and towns of Anantnag, Baramulla and Sopore. However, by 13th May part relaxation in curfew was possible in Srinagar, and in rest of the Valley the situation was well under control. As part of the pre-poll induction of forces which had started arriving, the presence of Central Reserve Police Force troops came in very handy in the maintenance of law and order situation. However, the fact remains that in spite of Pakistan's propaganda machine working overtime, the people of the Valley had in their collective consciousness realized that this mischief and act of sacrilege was a deliberate action on the part of the foreign terrorists headed by Mast Gul under instructions from Pakistan and that the security forces were in no way involved in it. The latter could only be blamed, in an indirect manner for not having been successful in neutralizing the terrorists holed up in–side the shrine. Had the people of the Valley believed otherwise, it would have been impossible for a few additional battalions of the Central Reserve Police Force to control the collective anger and uprising of the people if they had ever felt that the security forces had a hand in the destruction of the Charar-e-Sharief. Those who know the Valley and its people and also the way the agitations had taken place when the Holy Relic became missing for a few days during 1963 from Hazaratbal shrine can very well imagine reaction of the people of the Valley if they had reached to the conclusion that Charar-e-Sharief was not destroyed by the terrorists and the security forces had a hand in fiery devastation of the shrine. That the population of the Valley had reached the right conclusion was further confirmed when Mast Gul surfaced in there, sometime later and was accorded a hero's welcome in Pakistan, sponsored by Pakistan government and its media.

In spite of the incident of Charar-e-Sharief and subsequent disturbances, the poll preparations continued. A meeting of the Returning Officers of the constituencies in the Valley was convened on 20th May, in which a detailed briefing was given to by the State Chief Electoral Officer and other senior officers in charge of law and order. It was evident that while a good number of officers were prepared to contribute for the success of elections, some of them were apprehensive about their personal safety and security of their families. While four senior officers working as Returning Officers came to Additional Chief Secretary (Home) requesting for enhancing their personal protection, next day

Deputy Commissioner of Anantnag said that in case he was forced to work as a Returning Officer he would rather go on leave and ask for a change of posting.

The procurement of defence stores, putting up of transit camps for the convenience of all arriving Central para military forces and requisition of vehicles continued at a hectic pace. Even though no date for the elections had been fixed, these were still expected to take place towards the end of June or beginning of July.

As mentioned earlier, T.N. Seshan, Chief Election Commissioner, came to Srinagar for on the spot study on 27th May and met Advisors to the Governor, Chief Secretary, DGP, Additional Chief Secretary(Home) and senior officers of Central para military forces and intelligence agencies. He was also briefed by the Corps Commander based in Srinagar. The Chief Election Commissioner also held a round of discussions with various political parties and leaders and returned to Delhi the same day. After a couple of days it was revealed that the elections were postponed indefinitely and that these would now be possibly held any time during October/November. With this, the first round of preparations for holding of Assembly elections came to an end. Even though no specific reasons were given for this change, it was evident that this was due as much to the post Charar-e Sharief disturbances as because of unlikelihood of participation of broad spectrum of political elements in the proposed elections. Some of the major political parties had opposed the idea in their meeting with Seshan.

The postponement of elections gave a much-needed breathing space and more time for better planning and mobilization of resources. This included further fine-tuning of security classification of the polling stations, re-assessment of forces required and phasing of elections. Greater attention could be paid to the ground level problems of stationing the troops once they moved in and to cater to their basic requirements of accommodation, food, water, electricity, etc., as well as their organized movement from Jammu and Srinagar to their subsequent deployment. Although some of the troops that had come for the poll duties returned to their original locations, the pre-poll force of 176 coys of Central para military forces, however, stayed back. These were utilized for further improving the security situation by undertaking anti-terrorist operations, strengthening the existing security grid as well as manning important points and installations. Earlier only one Company each of Central Reserve Police Force was available to the district SPs for augmentation of their law and order reserve. With the arrival of the additional pre-poll force, the Special Operations Groups of the State police became more effectively operative. Consequently, two battalions were earmarked for Srinagar city and one each for Baramulla and Anantnag. These proved a big asset to the State acting as a catalyst in the form of additional trained manpower and enabled the State police to stand more firmly on its own feet and meeting the terrorists' challenge on its own steam.

Nothing much of consequence happened during the month of June except that Lt.Gen. M.A. Zaki (Retd), who was functioning as security advisor to the Governor, tendered his resignation on 22nd June. It was widely believed at that time that unlike Hazaratbal incident where there was no dearth of claimants for the credit of successful end of the siege of the shrine, like all failures, no body was prepared to take responsibility for the failure to save the shrine of Charar-e-Sharief and that General Zaki was made the scapegoat by the establishment. The next day Lt. Gen. D.D. Saklani (Retd) who was already functioning as one of the four Advisors to the Governor and looking after the departments of Tourism, and Information also took over as Advisor in charge of security. Soft spoken General in his usual unobtrusive and methodical ways quietly beefed up the security apparatus of the State, and coalesced the police, army and CPMF as well as the intelligence agencies into a highly effective and cohesive group, deeply committed to the task at hand.

After the destruction of Charar-e-Sharief, the ISI tried to create further stumbling blocks in the efforts to normalize the situation by abducting foreign tourists in the months of June and July.

On June 7, 1994, two British nationals, namely, David Nackay and 14-year old Kim Housego were abducted from Pahalgam (Aroo) by terrorists of Harkat-ul-Ansar. However, both of them were released by the terrorists unharmed on 23rd June. Hitherto unknown terrorist outfit Al-Faran kidnapped four foreign tourists, namely, D.F. Hutchings and John Childs (US), P.S. Wells and K.C. Monighan (British) on July 4, 1995, from Lidderwat Pahalgam. On 7th July, the outfit abducted two more foreigners, namely, Dirk Hasert (German) and Ostro Hans Christian (Norweigian). The next day one of the abductees, John Childs (US), escaped from the clutches of the terrorist outfit and was rescued by the security forces who were searching for the foreigners and airlifted him to safety. The outfit demanded release of some hardcore terrorists which was not accepted by the Government. On 13th August, the dead body of abducted Norweigian tourist Ostro Hans Christian with severed head was recovered from Panzmulla in Anantnag district. Several appeals were made by political, religious and other organizations including the Government to set free the hostages on humanitarian grounds but the outfit did not pay any heed and continued to hold four foreign tourists as hostages. It is believed that they have been killed by the terrorists, though their dead bodies have not been located so far.

Immediately after the conclusion of the annual Amarnath pilgrimage, the preparations for elections to the Legislative Assembly were resumed with a meeting in the Ministry of Home Affairs on August 29, 1995, and the threads of conceptual planning, arrangements and logistic provisions were picked up from where these were left three months earlier. M.S. Gill, one of the Election Commissioners, visited Srinagar and held discussions with the Chief Secretary, the Chief Electoral Officer as well as senior functionaries of the State government, Central Reserve Police Force and intelligence agencies. He was informed that insofar as electoral arrangements were concerned, a lot of headway had been made. He also reviewed the position with the political parties.

Several writ petitions had been filed by various interested parties against the new Delimitation Order. However, there was no order from the courts, restraining the Government from not acting on the Order of the Delimitation Commission. EROs/AEROs stood appointed by the Election Commission for all the newly delimited 87 constituencies. Electoral rolls corresponding to January 1, 1995, as the qualifying date had been published by the EROs/AEROs on May 26, 1995. Returning Officers (ROs) and Assistant Returning Officers (AROs) had also been appointed by the Election Commission for all the 87 constituencies. They had been provided with copies of Handbook for Returning Officers, copies of relevant Act and Rules and requisite forms needed during the period of nominations. Briefing sessions were held with them at Jammu and Srinagar in May 1995. Fresh lists of polling stations for all the 87 constituencies had been prepared and were approved by the Election Commission. Some minor changes proposed by the District Elections Officers were examined and incorporated. All the election material needed for the polls, including paper for ballot-papers had been procured. Printing of forms and envelopes had also been done. All serviceable ballot boxes in stock had been serially numbered for all districts. One thousand new big size ballot boxes had also been procured and got serially numbered to meet the requirement of larger number of voters. Repairs and repainting of boxes had also been undertaken. Arrangements had been initiated to build up stocks of essential commodities for use during the forthcoming winter period, keeping in view additional demand which would be generated due to conduct of elections. Poll parties were being constituted for all the districts in Jammu, Kashmir Valley and Ladakh regions. For the Valley, a request had also been made to the Department of J&K Affairs to provide staff from outside the State as a contingency plan, if any problem arose in detailing local staff on election duty.

Insofar as the requirement of CPMFs was concerned the demand was pegged at the same level as it was during the earlier attempt, in addition to 176 Companies already available for pre-poll duties. However, there were certain major constraints that the Election Commission was apprised of. These included, non-availability of requisite number of bullet proof vehicles as well as arrangements that were still required to be made for bringing polling personnel from outside the State for conduct of polls in Kashmir division as well as in Doda district of Jammu region. Also due to the approaching winter a new requirement had arisen for making adequate arrangements for winter clothing and bedding for the additional troops as well as the polling personnel. This could run into thousands of arctic tents, large number of bukharies, sleeping bags and requisite stocks of hard coke for keeping the troops warm. At an average the additional clothing requirement for one Company worked out to fifty each of mattresses and snow goggles, one hundred each of sleeping bags, coat parkas, balaclava caps, woolen trousers and snow boots, etc. Procurement of this large quantity of special clothing and equipment was to be one of the major constraints being felt at that time.

By the first week of October the State government assessed that the security situation was conducive for holding of elections to the Legislative Assembly. However, political management needed greater attention to ensure adequate participation in the electoral process. The demand of National Conference for greater autonomy to the State, a pre-requisite for the participation of the party in the elections, dissensions and differences within the State unit of Congress-I and efforts for involvement of moderate elements in the Hurriyat Conference and some of the terrorist outfits in the electoral process needed greater and more focussed attention of the Central government. Taking all relevant factors into consideration, the State government felt and recommended that the elections could be held during the month of November and proposed a four-phase poll spreading over seventeen days. At the same time, it was also recognized by the state administration that irrespective of when the elections are held the Pak game plan would be to disrupt this process. For this it would endeavour to escalate violence and create disturbances. Even from this point of view, holding of elections during winter months was considered more prudent. However, the most difficult aspect was not the management of security issues but administrative and logistic arrangements.

At the political level, during the month of October, increased political activity was witnessed both in Srinagar as well as in New Delhi. The focal point of these efforts was to bring around Dr. Farooq Abdullah and his National Conference to participate in the elections as also to pep up and reorganize the Congress-I. Prime Minister P.V. Narasimha Rao as President of All India Congress Committee took the matter directly in his hands to tackle both these issues. Although he was not able to resolve the internecine problems within the State unit, his efforts to bring around the National Conference to join the elections did appear at one time heading towards success. He issued a much awaited statement from his foreign visit to Burkina Fasso in the beginning of November 1995. This statement was expected to yield positive results in the political circles as it was expected that the Prime Minister would indicate the contours of greater devolution of powers to the State as was being demanded by the National Conference. However, he only indicated the willingness of the Central government to consider cosmetic changes like rechristening the Governor of the State as Sader-e-Riyasat and Chief Minister as Prime Minister and said that further course of action would be decided by the coordination committee in consultation with the elected representatives of the State. This generated considerable discontentment amongst the political circles in the State, particularly the National Conference leadership.

Full Election Commission comprising the Chief Election Commissioner and the two Election Commissioners undertook another visit to Leh, Srinagar and Jammu in November 1995, reaching Srinagar on 8th November. The exercise of consultations and discussions with the political parties, state administration, law and order authorities, central security and intelligence agencies etc., was more elaborately repeated. A slight improvement in the attitude of political parties was noticed with a couple of political parties actually wanting conduct of elections. A notable opposition came from the National Conference, which was categorical that the ground conditions were not conducive for holding of polls. The Commission left for Delhi on the 10th. The

National Conference working committee formally decided on 9th November not to participate in the elections as its demand on autonomy had not been agreed to by the Centre. After deliberating upon all the connected matters at length, the Commission declared through a press conference held in Delhi the very next day that they were not recommending the holding of elections to the Jammu & Kashmir State Assembly at that stage as the ground conditions were not conducive for the exercise. By this time, holding of elections in the State had not only become an imperative political need, it was also seen to be a matter of government's prestige. However, the Election Commission were obviously more interested in holding a credible election. In the meanwhile, the general elections to the Parliament scheduled for early summer of 1996 were approaching fast.

In view of the yet another postponement of the elections, the President's rule which was last extended for a period of six months on July 17, 1995, had to be further extended for another six months in January 1996. Also due to the postponement of the elections and approaching winter, there was pressure from the commanders of the Central para military forces to request for de-induction of their troops from the State to their base headquarters. In spite of the efforts by the State government and law and order authorities to the contrary and forceful assertions that presence of at least 176 Companies on pre-poll election duties was bare minimum requirement to keep the heads of the terrorists down in order to ensure appropriate climate for the conduct of elections next May, 64 Companies were pulled out denuding the pre-poll level of forces to 112 Companies. With this limited force the State authorities had to manage the difficult task of not only maintaining the edge that had been acquired over the activities of the terrorists but also ensuring security of political leaders and activists who, in the wake of preparations for the conduct of elections twice during 1995 had become active once again after lying low for the past six years.

In March 1996, the schedule for Parliamentary Elections in the country was announced by the Election Commission. The statement also mentioned intentions of the Election Commission to simultaneously hold elections to the Parliamentary seats in the State of Jammu and Kashmir. A few days later, the three-phase schedule for elections to the Parliamentary constituencies was notified. For the six Parliamentary constituencies of the State, three sub-phases were decided. The elections for Jammu and Ladakh seats were to be held on 7th May, coinciding with the third and the last phase for the rest of the country, for Baramulla and Anantnag on 23rd and in sub-phase three, elections for Srinagar and Udhampur constituencies were to take place on May 30, 1996. Immediately after the announcement of Parliamentary elections, and as had happened on earlier occasions, ISI prompted its terrorist organizations to engineer another nefarious incident with a view to forestall the third government attempt to enable the people to exercise their franchise in the State after a lapse of seven years.

On March 24, 1996, a group of JKLF terrorists led by their self-styled Commander-in-Chief Basharat Raza, armed with weapons, tried to force their entry into the Hazratbal shrine. The JKAP guard posted at the shrine asked the terrorists to get frisked which the latter refused and resented and fired on JKAP personnel which was returned. During the firing nine terrorists, including their Commander-in-Chief, were killed. One SI, one ASI and three constables of the JKAP guard also received bullet injuries. The Sub-Inspector later succumbed to his injuries. In the melee which followed the incident of firing, some armed terrorists managed to enter the shrine premises. Some dead bodies of the terrorists lying outside were also carried inside the shrine by these terrorists. Upon this the security forces laid a cordon and asked the holed terrorists to surrender but instead they moved out of the shrine to a nearby building, and threatened the respectables of the area who mediated. Thus, even though threat to the shrine came to an end on 26th March, the presence of terrorists in the vicinity continued to be a cause for concern prompting the security forces to further increase their pressure on the terrorists. However, on 30th March early in the morning J&K Police cordoned off the building in the occupation of JKLF terrorists and asked them to vacate it and surrender with their weapons. Three terrorists surrendered in response to the call. In addition, three women and two children came out of the building. Thereafter firing by the terrorists started from the house, which was returned. In the exchange of fire, 24 terrorists inside the building were killed and 8 AK rifles recovered. Six jawans of J&K Police also received injuries. The resolute and effective handling of the incident enabled the authorities to get rid of terrorists in the vicinity of Hazratbal shrine.

The State government constituted a high powered committee to further strengthen the security of Hazaratbal shrine and areas around it as also issued instructions for mounting fullest vigil to forestall any further attempts by the terrorist outfits to put obstacles in the conduct of forthcoming elections.

5

The Preparations

The announcement of the schedule for Parliamentary elections created a flutter and caused a flurry of activity in the political circles, main political parties and certain smaller outfits. Although low key political activities had been continuing almost unabated in Jammu and Ladakh regions, some progress in this direction was made during 1995 in the Valley also. A few of the political leaders, mostly belonging to National Conference, who had stayed away from Kashmir during the last six years, had started returning to the Valley. The State government had made requisite arrangements for their housing, security, transport and other facilities to facilitate the revival of the political climate in Kashmir. The legislators' hostel in Srinagar was renovated and secured for exclusive use by political personalities. In addition certain government buildings were earmarked for this purpose as also a couple of hotels taken on hire in security zone areas. The beginnings of political stirrings in the Valley were further stimulated by preparations for the conduct of the Assembly elections during 1995. However, three main factors defined and circumscribed the re-emergence of public men on the scene as also expected public participation in the political resurgence. The first was the demand of the National Conference for greater autonomy to the State within the Indian Constitution as a pre-requisite for its participation in the electoral process. Unresolved dissensions and differences within the State Congress Party was another important ingredient affecting the political climate. Serious efforts at various levels were made for involvement of the moderate elements amongst the Hurriyat Conference and terrorists aimed at their participation in the electoral process.

One of the evident failures of the terrorist movement, over the past years had been the absence of the emergence of political leadership which could strive to channelise and represent the aspirations of the people of the State, particularly of the Valley, projecting itself as a viable alternative to the traditional political elements which the overground terrorist outfits were trying to discredit. The apparent reason for this was that the ISI, while organizing terrorism in the State, had followed the Afghanistan pattern. Consequently, a surfeit of groups were created with each acting independently, reporting only to its handler across the border. Thus the armed wings of various outfits were dictating to, rather than taking instructions from their respective front organizations. Therefore, stunted growth of political elements in their ranks was inherent in the situation. The All Party Hurriyat Conference, claiming to be the focal political point of all secessionist and disgruntled elements, was at best a loose collection of disparate elements collected together more on a negative platform of questioning the State's accession to India rather than any constructive political programme. Therefore, on the political scene with none of the APHC leaders having significant following amongst the people, the field was still open to the traditional political parties and personalities even within the Kashmir Valley.

Apart from BJP's influence in isolated pockets in Jammu region, Congress and the National Conference had remained the only two major political entities in the politics of the Jammu and Kashmir State. These were expected to play a very significant role whenever the democratic rule was to be restored in the State. Traditionally the Congress had been more dominant in Jammu and Ladakh regions, whereas, the National Conference held its sway in the Valley. However, the influence of these two parties was not necessarily confined to any geographical area and they had the capacity and potential to influence and win the confidence of significant sections of the voters in all the three parts of the State, provided they could put forth an imaginative political agenda, ensure motivated and dedicated cadre and effective leadership. During the first six years of disturbances almost the entire leadership of Congress and the National Conference had either remained dormant or migrated to Jammu.

With the improvement in the security situation and significant turn in the mood of the people, important leaders of National Conference and Congress were offered government accommodation, security and transport facilities and encouraged to return to Valley and re-establish their contacts with the public. The aim was to make them feel safe enough to resume political activity which was a pre-requisite for starting of political process leading up to holding of the Assembly elections and forming of a democratic government. Still except for brief stirrings during May-June and then again in October-November 1995, when holding of elections became a distinct possibility hardly any effort was made by them to channelize the aspirations of the people and their yearning for the return of democracy. In the name of political activity some rallies and meetings were organized in Jammu and Ladakh regions with practically nothing happening in the Valley, in spite of considerable improvement in the security scenario.

The Congress had also to cope up with its intra-party squabbles and dissensions within its ranks. The leadership of State unit as well as the party high command had failed to resolve this malady thereby reducing its effectiveness even in areas where it traditionally enjoyed a greater advantage. On the other hand National Conference, with its stand against the Assembly elections in November 1995, and insistence on greater autonomy, had been able to recapture some of its ground in the Valley. Still it was not clear whether the party could build upon the foothold it had gained and also whether it would be willing and prepared to participate in the ensuring electoral contest.

The intra-group rivalry amongst the terrorists and the emergence of counter terrorist groups had also become a relevant factor in the emerging political climate. It had, on the one hand, appreciably curtailed the once considerable striking capacity of the insurgents and on the other hand inculcated political aspirations in the hearts and minds of the former terrorists. However, in the absence of a strong rallying point for a composite political outfit representing the political ideology and aspirations of these former insurgents, their personal influence and ambitions were too scattered and limited to make any dent in terms of forming a cohesive political structure. The most well- known persona from amongst them who emerged was Kuka Parrey but his influence too was confined to a few villages around his residence. This was the broad political scenario prevailing at the time of the announcing of schedule for the Parliamentary elections, which set in motion a high degree of all round activity in the administrative echelons both at the Centre as well as the State. The entire machinery was put into top gear.

The Conceptual Planning

With the general elections to the Parliament nearing, it had become abundantly clear that there was no intention of any concerned quarter that J&K State would be again excluded through another amendment in law as was done during 1991 general elections. Therefore, a flurry of activity had commenced on the following tracks to make the electoral process more effective:

- Amending the laws to provide for harnessing the employees of Government of India, other State Governments, Public Sector Undertakings, Autonomous Bodies and even Commercial Banks and Financial Institutions so that list of employees could be prepared by the Ministry of Home Affairs and the services of these employees would be placed at the disposal of the Election Commission of India for conduct of polls and counting of votes, if adequate local manpower was not available in the Valley of Kashmir as also to provide for a special scheme of voting for the Kashmiri migrant electors;

- Organizing and providing adequate security forces and security arrangements together with the logistics for ensuring safety of the polling stations, polling materials and polling staff together with security of the candidates, their elections and polling agents, workers and electors in general;
- Preparation of all the requisite notifications and orders and establishing a coordinated mechanism of providing electoral rolls, movement and transport of ballot papers and elections material, boarding and lodging of the polling staff, storage of election material, arrangement for escorted movement of ballot boxes after polling, their storage under safe custody and counting arrangements; and
- Creating legal provisions for a special set up of election officers anticipated to meet the ground conditions.

The new legal provisions required careful thinking and drafting in a time bound manner. This had to be handled by the election department working under the direct control of Election Commission of India and duly supported by the State Government which had to make necessary formal recommendations to the Government of India, seeking Commission's approval and issuing the statutory notifications. All the legal amendments were processed in time with a clockwork precision and the requisite amendments were gazetted after obtaining the assent of the President of India. The following amendments and notifications came into existence.

President's Act no. 3 of 1995–

Replaced the old Section 61 of the Act which provided for countermanding of the election in case of death of any contesting candidate. The new Section 61 provided that the death of any contesting candidate would not result into countermanding of election. It was also provided that only in case of death of a candidate set up by a recognized political party, polling shall be adjourned and the concerned recognized political party would be asked to nominate a substitute candidate and a fresh date of polling would be notified.

President's Act no. 4 of 1995 resulted into–

i. Insertion of Section 9A under which Chief Electoral Officer, District Election Officers etc., shall be deemed to be on deputation to the Commission during the period of elections;

ii. A proviso was added to Section 33A enabling the Commission to appoint the same person to be ARO for more than one constituency;

iii. Section 36A was inserted to enable the District Election Officers to establish the polling stations outside the territorial limits of a constituency and to enable the Commission to notify class of persons who would not be in a position to give their votes in the polling stations set up within the territorial limits of the constituency;

iv. Section 39A was inserted to provide that Returning Officers, Presiding Officers etc., shall also be on deputation to the Commission during the conduct of elections;

v. Section 68A was inserted to provide for adjournment of polling and countermanding of elections in case of booth capturing;

vi. Clause (c) was added to Section 70 to provide for use of postal ballot facility by the migrant electors; and

vii. An explanation was added below Section 85 to exclude expenditure incurred by a political party from the ceiling prescribed in respect of the individual candidates.

President's Act 1996 provided for the following:

i. Section 41(d) was amended to provide that the polling day could be fixed by the Commission after 14 days counted from the last day of withdrawal of nominations instead of minimum 20 days existing earlier;

ii. Section 142A was inserted to define the offence of booth capturing and to provide punishment for the same;

iii. A proviso was added to Section 44 (1) stipulating that a candidate not set up by a recognized political party was not to be deemed to have been properly nominated unless his nomination paper was subscribed by 10 proposers being electors of the same constituency; and

iv. Section 45 was amended to increase security deposit of each candidate to Rs. 5000 (Rs. 2500 in case of candidates belonging to Scheduled Castes).

The amendments in the Act resulted into corresponding comprehensive amendments in the Conduct of Election Rules. A self-contained Part III (A) was added to the Rules to provide for a comprehensive scheme of voting by the Kashmiri migrant electors. The modifications made in the Act and the Rules also resulted into notifications of comprehensive guidelines and instructions from the Commission about the manner in which the provisions of the new Rules were to be implemented by all the concerned officers of the election department.

While the State government wanted the Parliament elections and the general elections to the State Assembly to be held simultaneously, the Election Commission, relying on their own assessment of the ground conditions, did not subscribe to this viewpoint mainly on the consideration that the biggest political party of the state, namely, the National Conference whose cadre had borne the maximum brunt of selective killings at the hands of the terrorists had declined to participate in the elections. The Election Commission were not sure whether all arrangements of security promised by the Government of India and the State Government together with arrangements for procuring cent per cent manpower from outside the State to actually conduct the polls would culminate into credible amount of polling. Therefore, they decided not to recommend simultaneous conduct of elections to the State Assembly in terms of the Jammu & Kashmir Representation of the People Act while the recommended schedule of Parliamentary elections sent to the President of India included Jammu & Kashmir in strategic third, fourth and fifth phases. Parliamentary elections in the rest of the country were to be completed in three phases and a part of the third, the fourth and fifth phases were meant to cover parliamentary constituencies from J&K (two in each phase). This phasing ensured that even if the elections to any of the six seats of Jammu &

Kashmir would run into difficulties, the results of general elections to the Lok Sabha would not be affected and completion of general elections would still be notified. This also facilitated the deployment of central para-military forces which would move from other regions or States to J&K for deployment after the first two phases at the national level would be over.

The notification for holding Parliamentary elections in the country was issued on March 9, 1996. The third and the last phase of polling in the rest of the country was scheduled for May 7, 1996, and included polling for two parliamentary constituencies located in Jammu & Kashmir, namely, Jammu and Ladakh which were considered to be quite safe from the point of view of terrorism related law and order and security arrangements, deployment of manpower, electioneering by the political parties and their candidates. In the fourth phase of polling, parliamentary constituencies of Baramulla and Anantnag were scheduled to go to polls on 23rd May, 1996. The last phase of polling was scheduled for the remaining two constituencies of Srinagar in Kashmir Valley and Udhampur in Jammu region on the 30th May. Because of a large urban component of Srinagar Parliamentary constituency having been infected by terrorism, apprehended to cause low voter turnout, it was included in the last phase. The Udhampur Parliamentary constituency of Jammu region comprised three districts of Kathua, Udhampur and Doda. While Kathua and Udhampur were by and large free from terrorism, the sparsely populated vast hilly and forested district of Doda suffered from wide-spread terrorism. Hence keeping this Parliamentary constituency also in the last phase was calculated to facilitate adequate deployment of CPMFs into Doda district after they would be free from the adjoining Anantnag Parliamentary constituency located in South Kashmir. The forces deployed in Baramulla constituency were to be side-stepped and located in Srinagar constituency during the last phase of polling. It was also envisaged that since comparatively low polling was already anticipated in Srinagar and parts of Udhampur constituencies, keeping polling there in the last phase could have a positive effect of better polling in the earlier phases on the voter turn out of these two constituencies.

As mentioned earlier the polling in respect of the Parliamentary constituencies in Jammu & Kashmir was so scheduled that the general elections of Parliament were to be concluded without waiting for completion of polling, counting and declaration of results in respect of these constituencies. The simultaneous notification for election to all the Parliamentary constituencies of the Lok Sabha and conclusion of the elections without waiting for the poll results of Jammu & Kashmir caused some consternation amongst a few political parties and activists who objected to a very very long waiting and campaigning period between the last date of withdrawal of the candidature and the day of polling. Thus the candidates for Jammu and Ladakh Parliamentary constituencies had a campaigning period of about 30 days. Srinagar and Udhampur Parliamentary constituencies had the longest campaigning period of over 50 days. It was argued that declaration of results in the rest of the country would influence the poll pattern in respect of constituencies located in Jammu & Kashmir which would be taken up for polls even after counting in respect of other constituencies all over the country would have already begun or completed. Some of the political parties even went to the court on this issue but their contentions were not upheld.

The Election Commission's instructions on setting up of the polling stations included adequate publicity of their locations and no change could be affected without the approval of the Commission once the list of polling stations was approved by the Commission and notified by the concerned District Election Officer. However, due to exigencies connected with terrorism situation, in respect of Jammu & Kashmir, the Commission made the following two major concessions:

- The District Election Officers (Deputy Commissioners) were given the authority to make a last minute change in the location of the polling station or even shift the polling station midway through the polling in the same locality if the polling station was threatened by any terrorist action. The Election Commission was to be kept informed in such eventuality; and

- In case of destruction of a polling station building and in the absence of another suitable alternative building in the locality, the District Election Officer could immediately set up a polling station in a tent or a truck or a similar vehicle which was to be stationed in the area.

Though the need for setting up a polling station in a truck or motor vehicle did not arise, the provision for change of building proved very useful in several cases.

The most important part of the planning process was to determine the requirement and availability of additional Central para-military forces, their induction into the State and further deployment for duties during different phases of the election as well as return to their bases leaving behind requisite force level to take care of the post poll security arrangements. Equally important was the requirement for getting almost ten thousand employees from outside the Valley and other states as polling parties since it had become almost clear that the State government employees on one pretext or the other were not likely to take part in the elections. Then, there was a huge task of coordinating large scale movement of security forces and polling parties to pre-identified locations and keeping them together during the election period followed by disengagement and return to their respective locations, all under the constant threat of violence and terrorist strikes.

Various aspects of logistics, including the planning and preparation for providing medical facilities to the additional security forces as well as polling parties had to be planned and catered for. The State government had already informed the Ministry of Home Affairs as well as Defence Ministry that there was a possibility of terrorists giving a threat to the government employees and keep them away from doing their normal duties affecting the essential services during the election period and had also made a request to cater for the services of defence personnel and equipment for maintenance of essential services like, water, electricity, food, supplies and health care, etc.

Arrangements had also to be made for acquisition of at least one hundred bullet proof vehicles, three hundred gypsies, hiring of over 3500 vehicles, stocking of POL for such a large fleet. There was also huge requirement for defence stores like CGI sheets, ballies, sand bags, bricks, etc., and movement of stores from one location to another along with that of central para-military forces units and sub-units. Then there were ancillary requirements of arms, ammunition, bullet proof jackets, sleeping bags, tents, etc., which had to be procured or borrowed from the ordnance factories, civil suppliers or from the holding stocks of the army and central para-military forces reserves.

Security of candidates and important political leaders as well as government functionaries had to be meticulously planned. Any laxity or mishap in this direction, particularly with respect to political personalities would have had serious repercussions on the government's efforts to successfully complete the electoral process that had been set into motion. Maintenance of essential services and availability of essential commodities were other issues demanding attention of the administration. It had been envisaged that instead of making last moment efforts in this direction it was more prudent and practical to build up sufficient stocks in advance of essential commodities by using all available storing spaces and capacities as also making foolproof arrangement for maintenance of essential services including the contingency plans in the event of failures or sabotage.

Last of all, a coordination mechanism was required to be put in place which was to constantly monitor day-to-day progress for the important parameters that had been carefully worked out and undertake mid-course corrections, if required. This was to be done at three levels, firstly within the various layers of concerned departments, then the coordination at the State level which could either take place in the meetings of the Unified Headquarters or under the guidance of the Chief Secretary. At the apex level some of the important issues were to be monitored, almost on continuing basis in different ministries of the Central government in New Delhi in which the nodal coordinator was the Department of Jammu and Kashmir affairs in the Home Ministry.

Collecting Wherewithal

While the announcement of Parliamentary elections in the State, in tandem with the elections at the national level, was welcomed across the political spectrum within the country as well as in Jammu and Kashmir, a discordant note was struck by the National Conference on 29th March, when it announced its decision not to take part in the forthcoming elections. One of the top State functionaries had a dinner meeting with Dr. Abdullah, President of National Conference, at latter's residence on Ist April, but failed to persuade him to change his mind. Dr. Abdullah, however, hinted that his party may not be averse to contesting the Assembly elections whenever they were conducted. Also as expected the Hurriyat Conference gave a call for election boycott and appealed to the people and the government employees to refrain from taking part in the elections as well as electoral process. Significantly this call was issued on the Eid Day on 29th April, during a large prayer congregation. However, on the administrative side, events started moving fast with almost every department striving hard to contribute towards success of the electoral endeavour. A meeting of all the Deputy Commissioners was held on 9th April, and the brainstorming session continued the whole day to discuss various aspects relating to the preparations and the difficulties that were likely to be encountered during the elections. This meeting was attended by the Chief Secretary and heads of the army and central para-military forces as well as intelligence agencies, and all the issues were discussed threadbare so as to ensure that no one left the meeting with any doubt in respect of his sphere of activities or areas of responsibility. Four days later a multi-disciplinary team from the Centre headed by Special Secretary, Department of Jammu and Kashmir Affairs in the Home Ministry, came to Srinagar. It was a very useful interaction between the State and the Central Government representatives wherein important issues like availability of additional forces, polling parties, transport arrangements and requirement of additional financial resources to the State for the conduct of elections were deliberated upon in detail and loose ends tied up. This was followed by a two-day visit to the Valley by the Union Home Secretary a week later for taking review of the arrangements being made, discussions with various officers and heads of organizations. He also visited and held district level meetings at Kupwara, Baramulla and Anantnag.

Force: When the Assembly elections were being planned for during 1995, the State government had recommended a five-phase polling spread over nineteen days during the summer and changed this schedule to four-phase elections spanning seventeen days during the month of November. However, with the schedule for Parliamentary elections being confined to a three-phase electoral exercise from 7 to 30th May, for seats in J&K, the requirement of security forces had to be re-worked out. The state law and order authorities in their discussions with heads of various agencies in the Unified Headquarters had asked for the induction of over seven hundred companies of central para-military forces, in addition to the troops available already for pre-poll duties. Keeping in view the requirement of these forces in other parts of the country and also the need to quickly redeploy them in the State, the Ministry of Home Affairs expressed its inability to spare no more than five hundred companies. After considerable discussions and re-working of the requirement, this figure was revised to around 550 Companies which included major component of approximately 250 Companies of CRPF and 200 Companies of BSF. Some compliments also came from the Indo Tibetan Border Police, Punjab Armed Police, Central Industrial Security Force, Railway Protection Force, etc. At the peak level of deployment a few training reserve companies of BSF were also used for polling duties. Of this force, maximum deployment was made in phase three, particularly in upper reaches of Udhampur district and entire Doda district where, large tracts of inaccessible area were infested by terrorists. The requirement of security forces was not so heavy during the first phase of election for Jammu and Ladakh constituencies.

As mentioned earlier, the responsibility of coordination of all central para-military forces activities in the State was entrusted to the Additional Director General of CRPF, North West Zone, and the officer directly given charge of coordinating all movements and logistics was the IG CRPF, J&K. Under his overall supervision an elaborate command, control and communication structure was set up. At the apex level, the IG Operations CRPF Jammu and Kashmir, A.S. Gill, was nominated as coordinator for elections. His job was to liaise with the State authorities and various security agencies, including army, to plan smooth and incident free induction and deployment of security forces in time, to work out the kind of force and its strength in each segment, to ensure proper demarcation of the areas and deployment of road opening parties in coordination with the army. He was also to identify and establish transit camps for troops on move at Jammu, Srinagar and in certain district headquarters, to procure defence stores from different sources, bullet proof jackets and tents, etc, tying up and matching polling parties with troops as well as ensuring proper communication network and de-induction of troops and polling parties after elections. It was also incumbent upon this officer to work out the need as well as procurement of logistic requirements such as POL, ration, firewood, etc., for all the central para-military forces and to prepare comprehensive medical plan to cater for other contingencies.

Zonal Commanders of the rank of DIGs were earmarked for these districts. Six Zonal Commanders were nominated and located at Srinagar, Baramulla, Anantnag, Poonch, Jammu and Doda. Their jurisdiction was generally co-terminus with that of the Range DIGs, except Zonal Commander, Jammu, who was looking after the districts of Jammu, Kathua and Udhampur. Zonal Commanders were expected to liaise at a senior level with the Army/BSF/ITBP, etc., and Police authorities, provide guidance to the Nodal Officers, and generally supervise the troops deployed in their area. Their primary job was to ensure timely movement and deployment of troops and polling parties both to the polling stations and their return. Close liaison with the Army/BSF for area domination, ROPs, etc., on all days of force movement and election day was one of their important tasks.

One Nodal Officer for each district in the rank of Commandant was nominated. He, under the overall supervision of the Zonal Commander, was to liaise with the District S.P. and District Magistrate for working out the force requirement, movement of troops within the district, deciding their places of stay, etc. He was also responsible for supervising the distribution and dispatch of polling materials and sending all required information before, during and after the elections to the headquarters.

Officers of the rank of Deputy Commandant and Assistant Commandant were nominated as Assembly Segment Officers for each segment including the segments of other CPMFs. These officers were to be sent in advance to their areas to visit selected campsites and see their location, act as guides for incoming troops, see all polling stations and deploy troops at these when they arrived. They were to collect the polling parties from Srinagar/ Jammu on arrival from outstations, take them to their respective districts and further distribute to the campsites after properly matching them with the concerned troops. They were also to keep in touch with the local army authorities, get the campsites and polling stations sanitized by them before the arrival of the troops. On the day of elections, they were expected to man joint control room consisting of communication officers from Army/_BSF/ ITBP/ CRPF, etc., and were expected to pass on timely information on security related matters and polling to the concerned authorities.

Two unified control rooms (UCRs) were established–one at Srinagar and the other at Jammu. The UCR at Srinagar was to function under two officers in the rank of Additional DIG Police –one to lookafter logistics and the other operations.

Because of the large-scale deployment and movement, both logistics and operations were a gigantic task. The officer incharge of logistic had to work out the logistic requirements of all Companies deployed and items like scale ammunition/arms, BP jackets, ECC clothing, generators, water tanks, tentage, defence material, POL, ration, transport and other operationally essential items like night vision device. An officer of the rank of Addl. DIG was nominated to be in charge of logistic arrangements.

The Addl. DIG in charge of operations was responsible for all movements, deployment, establishment of transit camps, campsites, distribution of polling materials, distribution and matching of polling parties, liaison with army, move to polling booths and return, depositing of ballot boxes and inter-phase movement.

A control room was established under the charge of a Commandant with adequate number of DCs/ACs to function round the clock under the overall supervision of Addl. DIG (Ops). All election related communication, especially those related to movement of troops and polling parties was done through this control room. It was to act as a central nodal point for interaction with the field troops and the senior officers in the UCR so as to ensure smooth conduct of elections.

A unified control room under the command of DIG Police was also set up at Jammu. As all the troops coming by road/rail were to report first at Jammu and then to be moved to the respective districts after being equipped at Jammu, the role of this UCR became very vital. The large scale movement from all over the country, with its inherent problems of not being strictly able to stick to schedule, necessitated setting up of transit camps to accommodate over 100 Companies at Jammu and Udhampur. As the State Government was not able to provide suitable accommodation for these troops, temporary camps had to be established at seven different locations in Jammu and at Udhampur under tentage. Reception centres at railway station and on highways for troops coming by road had to be opened. The hired transport was expected to reach before the troops at Jammu, to be further distributed to the arriving Companies. Because of the limited time given to the troops for movement, the entire force had to be fully equipped and moved within twenty-four hours from Jammu to the Valley. The movement to Jammu had to be staggered because of the lack of space there. It was planned that not more than forty-fifty Companies should reach Jammu on a particular day so that their equipping and further movement to the Valley could be properly managed. This, however, would have posed practical problems because of the unsurity of train movements. Hence the need for creating a greater transit capacity at Jammu and Udhampur. It was thus planned to move troops, arriving at Jammu before noon, to Udhampur. This was also to help stagger the movement of these Companies on the next day to the Valley to prevent congestion on the highway. It also necessitated tying up with State authorities to enforce one way traffic on days of heavy movements of troops on Jammu-Srinagar highway.

The role of UCR at Jammu was thus vital to the entire election process as without timely equipping and movement of these troops and ensuring their arrival at Srinagar as per schedule, the entire election process could have been in jeopardy.

Since bulk of the troops was to come by rail and road to Jammu and from there the movement was to take place to the Valley, the CRPF had also to coordinate with other central para-military forces regarding their reception and accommodation at Jammu. For troops arriving by trains, reception centers were set up at Samba, Bari Brahamana and Jammu railway stations. This was done for the reasons of administrative convenience as well as to avoid over concentration of troops at one location – a usual security precaution required under the circumstances. For the forces coming by road a camp was set up at Kunjwani at the outskirts of Jammu city. All these facilities were to be manned round the clock by reception parties. In charge of all the reception parties was a gazetted officer provided with wireless sets who was to keep track of the arrival of troops by train or by road, arrange for their stay and other administrative facilities as also making available transport, movement to designated areas/transit camps. Transit camps were established at Bari Brahamana, Ismailpur, Greater Kailash, Nagrota and Jhiri on the outer peripheri of Jammu city where requisite number of tents were put up with water, electricity and sanitation facilities. The State police under the overall in charge of IG Jammu coordinated these efforts and provided all the requisite help to CRPF.

Personnel for Election Duty: In view of the likelihood of the State employees not taking part in the electoral process. The State government decided to create a separate cell in the

Secretariat to be headed by a senior officer who could work in close coordination with the Department of Jammu and Kashmir Affairs in the Home Ministry for requisitioning the services of polling staff from outside the State. For this purpose, lot of logistical efforts, high degree of skill and effective coordination was involved. N.R. Gupta, Commissioner & Secretary, Department of Education, Jammu and Kashmir, was nominated to do this job and appointed as the Special Coordinator with specific assignment relating to issues regarding the polling personnel from outside the State. This measure required preparation of lists of all the employees from different departments and ministries of the Centre and neighbouring states and arrangements for their transport, boarding and lodging and dovetailing all their arrangements and movements with the security forces in order to ensure the safety of the polling parties as well as their effective functioning. The Special Coordinator along with a small team held discussions with the concerned officers of the Department of Jammu and Kashmir Affairs and started compiling lists of staff that could be deployed in the Valley out of the names that had been forwarded by different ministries of the Central government as well as some of the State governments. Based on these lists different groupings were made on the basis of age, qualification and status – taking care to avoid deployment of officials beyond the age group of 45 years. While preparing the lists, care had to be taken to put as many employees from the same State or department as possible at the scale of five personnel per polling station with at least Presiding Officer or one of the officials to have the capability of reading Urdu script. These lists were prepared and computerized in such a manner that information about any staff member from a ministry or a state could be extracted within minutes, including projected location on a particular date for onward transmission, or monitoring as and when required. The actual figure of total staff deployed exceeded ten thousand men drawn from eighteen ministries and forty-eight departments of Government of India as well as states of Himachal Pradesh, Haryana, UP, Delhi, Andhra Pradesh and Madhya Pradesh.

Due to special requirement of movement of polling parties with the security forces units and sub units a special software was devised so as to ensure recording of every official from any ministry and department and the polling station(s) where he had to be deployed alongwith the details of para military unit. For this each ministry, state and each polling party was assigned a separate number which was linked to the constituency number and the polling booth number of the particular station with a number of the security force unit for that particular polling booth.

It was decided that the employees drawn from outside the state would be provided an insurance cover of Rs. 5 lac in case of death. Movement of polling parties was planned in a manner to ensure their arrival latest by five days prior to beginning of phase-two of the elections. The preparation of these lists of the polling parties had to be done in close coordination with IG Operations CRPF Jammu and Kashmir whose staff was making identical lists indicating type of force, its strength, location, number of polling booth, etc. These two lists were then compared, matched and finalized.

Arrangements were also tied up between Special Coordination and the Department of Jammu and Kashmir Affairs, with the Indian Airlines and Indian Air Force authorities for airlifting of the polling personnel from Jammu/Delhi to Srinagar and back. For this purpose a detailed schedule was prepared indicating the capacity of each aircraft and the polling staff from each ministry/state that was to be transported in each flight, and lists given to the Divisional Commissioners of Jammu and Srinagar as well as to all the Deputy Commissioners. Since there was a limited capacity at the Srinagar airport for all the incoming flights, the air force station at Awantipura was also utilized. The schedule of flights, to and from, was drawn up and it was co-related to the arrival of the polling parties in each flight, and arrangements made for their reception, meals and accommodation, at the airports.

Logistics

Because of the conditions prevailing in the Kashmir Valley at that time it was not considered feasible to entrust the work of printing of ballot papers to Srinagar Government Press. Therefore, all the ballot papers were printed at the Government Printing Press at Jammu. Under the rules, printing of the ballot papers for a constituency is to be arranged by the concerned Returning Officer who is also to ensure distribution and dispatch of the ballot papers to all the polling stations strictly in accordance with the guidelines of the Commission. It was not possible for the individual Returning Officer to maintain liaison with Government Press at Jammu on day-to-day basis or to physically come to Jammu for arranging printing of ballot papers and their lifting after due verification and counting. To overcome this technicality, additional AROs, one each for the three Parliamentary constituencies of Kashmir, were nominated out of Jammu based officers exclusively for making arrangements for printing of ballot papers based on the final list of candidates which would be faxed by the Returning Officers. The arrangements for proof-reading of ballot papers, verification of machine-numbering, physical counting and taking delivery in locked and sealed steel-trunks were made by these especially designated AROs with the help of their local subordinate staff. The ballot papers were then transported under proper armed escort and under absolute secrecy of their movement through over 300 kms. of hilly route, between Jammu and the prescribed destinations for delivery to the concerned Returning Officers and Assistant Returning Officers in charge of individual assembly segments. The special AROs in charge of ballot papers who traveled from Jammu to various destinations in the Valley for proper delivery of ballot papers were required to obtain a proper receipt and deposit the same in the office of the Chief Electoral Officer at Jammu who would immediately cross check the delivery with the concerned Returning Officer. Temporary storage of ballot papers and election material was arranged in secured buildings which were properly guarded by the para-military forces. The election material and the polling parties were transported under armed escort from these secured places on the date of polling and in some cases one or two days earlier depending upon the distance up to the polling stations and topography of the area.

One of the main components of logistic requirement was requisitioning of over 3500 commercial vehicles of different capacities for transportation of CPMFs, polling parties and attendant administrative arrangements. Most of these were to be requisitioned from outside the Jammu and Kashmir State as the transport operators within the State were scared of providing their vehicles for election purpose. The need of the transport to the central para-military forces was worked out at the rate of one light vehicle, three medium vehicles and five heavy vehicles to all incoming companies immediately on arrival from the pool of vehicles so requisitioned from the States of UP, Haryana, Punjab, Delhi and Rajasthan. Each State from where vehicles were to be hired was provided with a nodal officer of CRPF who was to liaise with State Transport authorities and ensure dispatch of all vehicles to Jammu for further allocation to incoming troops.

The POL arrangements for these vehicles were made by specially appointed officers. As a contingency measure in case of POL supplies getting disrupted in the Valley during the elections two thousand barrels of two hundred litres capacity each were borrowed from the army. It was also planned to hire twenty oil tankers from the Indian Oil Corporation which were to be stationed at various district headquarters and moved from place to place depending upon the need. As backup arrangements fifty oil tankers were borrowed from the army and kept fully laden to be used by the central para military forces. At the ground level each company was provided with four to five barrels filled with POL and also given special advances for on spot purchase of these products wherever locally available.

All items of ration, including wheat, rice and sugar were purchased one month in advance at Jammu and distributed companywise on their arrival. This was necessary to tide over any disruption in the supplies in the Food Corporation of India (FCI) and State food and supplies Department outlets. Similar stocking was undertaken at Srinagar. Bulk purchases were also made in respect of dry ration items, pulses, condiments and hard vegetables through wholesale dealers at Jammu.

Troops were required to be equipped with other items of operational and administrative necessity. CRPF centre at Bantalab, Jammu, was made responsible for supply of these items, which included B.P.jackets, flexi tanks, sintex tanks, generating sets, tents, operational scale arms/ammunition and night vision devices. The scale for distribution of each of these items was carefully worked out. Some items like tentage, generating sets, B.P. jackets, flexi water tank, empty barrels, ration, sintex water tanks were moved to Srinagar in advance and a Commandant was made responsible for distribution of these items for troops which could not get these at Jammu or on their direct arrival at Srinagar.

A transit camp for fifty Companies at District Police Lines, Udhampur, was established and the Commandant of the battalion, was made responsible for this. It was felt necessary to establish a transit camp at Udhampur to decrease the congestion at Jammu and also to stagger the movement of troops to the Valley so that the pressure on the highway could be reduced.

As per the proposed phasing of elections, the first phase in the Valley was to take place in Baramulla and Kupwara districts. Because of the heavy movement of troops from Jammu and the consequent likely blockages and also possible land-slides, it would not have been possible for the troops to reach Baramulla/Kupwara on the same day. It was, therefore, decided to have Transit Camp facilities in the Valley for fifty-five Companies –fifteen at Anantnag, ten at Awantipur, five at Pampore and twenty-five in Srinagar for night halt of troops.

For housing such a large number of troops and polling personnel, arrangements were made for acquisition and taking on loan of over one thousand EPIP tents and over two thousand tents of eighty kilogram capacity. In addition five hundred tents which were procured by the Divisional Commissioner, Jammu, for use by migrants were temporarily diverted for election purpose. Arrangements were also made to procure, on emergency basis, sixteen thousand bulletproof jackets to be used by the polling personnel and the CPMFs.

The Food and Supplies Department of the State Government kept a constant watch from the beginning of April till the Parliamentary elections were completed about the stock and availability of POL and other items of essential supplies both at Jammu as well as at Srinagar. All tankage and storing capacity available at the State capitals and the district headquarters were fully utilized to ensure uninterrupted availability of these items to the security forces as well as local population during the period. Minimum level of requirement of these commodities was worked out and maintained at all times. For example, the requirement of Srinagar district for central para-military forces during the elections period was estimated to be 550 KL of diesel, 22 KL of petrol and one kilo litres of kerosene oil, with firewood requirement pegged at 6212 quintals. The requirement of rice was estimated to be 1200 quintals, atta 2397 quintals and sugar 357 quintals. Similar details were worked out and catered for in respect of districts and provisions made accordingly. The stock position and movement of essential commodities was monitored on daily basis by the departmental heads at Jammu and Srinagar, bi-weekly at the Unified Headquarters and on weekly basis by the Department of Jammu and Kashmir Affairs in the Home Ministry at New Delhi.

Medical Arrangements

In view of the terrorists' call to the government employees, threatening them to stay away from the electoral process, elaborate alternative arrangements were required to be made to provide health cover facilities to the additional security forces as well as polling parties coming from outside the State.

The Health and Medical Education Department of the State Government, in consultation with Ministry of Home Affairs, and Director, Emergency Medical Relief, Government of India, formulated a detailed action plan for this purpose. It envisaged a three-tier structure of medical facilities - centrally located at Srinagar followed by eight district teams, and at the ground level providing one mobile medical unit to each of the security forces/ polling parties camps in the field.

The super specialists, specialist doctors, paramedical staff were arranged by the Ministry of Health and Family Welfare mainly from the institutions in Delhi i.e. All India Institute of Medical Sciences, Ram Manohar Lohia Hospital, Lady Harding Medical College, G.B. Pant Hospital, Hindu Rao Hospital and the like as well as drawing some complements from the Central Government Health Scheme (CGHS).

At the apex level, the facilities of Army Base Hospital in Srinagar were to be used in case of emergencies, otherwise five specialist teams were organized and positioned in the Kashmir Nursing Home, a medical institution located in the security zone of Gupkar Road, Srinagar. Each team comprised one orthopedics surgeon, one physician, one surgeon, one anesthetist, resident doctors, one X Ray technician, one laboratory technician, one operation theatre assistant, nursing orderlies and safaiwalas. Super specialist teams consisting of one neuro surgeon, one cardio-thoracic surgeon, two anesthetists, five resident doctors and complementary nursing staff were also placed there. In addition two super specialist teams were positioned at the two main hospitals of Srinagar, Shri Maharaja Hari Singh Hospital and Sher-i-Kashmir Institute of Medical Sciences. Local doctors and officers were placed at each of the institutions to ensure proper liaison with the State government agencies and other administrative back up. The boarding and lodging arrangements in respect of these teams along with the Srinagar district group were made under security cover in hotel Welcome on the banks of Dal Lake. Two floors of this hotel were booked for this purpose.

For the districts, eight self-contained teams of specialist and general doctors were constituted with one team each for six districts of the Valley, one for Doda district and one team was kept as reserve at Srinagar. The boarding, lodging and security of these teams were taken care by the district authorities and each Chief Medical Officer of the district was made nodal officer for the purpose of ensuring proper functioning of these groups as well as other mobile teams operating in the district. At the ground level, and in addition to the medical units operating all over the Valley at the locations of various army and para military units and sub-units, 150 mobile medical dispensaries were created. For this purpose 150 vehicles, trucks and matadors, were hired from outside the State and fitted with stretchers and first aid kits, blood transfusion facilities and the like. These were manned by one hundred and fifty medical assistants specially engaged on contract basis from Jammu for a period of one and a half months from Ist May to 15 June, 1996, on, consolidated lump sum payment of Rs. 6000/- along with free boarding and lodging facilities, insurance and other facilities at par with polling parties and a promise of priority in government employment. These mobile ambulances as well as medical assistants were made into functional teams in Jammu and from there attached with the security camps at locations where no such facility had existed on the ground.

Keeping in view the possibility of local medical equipment and stores not becoming available in case of emergency, the district specialist teams were equipped with alternative set of resources which included – oxygen cylinders 200, nitrous oxide 200, portable E.C.G. machines 30, boyles apparatus 10, and portable X-ray machines 20, ventilators 10, diesel generating sets 10, medicines worth rupees one crore. Approximately a sum of rupees five crores was spent on these stores and equipment. The government also decided to provide one month's salary as honorarium to the entire staff and 50 percent of the honorarium was paid in advance before their departure from Delhi to Srinagar with one and a half times of DA. In addition, it was also decided to make ex-gratia payment of rupees five lacs in case of death besides providing medical cover, transportation, boarding, lodging and insurance cover.

One control room was established at Nirman Bhavan in New Delhi in the Union Ministry of Health where day-to-day activities of this parallel set up were monitored by Director General Health Services. At the State level similar daily checks were made by Secretary, Health and Medical Education Department, who was assisted by the State Coordinator Dr. Muzaffar Ahmad, throughout this period of one and a half months. The entire set up worked with clock work precision and with efficiency. Though not much work came the way of district and super specialist teams as fortunately the whole electoral process went through without major security related incidents. However, one hundred and fifty mobile medical teams did a commendable job of providing health cover to a large number of security personnel and, polling parties all across the Valley. The terrorists did manage to fire a rifle grenade at the Welcome Hotel in Srinagar where the specialist teams were staying but it caused only minor damage to the building with no loss of life or injury. No complaints were received from members of the medical teams regarding any lack of boarding and lodging facilities to them except one protest was registered from the residents of Hotel Welcome. They said that their rooms had not been swept by the hotel staff but on investigation it was found that due to a local call of strike the hotel employees had not turned up on that day. It was interesting to find that the group which had complained was that of safaiwalas brought from Delhi as part of the medical teams. Obviously, they were not prepared to clean their own rooms themselves.

Air Effort

The need for helicopters was felt for transportation of polling material and polling parties in certain cases, airlifting of security forces to far-flung and inaccessible polling stations. These flying machines were also needed for casualty evacuation as well for administrative supervision of election related arrangements. However, the availability of helicopters being limited with the Air Force, a very judicious requirement had to be worked out and a minimum need-based requisition for helicopters was placed with the Defence Ministry on the following basis:

1. For Logistics/Supervisions:

(a) Ex-Udhampur/Jammu:
One MI-17 & One Cheetah = 27 May to June 2, 1996.

(b) Ex-Srinagar:
One MI-17 & One Cheetah = 20 May to 26 May, 1996.

These helicopters were required to be made available to the State Government as standby facility for the period requested. These were to be used for carrying election material/personnel to areas like Gurez, Tangdar, Machil, Keran, etc., in the Valley and Marwah-Warwan belt in Doda district.

2. For Casualty Evacuation:

(a) Ex-Jammu:

One Cheetah = 3 to 10 May, 1996.

(b) Ex-Udhampur:

One Cheetah = 27 May to 2 June, 1996

(c) Ex-Srinagar:

One MI-17 & One Cheetah=20 May to 2 June,1996.

These helicopters were to be used on "as and when required" basis on a requisition made by the State government or by the officers nominated by State government to make such requisitions.

Coordination and Field Visits

With movement of troops and polling personnel taking place simultaneously on a very large and unprecedented scale, effective coordination mechanism had to be put in place to ensure that nothing went wrong, and all arrangements planned for were made on time and tasks formed out to different departments and agencies were carried out well and on time. The main nerve centre and the apex coordinating body at the State level was the Unified Headquarters which practically met each morning under the supervision of Advisor (Security), Lt. Gen. D.D. Saklani (Retd). During these deliberations implementation of decisions taken and progress made on the issues raised during the previous meeting were reviewed, new developments taken note of and any outstanding issues or items of disagreement or friction between different agencies were ironed out. These discussions were further carried out in smaller groups, at informal level either in different offices or over occasional meals.

A core group consisting of Advisor (Security), Additional Chief Secretary (Home), IG Operations CRPF and range Divisional Commissioners/IG Police were formed to visit each district headquarters and far flung areas of importance to guide, oversee and review security and election arrangements. This group, making use of helicopters, was able to visit all requisite locations starting from Leh and Kargil on 18/19 April, Rajouri-Poonch the next day. On Ist May, the coordination meeting took place in Kupwara and Baramulla, followed by Doda, Kishtwar and Marwa-Warwan Valley the next day. On 13th May, the Core Group visited Gurez and Tangdhar sectors of Kashmir division. The arrangements at Uri and Bandipur were reviewed on 17th May. The last visit of the Core Group took place to Kathua and Bani on 28th May. During these visits security arrangements as well as administrative arrangements for elections were reviewed in the presence of seniormost army, CRPF, police and civil officers of the area. Wherever available, the observers of the Election Commission were also requested to participate and their views taken note of. Since the visits were announced in advance these also provided an opportunity to the candidates taking part in the elections and the local political leaders to put forth their views and requirements.

Almost at all locations the local officers and commanders had done well in planning and making arrangements for smooth conduct of elections. These were particularly impressive in Gurez and Tangdar areas where due to paucity of appropriate local accommodation, the security forces deployed there had voluntarily vacated considerable part of their living accommodation to house the polling parties as well as additional central para-military forces. At all locations, a special feeling for the security and comfort was noticed in respect of the polling personnel. It was generally felt that whereas the army and central para-military forces were trained and equipped to face terrorist violence and live in harsh conditions, the civilian officials coming for polling duties were neither mentally prepared nor physically trained to face difficult situations and therefore, there was a need to take special care of them.

The most important aspect of election arrangements related to the security of the contesting candidates which were 110 in number and also important political leaders canvassing for their party candidates. Guards were provided at the respective residences of the contesting candidates and leaders. They were also made available provided with, to the extent possible, bullet proof vehicles as well as escort vehicles with adequate police, CRPF guards while on move. Guards were also provided at the MLAs Hostel and other guesthouses at Srinagar and district headquarters where the candidates and the political personalities were staying. In addition, adequate security at public meetings was also planned and taken care of under the supervision of the respective district SPs.

The security arrangements for candidates and the officers connected with overseeing the electoral process were broadly made as follows. In Kashmir Valley each candidate was provided a BP car, two BP escort vehicles, two PSOs and one platoon of CRPF, out of which one section was used as residential guard and two sections of troops were earmarked for doing escort duties. Detailed instructions were issued by IG Security in respect of each candidate. A typical example of such details in respect of a candidate is given as under:

"Sh. Bashir Ahmad Takroo S/o Gh. Nabi Independent Symbol–Clock

Place of stay	Tele Nos.	Blood Group	Election Agent	Next Kin	Security
Mla Hostel Room No. 225	452346				
PSOs Name			Transport Veh. No.		Driver
CT Ab. Rashid 160/8th BN			BP CAR 2464		Chain Singh
Ct Noor Mohmad 834/14th BN			GYPSY 2455		Sushil Kumar
			GYPSY 299		Mohammad Shafi

In Jammu province and Ladakh all candidates were provided residential guards and PSOs. Candidates of recognized political parties and chiefs of these parties were provided Z category security cover in Jammu and Udhampur constituencies. All candidates visiting Doda were given a BP car and armed escort. Similarly all candidates and political leaders of importance going to Poonch and Rajouri districts were made available armed escort. Both in the Valley as well as in terrorist infested areas of Jammu region road opening parties were organized as per the movement plans of the candidates and places of election meetings were secured well in advance. Adequate security arrangements were made for Election Observers, Returning Officers and Assistant Returning Officers, etc. Similarly security was provided at the places of reception, travel and stay of polling personnel as well as medical staff coming from outside the State.

The preparations for conduct of Parliamentary elections started in the third week of March and continued at a feverish pace for the next month and a half. In spite of a number of problems, hitches and omissions the necessary arrangements were finalized in time and as the date of polling neared, almost every member of the large team, which was working hard so constantly and in a coordinated manner, felt confident of the success of the individual and combined efforts.

6 The Juggernaut

Phase-I of the election was to take place on 7th May, with polling scheduled in Ladakh, comprising Leh and Kargil districts, as well as in Jammu Parliamentary constituency which included the districts of Jammu, Rajouri and Poonch. In Jammu, Leh and Kargil districts not much additional force was required for law and order and polling duties and it was possible to take care of smooth conduct of elections with the forces already locally available in the pre-poll phase with very small additional component required. However, the situation in the hilly areas of Rajouri and almost the whole of Poonch district was as disturbed as some parts of the Valley and therefore, needed much larger number of additional troops to be deployed for area domination, the security of camps and polling booths as well as to instill a sense of security and confidence amongst the local population. Since this phase also coincided with the last phase of the elections in the rest of the country, the availability of additional forces was a problem, as movement from their respective station of deployment could not be ensured simultaneously. Therefore, a large component of the forces for Rajouri and Poonch districts had to be got from the CPMFs already deployed in the neighbouring states of Punjab, Himachal Pradesh and Haryana where polling had been so planned that it had concluded in the earlier phases, as well as the additional manpower of the Punjab Armed Police that could be spared by the Punjab government.

The movement of bulk of the forces which was to take part in the second and third phases of the Parliamentary elections and were mostly meant for the Valley, commenced only after the conclusion of last phase of the election in the rest of the country on May 7, 1996. Elaborate administrative and logistic arrangements were planned for and put in place for orderly induction, deployment and deinduction of this huge force exceeding five hundred companies which were moving, simultaneously by road, train as well as by air.

Transit camps were established at Jammu and Udhampur for the troops coming by road and trains. Adequate arrangements to ensure supply of water, electricity and sanitation requirements of this massive force was completed mainly by the CRPF with help from the State Police. Further difficulties for the organizers of the transit camps were compounded by untimely rains and high winds which lashed the region during the first week of May upsetting the efforts already made, requiring re-establishment of some of these facilities all over again.

The troops started arriving in Jammu from 3rd May onwards and after being provided with rations, POL and transport component as well as rest in the transit camps, were dispatched to the districts of their duty stations. Sixty-two companies were airlifted directly from the North-East by the Indian Airlines planes and landed at Srinagar and Awantipura airfields. The troops landing at Awanipura were utilized for deployment in Anantnag Parliamentary constituency and those landing at Srinagar were deployed in Baramulla constituency. The logistic and administrative arrangements for them were made near these two airfields. On landing the men were welcomed with a hot cup of tea or a hot meal, depending upon the time of their arrival, before their onward move to respective camps. For the troops which landed in the afternoon arrangements were made for their stay during the night near the airfield itself as the night movement of troops was being avoided due to security reasons.

In the Valley also, the weather was bad particularly during the second half of May. High winds and rains pushed the temperature unusually low and it suddenly became very cold for the month of May, making it difficult for the troops to stay under tents as the ground had become wet and soggy. Men, therefore, had to be hastily shifted and squeezed into whatever built up accommodation was found near the camp sites. This also created sanitation problems as deep trench latrines became non-functional at most of the campsites.

The nodal officers stationed by the CRPF in each district had in advance surveyed the campsites in their areas of responsibility, including polling booths to ensure smooth deployment of forces. They had also identified the accommodation available for camping and deployment of troops at various locations and in case sufficient accommodation was not available the requirement of tents at each place had been worked out and stores procured as well as camps erected at locations which were secured well in time. The type and condition of roads in the locality, easy availability of safe drinking water and electricity as well as deployment of army/CPMFs already in position for area domination had been listed out in details. The nodal officers had also prepared detailed road maps showing the location of each campsite, polling booth and their link with the district as well as smaller administrative headquarters. All this information was provided to the units arriving from Jammu and Srinagar so that immediately on arrival they were in the know of exact campsites where they had to go and the roads to be followed and level of deployment at each polling booth and area around. In addition the information folder available to the commanders of the incoming troops helped in acquainting themselves to the general situation in the area, the threat assessment and the drill to be followed as well as the nearby units to be contacted in case of need. These instructions included general guidelines about the movement and deployment of troops for smooth conduct of elections, security drills to be followed, road chart, a list of important telephone numbers, etc. The brief also gave an overall security scenario and the intelligence inputs available, contingency plans in case of any major mishap by the terrorists in the respective areas, drills to be followed in dealing with improvised explosive devices (IEDs), details of communication network as well as the medical facilities available during the move to the campsites, in the nearby units as also the chain of evacuation to different hospitals in case of need. A note in Hindi was also circulated to the Platoon Commanders highlighting the kind of activities undertaken by the terrorists and steps required to avoid these threats particularly for security of the camps and polling booths during night as well as patrolling for area domination.

The troops started arriving about fifteen days before the date of polling in the Valley, which was to start from 23rd May and, therefore, it was necessary to accommodate them in camp- sites of three to four companies each at different places in the districts of Pulwama and Baramulla around areas where these were to be deployed. The nodal officers of each district had in advance identified these locations and efforts were made to locate camps at such places so that the troops did not have to move more than ten kilometers to reach their polling booths. The troops after arriving at the campsites could have a few days to rest and reorganize themselves with area familiarization, patrolling and all round domination within a radius of five to six kilometers from the campsites. Extensive patrolling was undertaken in coordination with local army units deployed in the area and they were also to provide road opening parties for the troops coming on later days and also for their movement from the campsites to tehsils, sub-divisional and district headquarters for collection of polling materials as well as move to the polling booths.

By the time polling personnel started arriving, almost the entire force had reached the Valley and were able to move into the campsites, dominated the area around and got ready to receive the polling personnel and take them under security cover from the airfield to the campsites.

Arrival of Election Personnel

A total of 10555 men, five persons per polling station, were brought from outside the State for conducting the elections. Only a few hundreds came by road from Jammu as well as neighbouring states and these were mostly Urdu knowing persons. Almost ten thousand persons were airlifted to Srinagar and

Awantipura airfields from Delhi over a period of four to five days. According to the induction plan, the persons required to go to the farthest places were brought in first from Delhi. The designated polling personnel were first collected in Delhi where they were given two days training in the management of polling stations and handling of polling material as well as briefing about the administrative arrangements plus security cover that was to be provided to them during their polling duties. As expected there was a lot of reluctance and apprehensions in the minds of the officials nominated to perform these duties and right till the end, a number of them made efforts to avoid going to the Valley. At the reception end lot of arrangements had to be made, particularly in Srinagar and Awantipura airfields. It was planned that the polling personnel would be received at the airfield by officers of the respective units with which they would be staying along with transport already earmarked for their conveyance. On arrival the men were to be given a hot cup of tea or coffee and packed lunch in case of their arrival before noon and a hot lunch on their landing after 12 O'clock. After taking tea and lunch each one of them was issued a bullet proof jacket and transported to the campsite under escort. These moves were so planned as to ensure that the polling parties reach their campsites before sunset.

For the polling personnel arriving at the airfield after 2 p.m. arrangements were made for their stay near the airfield for the night to ensure that no movement of polling personnel or the troops after hours of darkness takes places as the road opening parties were in place only from sunrise to sunset. For this purpose some structures were vacated by the troops residing near the Srinagar airfield and they were converted into temporary transit camps by taking wooden cots, bedding, linen, etc., on hire from the camping agencies at Srinagar. The boarding and lodging arrangements for these people were made at Srinagar airport by JK Tourism Development Corporation under the overall supervision of the Divisional Commissioner, Kashmir, district administration as well as the Special Coordinator. Since hardly any build up accommodation was available near the Awantipura airfield two of the hangers were converted into makeshift living halls. Shamianas and tents were erected for making necessary arrangements for food and sanitation. Since inside the airfield no civilians were allowed to operate due to security reasons, these arrangements were made by the local army units located in the area. All the administrative measures made at Awantipura airfield were organized flawlessly. However, there were initial hiccups to start with in respect of the polling personnel arriving at the Srinagar airport but the situation improved after the teething problems of the first day and subsequently the arrangements of the Jammu and Kashmir Tourism Development Corporation came up to the required standard.

The polling personnel were airlifted in the Boeing aircrafts of the Indian Airlines as well as Indian Air Force planes of different varieties including IL 64, AN 12, AN 32 transport aircrafts. Over eighty planes landed at these two airfields during the period of three to four days. Since at Awantipura airfield only Air Force planes were landing, reception, night stay as well as onward movement to camps did not create many problems. However, at Srinagar airport not only the polling personnel were landing in Indian Airlines planes as well as Air Force aircrafts but the normal civil traffic in the Indian Airlines planes continued simultaneously. To make logistic management even more difficult, the landing and dispersal sites of civilian and Air Force aircrafts were at two different locations. Therefore, the administrative and logistic arrangements at the Srinagar airport both by the civil administration as well as CRPF required much greater effort and higher degree of coordination between various agencies. After encountering some problems on the first day a more effective coordination mechanism was put in place at Srinagar airport with Divisional Commissioner, Kashmir, and Deputy Commissioner, Srinagar, personally supervising all the arrangements during the next few days.

The first group of polling parties started arriving on 13th May, at Srinagar and Awantipura airfields. Their subsequent move to the respective campsites in the four districts went of smoothly. The next day also almost two thousand polling personnel landed from Delhi and were received and dispatched to onward locations as well as arrangements made for the night halt for some at these two airfields. By the evening of 18th May, all polling personnel had arrived at Srinagar and by next afternoon they were safely settled in their respective camp-sites. The Advisor (Security) accompanied by senior officers visited various campsites. It was heartening to see the high morale of these civilian officials. It goes to their collective credit that after initial display of fear and some irritation at the arrangements made at the airport, they admirably adopted to the damp and chilly weather as well as uncomfortable living conditions in the camps. Once they realized that they were part of a great endavour and unique effort to initiate the process of return of democracy in one of the most troubled spots in the country, a higher sense of duty and dedication to the national cause had clearly overtaken their feeling of discomfort and sense of danger to their personal security. It was a happy sight to see them very well mixed up with their comrades in uniforms. While most of them kept themselves occupied by reading, playing cards or listening to the transistors, some were seen helping the troops in preparing and serving meals and also helping them in making administrative arrangements. Both civilians as well as men in uniform had beautifully blended themselves into cohesive working outfits.

The process of identifying, listing out, training, airlifting and subsequent transportation to campsites had entailed extensive and deliberate planning and coordinated execution of administrative arrangements in great details.

When the polling staff finally arrived, everything was in place. All the agencies, paramilitary forces, Tourism Development Corporation, State Government and other related agencies were working in complete unison. At one occasion, one of the polling staff member's mother died and his family had requested for his presence at the cremation. Within ten hours, arrangements were made for his flight back to his home State and it was ensured that he was able to attend his mother's cremation. In all eight persons were called back from duty and returned for different reasons through regular Indian Airline flights. This became possible because while sitting in office, the authorities concerned could find out the polling party number, its location, the name of the employee, the ministry to which he belonged and the paramilitary forces which were deployed for that polling booth. During the stay of the polling staff in the Valley, not only the Ministries but also the families of the polling staff were making queries about their welfare. Based on carefully compiled centralized data bank by the Special Coordinator and regular flow of information from the field units and force headquarters, it was possible to provide accurate information about the welfare of these officials on a regular basis.

For collection of polling material and move to the polling booths, Presiding Officers of all the polling parties were moved under strong escorts to their respective material distribution centers which were located at the district, sub-divisional and tehsil headquarters to collect the material and move back to the campsites. From the campsites the Presiding Officers, along with the polling material and accompanied by rest of the polling party as well as the troops earmarked for that particular polling booth, proceeded to the polling site. The move from campsites to the polling stations was planned and staggered to ensure that the polling parties were in position two to three days prior to the date of election. Due to the possibility of terrorists having planted IEDs at the polling stations, these were sanitized through anti-sabotage check by the troops already dominating that area before the polling parties and force accompanied them moved to the polling stations. The purpose of sending them two to three days in advance was to make sure that they could properly sanitize and dominate the area so that there was no disruption by the anti-national elements on the polling day.

By the evening of 21st May, all polling material had been distributed and the polling parties along with escorts had reached their polling stations except a few polling parties who could not reach Gurez as the road was closed due to snow-slide near Rajdhani Pass. They were airlifted by the helicopter next day. During the entire exercise involving movement of additional forces to the campsites, reception and transportation of polling personnel to the camps, their subsequent journey for collection of polling material and to their respective polling stations went with clockwork precision and without any major mishaps. None of the polling personnel could be hurt by any terrorist activity. Only at one location in Shopian area of Pulwama district a polling patrol was attacked by terrorists in which one BSF jawan was killed. During the evening of 21st May, the Governor convened a special meeting of Unified Headquarters to take stock of arrangements made so far and expressed his satisfaction at the orderly and safe move of the polling parties and troops to all the polling stations.

Kaleidoscope

To make this massive administrative exercise possible required a huge effort in terms of planning, procurement and coordination between different agencies and departments of the State as well as Central Government. One of the main difficulties was to arrange a large number of vehicles for transportation of election candidates, political leaders as well as officers supervising the electoral process, in addition to thousands of vehicles required for the movement of security forces. Major problems were encountered in the acquisition of bullet proof cars and Gypsies. These were made in only one of the ordnance factories which had a very limited capacity as well as a long delivery period which did not suit the requirement of speedy acquisition of these vehicles. At least one hundred additional bullet proof cars and two hundred such Gypsies were needed. These were finally arranged by utilizing the experience of the Punjab administration which had faced similar situation in the past and it was found that some of the fabrication units in Punjab had acquired the expertise and the technical capabilities to make bullet proof cars. The final product was certainly not of the standard achieved by the ordnance factories but was good enough for the purpose these vehicles were required. In addition to the Punjab body-fabricating units, some commanders in the Valley also made use of the local talent available and were able to get a good number of Gypsies as well as some medium capacity vehicles reasonably made bullet proof. It is interesting to note that during the entire process of getting the vehicles bulletproofed in some of the local workshops no terrorist threatened or interfered with this process. Presumably they also did not want to antagonize the local business community by taking away the chances of furthering their business interests. However, more stupendous task was to hire and move over 3500 small and medium commercial vehicles, buses and trucks to Jammu and Srinagar for transportation of troops and polling personnel as also meeting their administrative requirements including medical cover. These were requisitioned from various states by their respective Transport Departments in a coordinated efforts monitored in the JK Affairs Department at New Delhi. Although the owners and drivers of these vehicles were paid handsomely, it did require lot of persuasion, cajoling and threatening by the respective State Transport Officers to get these people to come to Jammu and Kashmir during election period. Almost by a Herculean effort the requisite number of vehicles could be made available well in time.

The procurement and movement of defence stores like CGI sheets, ballies, sand bags, bricks, etc., in comparison was not that difficult a job and was performed well by the State police. These stores having been procured were further issued to different units on loan for the period of elections. Getting requisite number of sleeping bags for the polling personnel as well as over 16000 bullet proof jackets for the additional troops and polling parties did pose considerable difficulties to the CRPF. These were not available in the open market, certainly not in such a large quantity within the short time available. Ultimately, the problem was solved with a good gesture from the army which agreed to release these out of their reserve stocks to the CRPF. Lot of attention was also paid to upgrade the wireless network of the State police so as to ensure that even the smallest detachment was connected with radio communication. Successful efforts were made to integrate the wireless networks of army, CPMFs and police not only at Srinagar but also at the different district as well as formation headquarters to ensure quick sharing of information and speedy response of all the forces to meet a given challenge.

Over two hundred polling booths in the Valley were not connected by road and this necessitated the movement of polling parties and troops on foot ranging from a couple of hours to over a day long march. For this necessary arrangements for hiring of porters and ponies as well as security during the move had to be planned and put in place. Another exercise was made to reduce the number of polling booths and polling stations by clubbing them in the same building wherever possible and without putting the voters to inconvenience while remaining within the norms set up by the Election Commission of India governing the permissible distance between the population centers and the polling stations. For instance, where a double storey government office or school building was available and sufficient number of voters existed in the neighbourhood one polling station could be located at each of the floors. Such an exercise was necessary as more troops became available to guard the structure and dominate the area around. At few places where the government buildings were more than double storey up to three polling stations were accommodated in the same structure. This exercise was undertaken both in the Valley as well as in the hilly regions of Jammu region. This way, the 3050 polling booths in the Valley were set up at 1704 locations making security arrangements of the polling stations as well as polling process itself so much more secure.

In order to create proper atmosphere for the successful conduct of elections, intensification of security efforts was carried out to put greater pressure on the terrorists so that they were kept on the run and were not able to regroup or organize themselves to create a major mischief. Special operations were undertaken, based on locally gathered intelligence, and targeted strikes to flush out the terrorists, especially the foreign mercenaries.

The security of candidates and political activists was considered a matter of prime concern by the law and order machinery so as to inculcate a sense of confidence in them. This way they were able to participate in the elections without fear and apprehension of threat to their life. The contesting candidates, their residences and offices were guarded and necessary frisking and searches carried out of the people who came to meet them. Security cover was also provided in public meetings and special drills put in place for the movement of the candidates within their constituencies. All this required coordinated effort between the district administration, central para-military forces and the army units deployed in a particular area. Detailed guidelines were issued with regard to movement of election candidates, political leaders, other VIPs and holding of public meetings, by the State police authorities at various levels. Adequate arrangements for protection of polling booths were made, including anti-sabotage checks prior to occupying the designated buildings and structures. Comprehensive briefings were given right down to last jawan impressing upon the need to follow the security drill and the lessons which had been learnt over the years. Officers at all levels were impressed upon to visit the camps as many times as possible arrangements to oversee the arrangements and to ensure that the instructions issued were being carried out by the troops, and also to boost their morale.

The attitude of the State government employees in Kashmir Valley remained uncooperative and ambivalent during the preparations for conduct of Parliamentary elections, not so much due to boycott call by the APHC but more due to threat to their own lives. Various employee bodies had unmistakably told that they would not be taking part in the electoral process. That is why such a large number of polling personnel had to be called from outside the State. This was also a way of showing to the State employees that both the Central and the State governments were determined to carry the process of elections to its -successful conclusion with the hope that during the Assembly elections, which were planned in not too a distant future, the State government employees would be forthcoming to perform their duty. As an incentive for the State employees to take part in the elections, the government had announced one month's salary and special life insurance cover to those who did the polling duties. It was also decided that any daily wager who voluntarily took part in the election duty would be regularized, irrespective of his length of service-which ought to have been seven years in normal course. This did produce some positive results, although not to the extent expected, and those who reported for election duties were attached to the nearby camps housing security forces and polling personnel and were provided boarding and lodging till the election process was completed. On the day of polling, even though the complete polling parties had come from outside, wherever the local persons had reported for duties their services were utilized for the conduct of polls.

However, the State government was absolutely strict about its officers taking part in the electoral process. It was made clear that any refusal to do so could cost them their service. In almost all cases the officers did perform designated duties and very few were able to avoid taking part in the elections by using devious means and unethical practices like faking illness, etc. However, even senior officers were not averse to making efforts to avoid election duty and a few were willing to be nominated as Returning Officers or Assistant Returning Officers. The HODs and Secretaries were advised to not to undertake tours, outside the Valley immediately before and during the Phase-II and Phase-III elections so as to ensure supervision of their officers and their taking part in the elections. It was also decided by the Chief Secretary that senior local officers should go on TV and radio with an appeal to the employees to take part in the elections but all of them refused to do so expressing apprehension of threat to their lives and of their families saying that they would otherwise use their good offices and motivate their subordinates to participate in the elections. On the whole the conduct of officers of the State government, particularly at the higher level was encouraging and they did carry out the duties assigned to them well, and in certain cases with zeal and dedication.

On The Eve of Elections

With all the security, administrative and logistic arrangements put in place as per plans and on time, everything was set on the eve of the polls to see through the successful completion of an exercise which had taken months of hard work, in planning and execution. One of the most satisfying indicators about the success of this painstaking effort was the number of candidates who had shown the courage, determination and confidence in the system to file their nomination papers. One hundred and sixty four candidates in all had filed their nomination papers, out of which six were rejected and forty eight withdrew from the contest. There were finally one hundred and ten candidates left in the fray which included thirty seven for three constituencies from the Kashmir Valley. They were trying their electoral fortunes at the discretion of over forty two lac voters who were to cast their votes in 6191 polling stations across the State. In Srinagar district there were total eleven candidates, important ones being G.M. Mir (Magami) of Congress-I, Amarnath Vaishnavi of BJP and Farooq Ahmad Andrabi of Janata Dal. In Baramulla constituency Ghulam Rasool Kar, PCCI President, was representing Congress-I, Sheikh Mohammad Sadiq of Janata Dal and Diljit Singh of Panthers Party were amongst the ten candidates contesting elections; Anantnag constituency had in all sixteen contestants better known amongst them included Taj Mohi-ud-Din of Congress-I, Sarla Taploo of BJP and Mohammad Maqbool Dar of Janata Dal. Ladakh had only three candidates with Congress-I being represented by P.Namgial and BJP by Spalzes Angmo, the third was an independent. In Jammu region a total of seventy candidates were in the fray with thirty trying their luck in Jammu constituency; principal contestants being Mangat Ram Sharma of Congress-I, Sheikh Abdul Rehman of BSP and Vaid Vaishno Dutt of BJP. There were forty candidates from Udhampur constituency, important ones being Janak Raj Gupta representing Congress-I, Prof. Chaman Lal Gupta of BJP and Prof. Bhim Singh of Panthers Party. Amongst the political parties participating in the elections BJP, Congress-I, Panthers Party and Janata Dal had put up six candidates each, followed by Indira Congress (Tiwari) and BSP contesting two constituencies each. Of the independent candidates, three each were having affiliation to Awami Tehreek, Awami League and Aman Nawaz Conference. Three National Conference activists also contested elections as independents.

Close coordination and excellent rapport between the State administration, central para-military forces, army as well as intelligence agencies made them work in tandem to ensure a peaceful and almost incident free pre-poll process. Security of candidates and their families and also uneventful conduct of public meetings was managed by proper and imaginative use of the additional resources in terms of manpower, etc., that were made available for this purpose. In nutshell, a climate was created which was conducive to free and fair participation in the election where people at large could cast their votes without any threat or pressure from the terrorists. This feeling was further enhanced due to effective area domination and security of the polling stations right up to the polling dates. The public was also assured that the domination of security forces would continue to the extent required even after the Parliamentary elections had been completed.

The exertions of the security apparatus were successful in thwarting of attempts by the terrorists to disrupt the peaceful conduct of elections. They had made efforts to resort to various stratagems in furtherance of their nefarious designs. These included efforts to plant and explode IEDs at important locations, targetted strikes at the security forces particularly during their move from one place to another. Efforts were also made to disrupt the whole process by giving calls for general hartal and strikes by government employees. In addition to the general call of poll boycott issued by APHC on the Eid Day on 29th April, door to door campaign against participation in the elections was undertaken by the activists of the Hurriyat Conference. Important opinion leaders and village elders too were threatened at certain places with dire consequences if they took part in the elections. However, none of these tactics succeeded to dampen the spirit and wishes of a very large section of the population to actively participate in the process of restoration of democratic institutions in the State after a gap of seven years. In a way it was also an opportunity for them to send unmistakable signals to the outfits of the terrorists which had disrupted their normal life and peace of mind.

The State police played a very significant part in the entire process of planning, mobilization and management of the poll process. In fact right from the DGP down to the district S.Ps. they–were provided very important and vital links in ensuring availability of local expertise, resources and influence amongst the local population. The support to incoming forces and polling parties was particularly noteworthy at the district administration level where the Deputy Commissioners and the district S.Ps' worked as a well-knit team. In order to supplement the availability of manpower in Anantnag and Baramulla constituencies, additional strength of one thousand officers and jawans of the State police drawn from Srinagar and Baramulla districts and other wings were sent to Baramulla and Anantnag constituencies for election duties on 23rd May, and reverse movement was made for the elections in Srinagar constituency during the Phase-III on 30th May. Additional policemen were also mobilized by withdrawing such manpower as was possible from the training institutions, including the trainees who had completed half of their induction courses. The State police also contributed its mite by undertaking intensive operations against the terrorists through their respective district operation groups who targetted terrorists and their hideouts leaving very little room for them to maneuver and carry out their activities. In the final set of instructions issued by the Inspector General of Police, Kashmir Range, he called upon the officers and men under his command to put in their best for the successful conduct of elections exhorting, "The successful conduct of these elections is a national challenge and we must put our best leaving no stone unturned in achieving this objective. There is no scope for any complacency at any level. With dedication, combined and coordinated endeavour it is hoped that we will be successful in our mission. For this purpose, requirements by way of manpower, transport, equipment, accommodation and funds have been taken care of so that you will face no difficulty at all in completing this unbelievable task".

The stage was thus set for the electoral process to roll with elections in Phase-I taking place on May 7, 1996.

7 Parliamentary Elections

During the polling of Phase-I, the electorate of Jammu, Rajouri and Poonch districts in Jammu region and Leh and Kargil districts of Ladakh region went to polls. The polling was peaceful in both the constituencies. Whereas no mischief was expected in Ladakh region, it was apprehended that in all the three districts of Jammu region efforts could be made to disrupt the polling by interference from across the border in Jammu district and the terrorist activities in Rajouri and Poonch districts, particularly in far flung and mountainous regions. However, the security forces and the administration were able to ensure peaceful polling throughout the day. As per preliminary reports received at the end of the day Ladakh, which had traditionally returned very high percentage of voting, had intimated 80% voter turnout and Jammu constituency showed 50% polling. This was a good sign, particularly the peaceful conduct of elections in Rajouri and Poonch districts. With Phase-I completed satisfactorily all attention was now directed to ensure equally creditable polling during Phase-II.

As the preparations were being finalized for the conduct of Phase-II elections on 23rd May, V.P. Singh, former Prime Minister, came to Srinagar on 20th May, on a private visit. He was received and accorded all necessary facilities and security as was due to a person of his status. However, in spite of advice to the contrary he insisted on meeting Shabir Shah, one of the prominent separatist leaders. He was adamant and extended his stay by a day till the arrangements were made for him to meet Shabir Shah at a house in Barzulla locality in Srinagar city. His movement from a secured area through the town to Barzulla and return to the State Guest House at Cheshmashahi did create considerable hassles and tension for the State administration. Also while the final arrangements for conduct of Phase-II elections were being tied up, the Special Coordinator responsible for all arrangements in respect of polling parties was busy in giving shape to the plans for de-induction of the polling parties which was to commence from 24th May itself.

On 23rd May, polling for Phase-II in Baramulla and Anantnag constituencies also took place peacefully. Not a single polling station was disturbed by terrorists which was a happy and satisfying development. At the end of the day over 45% polling was reported, as per provisional figures from both Baramulla as well as Anantnag constituencies. The peaceful conduct of polls in Anantnag and Barmulla constituencies and very encouraging participation by the electorate of the four, out of six districts of the Valley, which went to poll during the day was a major success and, like all success stories, at the end of the day there were a good number of personalities eager to take credit for what had been achieved in a remarkable manner. Some of those vying for credit were only remotely connected with the polling and had practically contributed nothing to the effort that was made during the last few months. At the same time the Core Group of officers who were actually responsible for achieving this near miracle were busy in planning and preparing for the considerable amount of work that still lay ahead in the next week to ten days.

Since major part of the Valley was going to the polls in Phase-II, there was a lot of media attention focussed on the polling process on 23rd May. The print and visual media persons from all over the country as also from abroad representing all major newspapers, magazines and TV channels had descended on the Valley a few days before the polling date. Special arrangements had been made to facilitate their reporting of polling on that day through not only through regular briefing by the State Media Center but also by making available to them road transport and helicopter facilities so as to ensure that the media coverage was available not only in areas with easy communications but also in far flung and mountainous regions, particularly in Baramulla and Kupwara districts. The media persons who wanted to make use of these facilities were divided in five groups. The first group was taken by MI 17 helicopter from Srinagar at eight in the morning and brought back by lunchtime after covering Tangdhar, Kupwara and Bandipur sectors. The second batch of media persons was also airlifted and were taken on a round of Uri, Baramulla and Manasbal before getting them back to Srinagar. The third group was airlifted to Gurez, Kupwara, Sonawari/ Sumbal area and back to Srinagar. The fourth, a smaller group, was provided a Cheetah helicopter, which took them to Gurez, Kulgam and Pulwama before returning to Srinagar. All these groups, once they landed at particular location, were provided with a number of vehicles along with escort parties and they were free to go to polling stations of their choice. They were only requested that wherever they wished to go, subject to restrictions mandated by the Election Commission of India, they were free to do so provided they returned to the helipad for the return flight. The fifth party was provided road transport to depart from Srinagar and visit Anantnag, Aishmuqam, Bijbehara and Pampore areas before returning to Srinagar. Special arrangements were made for carrying their dispatches and transmissions to Delhi so that these could be used by their principals the same evening for broadcasting and telecasting and by the print media the very next day. A satellite uplink facility was established by Doordarshan at Srinagar which could be utilized for immediate transmission of the coverage.

Arrangements were made for delivery of news cassettes which were available till 1230 hours to be sent by Indian Airlines flight leaving Srinagar an hour later. In addition, a special courier flight of the BSF was operated from Srinagar at 1600 hours which was utilized for carrying cassettes of afternoon coverage to Delhi from where these could be transmitted to the requisite destinations all over the world. Special couriers were nominated by the State government to carry the cassettes and coverage material by each of these flights and subsequent dispatch to the different locations in Delhi was arranged by the Information Advisor to the State Government based in the capital. Doordarshan was also requested to make arrangements for wide sharing of their material by other agencies so as to ensure maximum projection of the election process. All these logistic and administrative facilities provided to the news persons proved useful in proper, adequate and correct coverage of the most important phase of the Parliamentary elections and by the end of the day the entire nation as well as major capitals around the world were made aware of the almost silent revolution that had taken place in the Valley where successful polls were conducted in four of the six troubled districts, an achievement which was considered to be almost impossible task by the skeptics within and outside the State.

The Pakistani propaganda machinery, particularly the State sponsored electronic media masterminded by its main anti-India propaganda agency, the Kashmir Media Services, tried its best to malign and run down the electoral success by insinuating baseless charges of coercion, intimidating and manhandling of local people and allegations of forcibly taking them to the polling booths. Also, as in the past, file shots from the archives and not relevant to the occasion were used freely on the PTV telecast. However, with the extensive and independent coverage through Indian and foreign media Pakistan's efforts to downgrade Indian achievement and obfuscate the successful conduct of the Phase-II of the Parliamentary elections did not cut much ice except, perhaps, with their local and captive audience.

After the elections were completed on 23rd May, the polling parties and their escorts, wherever logistically possible deposited the election material in the already nominated strong rooms and returned to their camps. Where the polling parties were at a considerable distance from the collection centers they spent the night at the polling station or the camp and deposited the material next day. May 24, 1996, was a day full of activities and complex pattern of large-scale movement of forces and polling parties. The number of polling parties required for the Phase-III of polling in Srinagar constituency was 939 as against 2111 in the second phase. This number was low because The external polling parties were required only for the Srinagar constituency comprising Srinagar and Budgam districts for the third phase; whereas for election in Udhampur constituency falling on the same day, local State government employees were to be used for polling duties. Thus 1172 polling parties became surplus and were required to be deinducted.

A detailed plan had already been prepared for deinduction of these polling parties during the three days of 24th to 26th May, from Srinagar and Awantipur airports. This was almost a mirror image of activity that had taken place at the time of induction. This put a tremendous pressure on the security forces particularly on 24th May, when six different kinds of movements were taking place; these included move from the polling station to campsites, from campsites to counting centers for depositing ballot boxes and polling material, return to campsites to collect remaining members of the polling parties and move with them to Srinagar/Awantipur where required for dispatch of polling parties to Delhi and then return from airports to campsites to join main body of troops. In addition, local polling parties from Jammu and neighbouring States which had come by road were sent under escorts to Jammu. Lastly, shifting of troops along with 939 polling parties to designated campsites for onward dispatch to the polling stations in Srinagar constituency by the nominated polling persons from Baramulla Parliamentary constituency as also similar movement of the troops deployed in Anantnag constituency to pre-determined campsites in Doda district and hilly areas of Udhampur district. Keeping track of this multilateral movement taking place almost in all directions was a complex task which could successfully be completed only by a very detailed advance planning, excellent communication network and close cooperation of all agencies and departments of security forces and civil administration. Concerned officers spent the entire day and well past the midnight on the 24th May, to monitor, coordinate and guide the permutations and combinations that were taking place at the field level and it was only during wee hours of the next morning that they could snatch a bit of sleep assured in the knowledge that yet another very difficult task had been completed successfully.

With the deinduction of surplus polling parties completed by 26th May, and the forces and polling parties having moved to their respective locations in Srinagar and Udhampur constituencies, the stage was set for the final phase of polling on May 30, 1996.

For this phase of elections the attention of the law and order authorities was particularly focussed in Srinagar city and certain pockets of Doda district where efforts by the terrorists to make a last desperate bid to disturb the elections was expected to take place. Srinagar city was extensively patrolled during the day and situation in Doda was constantly monitored by control rooms of security forces headquarters as well as Unified Headquarters at Srinagar. Like the earlier two phases of polling this day also passed without any major disruption taking place. During the day a few incidents of violence did take place in which one BSF jawan and one civilian lost their lives At another place in Batamaloo area of Srinagar city, an over-enthusiastic press reporter got into an altercation with a local BSF commander. The situation was amicably settled by intervention of senior officers and more sober members of the press community. By the evening preliminary estimates showed over 30 percent votes polled in Srinagar with over 50% voters registering their choice in Udhampur constituency. With the completion of Phase-III the entire process of Parliamentary elections in the Jammu and Kashmir State stood completed satisfactorily and convincingly. The verdict of the voters of the State and choice of their candidates had been deposited into the sealed ballot boxes.

Assessment

Notwithstanding all the doubts and suspicions, the response of filing of nomination papers was quite encouraging. As many as

183 nomination papers were filed by 164 candidates in the six Parliamentary constituencies. They included 113 independents. The remaining candidates belonged to eight political parties. After the last date of withdrawal, 110 candidates remained in fray. In comparison, figures for the number of candidates who contested elections to the parliamentary elections in 1989, 1984, 1980 and 1971 were 90, 85, 59 and 52 respectively. Recognized all India and regional political parties like Indian National Congress, Bhartiya Janata Party, Bahujan Samaj Party and Janata Dal along with a state recognized political party (Panthers Party) participated in the polls. INC won four seats, BJP and JD won one each. The voters turn out for the State was 49.02 percent. Out of total electorate of 44.51 lakhs, 21.82 lakh voters cast their votes. The percentages in respect of three constituencies of Kashmir Valley were quite respectable. Baramulla, Srinagar and Anantnag Constituencies recorded 46.62, 41.00 and 50.13 percent of polling respectively. These figures compare well with 48.28 percent polling recorded in respect of Jammu constituency which witnessed near normal political activity. Udhampur constituency which included the disturbed Doda district recorded 53.54 percent polling. Ladakh constituency which historically witnesses a tussle between its two districts of Leh and Kargil recorded a very enthusiastic turn out of 80.95 percent.

In Baramulla constituency, the lowest polling was recorded in Handwara assembly segment (24.63%) whereas the highest polling was registered in Uri assembly segment (67.59%). The city of Srinagar saw quite poor participation as was anticipated, with poll percentages varying from 14.27 percent in respect of Habba Kadal assembly segment to 28.03 percent in respect of Batmaloo segment. The polling figures included a large number of votes received by post from the Kashmiri migrant electors. In contrast, the two rural assembly segments of Kangan and Ganderbal within Srinagar district recorded 65.16 percent and 59.51 percent polling respectively. Polling percentages in all the assembly segments of Budgam district, part of Srinagar Parliamentary constituency, recorded polling between 60.03 percent to 66.94 percent. In respect of the Anantnag

Parliamentary constituency, the lowest polling was recorded from the assembly segments representing Anantnag town (37.74%) and Bijbehara (39.54%). The highest percentage of polling (60.39%) was recorded in Pampore assembly segment which is practically a suburb of Srinagar city, followed by Pulwama assembly segment (55.04%).

An interesting feature of the polling results was that the political groups floated by the surrendered terrorists militants and independents put together garnered an impressive 23.66 percent of votes polled as against 27.50 percent of INC, 19.63 percent of BJP and 17.62 percent of Janata Dal, but could not succeed in winning even a single seat.

For collection of the ballot papers from Kashmiri migrants, special arrangements had been made with complete cooperation of the postal authorities. Especially designed ballot boxes-cum-letter boxes painted with visible distinctive markings were kept in all migrant camps and other localities in and around Jammu and other towns of the region and at a couple of places in Delhi. The ballot papers were issued in advance to the migrant electors through the post offices. The Government of India had issued a special notification for postal delivery of the ballot papers without affixing of any postal stamps. On the days of polling, the postal authorities collected all the ballot papers immediately after the prescribed closing hours of poll. In respect of far-flung areas, the duty of carriage of the ballot papers in the sealed ballot box-cum-letterbox was performed by the officer in charge of the migrant camp. The ballot boxes-cum-letter boxes were carried by the postal authorities in their mobile vans to a special control room opened at Delhi and Jammu where all the ballot boxes were brought and emptied under the supervision of a senior postal officer. The envelopes containing ballot papers were sorted out constituency-wise. After proper counting of the number of envelopes constituency-wise, the postal authorities carried them by air to Srinagar for immediate delivery to the concerned Returning Officers well before the date of counting. In respect of other places not covered by the aforesaid arrangements, the ballot papers after recording of votes were returned by the migrant voters directly to the Returning Officer by post in the same manner as in case of the service voters.

The Election Commission's instruction about counting of the service voters also applied to the votes received from the migrants i.e. they were to be counted in the first round and results of counting were to be recorded before opening of the ballot boxes received from the local polling stations. The procedure resulted into some amusement as a particular political party not having any significant base in Kashmir Valley was announced to be leading after first round of counting. This arrangement was modified by Election Commission of India when the general elections to the Legislative Assembly were held subsequently and the ballot papers received from the Kashmiri migrants were mixed with the main lot of ballot papers taken out from the ballot boxes of the local polling stations before commencement of counting.

Notwithstanding the fact that full contingent of poll personnel had been called from outside the state, a good number of local government employees who had received training for conduct of polls came forward for taking up their polling duties. The district administration arranged for their boarding and lodging at the district and sub-district headquarters so that their further deployment would not be hindered by disruptive elements. Government of India had announced honorarium equivalent to one month's pay and an insurance cover at government expenses for all those employees who came to Kashmir from outside the State for doing the polling duties. On the principle of parity, a similar demand was made by the local government employees detailed for the election duties and the government conceded that demand. Instructions were issued to all the District Election Officers to give preference to the local employees for deployment at the polling stations and to keep an equal number of employees who came from outside the state as standby at each such polling station.

In the entire polling process the only jarring note was the counting process in A antnag which was delayed by two consecutive days and marred by violence within and outside the counting hall resulting in police firing and death of three persons. Notwithstanding the fact that certain unruly elements had entered the counting hall and created scene inside, the whole episode was ineffectively and unimaginatively handled by the Deputy Commissioner of Anantnag district who could very well have defused the situation by timely intervention and firm handling right at the time when the problem erupted. This incident once again emphasized the need to post seasoned and effective officers at sensitive and demanding assignments. Amongst all the Deputy Commissioners in the Valley this particular gentleman was the weakest and least effective administrator and had been kept there in spite of the recommendations for his removal by his immediate superior officers. Ultimately, the counting in Anantnag had to be completed by deputing special teams of counting officials from the Civil Secretariat Srinagar who resumed the counting on 3rd June, and completed it by their uninterrupted efforts towards the early hours next day. The employees of the Civil Secretariat, particularly those belonging to Jammu region played an important role in the counting process for all the three constituencies of the Valley.

Media Management

Right from the beginning of terrorism in the State, and along with the administration, police and judiciary, the terrorist outfits and their mentors made efforts to scare, browbeat and control the vernacular and local print media of the Valley. These newspapers from 1989 onwards became virtual mouthpieces of the anti-national organizations. A twin strategy of ceaseless criticism of the State and Central governments and eulogizing activities of terrorists was followed. Therefore, when the turnaround towards normalcy was achieved in 1995, it was only natural that sustained efforts would be made by administration to induce the return of the media to its original role of independent observers and impartial reporters of state of affairs in the government and the society.

In the run up to the May 1996 elections, and particularly in the backdrop of a barrage of adverse propaganda unleashed by

Pakistan, media management became a critical part of the overall strategy. The institution of Public Relations in Kashmir, like many others, had almost collapsed with considerable distrust and suspicion between the administration and the media. It is no secret that the local press which overwhelmingly comprised language papers, was willy-nilly playing in the hands of terrorists and the editors' job was painfully reduced to get their statements calligraphed, or typed in English and paste these on the pages of the newspapers. So terrified and apprehensive were the editors that they would desist from airing their views in front of their colleagues and staff even in their own offices.

The prevailing conditions in the Valley could not be better elucidated than a small box item that appeared on the front page of a popular Urdu daily, *Srinagar Times*. The editor had apologized to the terrorists for his inability to accommodate all handouts of 'Mujahideen' on the front page as per their diktats. This small item appearing conspicuously on the front page was, in fact, a mere tip of the iceberg of declining control of the editors in the prevailing conditions of terror in which Kashmir Press had unfortunately come to operate. The terrorists and the forces operating from Pakistan had come to exercise vice-like control on the local press, though none of the journalists would openly accept this fact for different reasons. The press was unwittingly providing requisite oxygen to the terrorist and secessionist outfits, much needed for their survival. By their actions, be it killing or the mere threats, which were perceived to be executionable, the terrorists tightened their grip over the susceptible segments of population and institutions, and media was no exception. It had over the years succumbed to their demands and diktats, howsoever unreasonable these might have been. In most of the cases though this was more due to expediency and for survival rather than any conviction of support to the cause that terrorists espoused.

With the terrorists thirst for publicity remaining unquenched despite getting the prime space in the press, the editors had, by and large, resigned to their lot. The newspapers had become devoid of any good reading material and were more often seen as 'propaganda sheets of terrorists'. The name of the government, be it the State or the Union, would generally appear in the local Press in the negative light. The administration had also reconciled with the coverage of its activities and announcements in the Jammu based Press and the Government controlled electronic media.

This was the overall print media situation in the Valley when major initiative was planned for restoration of peace through revival of the democracy. The change in the overall security situation in the Valley had a natural effect on the moorings of the media, which was doing tightrope walking in the changing situation. The things had started looking up in the second half of 1995, with the appointment of a new Director of information, K.B. Jandial, an outstanding officer, who took upon himself the task of turning the tide against all odds, with full support of the government, particularly the Home Department. It was a battle of wits and nerves, which was fought courageously and professionally and won in the most trying circumstances Kashmir had ever seen on the media front. The man who was picked up for this job in view of his commitment and public relations skills, started breaking the ice that had accumulated over the years on the government and Press relationship.

With an eye on possible elections in 1996, the administration in general, and Information Department in particular, started gearing up for the challenge on the media front. The strategy adopted by Punjab Government in a similar situation that had prevailed in the State in early nineties was also closely examined. Punjab Government had armed the District Magistrates with powers of seizure under provisions of the Criminal Procedure Code. The police and the administration used to chase the erring newspapers in every corner of the State and seize copies to prevent dissemination of the objectionable published material.

The strategy adopted in J&K encompassed various measures, which could be broadly categorized as public relations efforts, enforcement of legal provisions relating to press and prompt police action. Major thrust was directed to convince the editors that printing of objectionable material was prejudicial to the return of peace and overall welfare of the people of the state. They were requested and encouraged to voluntarily decide to say 'no' to it and help making environment congenial for the restoration of democracy.

The strategy revolved around the threat of forfeiture of newspapers carrying objectionable material as and when published, but first try to prevent publication of such material aimed at spreading fear and disaffection amongst government servants and general public. This included publication of threats and advertisements eulogizing slain terrorists, as such reports were detrimental to the public interest and return of peace.

Unlike in Punjab, Srinagar and Jammu cities were the only places from where major newspapers were being published and the Home Department accordingly delegated powers to the District Magistrates of Srinagar and Jammu districts to seize the newspapers carrying objectionable material. However, in practice, these powers were used only in two cases. The determined resolve of the government to act tough when required, a deft combination of coercive and persuasive effort and a dramatic turn in the situation in later days left hardly any need for such seizures. The hard labour that went into putting into practice the media management strategy did bear fruits.

Before touching the highly sensitive subject of enforcing legal provisions against the press with the objective of checking printing of seditious and other objectionable material prejudicial to interests of the State and public peace, it was essential to keep the Press Council of India, fully informed about the situation and seek guidance and support from it to enforce the law in the public good so that no body could later on accuse the Government of muzzling the freedom of the press.

Accordingly, a communication was addressed to the Chairman, Press Council of India, drawing its attention towards the publication of such material in the local newspapers and requesting it to exercise its influence and moral authority over the editors and make them to desist from indulging in such publications. Enumerating a long list of objectionable material that the local press had been publishing, the letter mentioned the fact that the J&K Government had been persuading the editors to desist from such writings but there had been no let up in such writings in the local newspapers that continued to threaten the public peace and abet terrorists' violence and secessionist activities. The Government did not wish to use coercive methods to prevent publication of material prejudicial to the public peace and security of the State and would like to use persuasive methods for the purpose.

The letter further mentioned, "We have also written letters to the editors of the leading newspapers listing the type of objectionable material that they have been carrying in their newspapers, and sought their cooperation. But there is no positive response to it. The Jammu and Kashmir Government would like the Press Council of India to deliberate on this issue and exercise its influence and authority over the editors and make them to desist from indulging in such publication. The Government would welcome any suggestion from the Council on this issue. Needless to say that security has been repeatedly offered to the media persons in case they feel threatened from the terrorists."

The Director Information was also simultaneously engaged in informal and formal meetings with editors of leading newspapers of the Valley, individually as well as collectively, and shared with them the concern of the government over continuous publication of objectionable material which attracted legal action almost everyday and impressed upon them to show courage and stand up against the interference of terrorists in the exercise of their right to freedom of Press. These meetings laid the ground for future relationship between the government and the Press in general. These unpublicized meetings revealed the state of mind of the editors and also palpable anxiety over their security. While sharing the concern of the State, the editors would express inability and helplessness to prevent publication of anti-State and pro-terrorist material.

The Director Information also apprised them of the legal provisions and the editors' bounden responsibility towards the society and sought their cooperation to provide to the readers constructive, useful and variety of material essential for benefit of the society. They were also told that in the atmosphere of the terror their newspapers might be inadvertently, promoting the alien cult of violence, which was neither good for the people nor for them and also retarded the return of peace and democracy in the State. It was also made clear that the government might stop advertisements to the newspapers that carry objectionable material.

It certainly wasn't easy to make the senior journalists see reasons and re-motivate them towards their professional ethics. However, as a result of sustained effort over a period of about six months, the journalists at least started appreciating that no government can be expected to be a mute spectator all the time to gross violations of the laws, for it had the bearing on the welfare of the people and overall situation in the Valley. The precipitative action could no longer be avoided especially when serious efforts were on for initiation of an electoral process. The message was loud and clear. The Government was determined, if required, to take action under law including sealing of printing presses. The local press was also fully aware of the dilemma between refusing to publish highly provocative and objectionable material and violation of relevant provisions of Ranbir Penal Code and J&K Criminal Procedure Code. The first impact of the prolonged dialogue was that the press began to exercise a little restraint in publishing obituaries eulogizing terrorists' and terrorist threats.

After a series of meetings with Director Information, a wrap up meeting of the editors was convened by the Additional Chief Secretary (Home) at Srinagar on April 10, 1996. The interaction took place in a cordial atmosphere, over tea and snacks, in a government guesthouse. While reiterating government's continuing commitment to the freedom of press, it was made clear that the government would no longer allow anyone to abet or promote violence, secessionism, communalism, ill will or hatred among various communities, derail electoral process and sought cooperation of editors and media persons to check this dangerous trend. The editors were also told in unambiguous term about the government's determination to hold elections and that atmosphere had to be created where nobody felt threatened while exercising right of franchise. They were also apprised about the spurt in the statements of Pakistan Prime Minister and other leaders across the border besides, and of the terrorists and Hurriyat leaders with common theme that elections would not be allowed to be held as obviously it ran counter to their interest.

In the meeting, the editors were repeatedly told that the government had been tolerating their objectionable writings as it always felt that the journalists were functioning under tremendous pressure and whatever was being published was not being done willfully but under coercion and threat. But now the time had come when such material needed to be prevented from appearing in the Press because it would affect the entire effort to hold election and to restore peace. The meeting concluded on a hopeful and positive note, from the governments' point of view. The senior editors in Jammu were also sensitized about these interactions.

On April 17, 1996, a letter was sent to editors of leading newspapers of Srinagar, formally 'advising' them to desist from publishing objectionable material. The letter listed reports that the Government considered as objectionable, like obituary advertisements of killed terrorists, threats to individuals, groups of people, government functionaries, policemen, political workers, etc., publishing interviews, statements, speeches and claims of terrorists, secessionists and banned terrorist outfits, publication of terrorists' calls for *bandh*, etc. The letter reiterated that the publication of such objectionable and subversive material in newspapers attracted action under Ranbir Penal Code and Cr.P.C. requiring initiation of criminal proceedings against the editors. It mentioned, "We are, however, aware of the security problem and the pressure of the terrorists and their outfits on editors for getting their statements published in newspapers. The government has, time and again, offered security to the Press. In case, you perceive any threat from the terrorists, you can approach the Inspector General CID/Security immediately for providing you need based security after proper assessment". The letter concluded with an exhortation, "Please extend your full cooperation to the government and contribute in curbing terrorist activities and violence and early return of peace, normalcy and communal harmony by avoiding publication of objectionable material ... I sincerely hope that there would be no occasion for the government to resort to legal recourse which will, of course, be the last resort".

Since the Information Department is a PR face of the government, this matter-of-fact letter was signed by the Deputy Secretary (Home).

The reaction was on expected lines. The editors in Srinagar convened an emergency meeting to deliberate upon the letter, which they considered as a 'threat to the freedom of the press'. Their reaction to the government's unprecedented move was though a guarded one. However, the reaction of the terrorists to the ban on publication of their threats and statements was more pronounced. The Hizbul Mujahideen on April 19, 1996, came out with a statement threatening 'retaliatory' ban on publication of government advertisements and handouts and threatened the editors of dire consequences in case they violate the diktat, warning 'the staff of such newspaper will be punished for their sin treating their act as treachery'.

The editors hurriedly gathered again in the evening to decide their course of action in the backdrop of government's resolve and terrorists' threat. Weighing the options available and in view of groundwork already done by Director Information they finally decided to suspend their publication from 21st April, and resumed publication of their newspapers only after the polling was completed on May 30, 1996. The administration appreciated that it was for first time that the editors took such a courageous step collectively. In a way they jointly refused to follow terrorists' diktat.

After suspension of the publication of Srinagar-based local dailies, a close vigil was maintained on the reports published in the newspapers in Jammu and outside the State so that the environment was not vitiated. Showing determination to implement the decision to prevent circulation of objectionable material in the Valley, the government seized copies of two outside newspapers, Awam, an Urdu daily on May 10, and *Kashmir Times* and *Dainik Kashmir Times* on May 12. Both these papers were carrying objectionable material.

While the government showed unprecedented resolve to take action to prevent objectionable press reports, it simultaneously opened a channel of communication. To regularly feed the Press about the activities of the government and the preparations for the election, daily briefings were organized by the Police and Army spokesmen, headed by Director Information This provided a forum for fruitful interaction between the media and the administration. The media persons were able to seek clarifications from the authorities. In spite of some deficiencies, the exercise proved to be of considerable benefit to both the government as well as the media.

Managing the local newspapers during May 1996 elections was, indeed, a major breakthrough keeping in view the blatant misuse of the local press by terrorists since 1989 Parliamentary elections which terrified the voters to the extent they did not dare to come out of their homes. The telling newspaper photo of a TV set kept in a trolley as prize for any one who would venture out to exercise right of franchise had proved disastrous for the polling in the Valley then.

But suspension of local newspapers was not enough. Other steps were also taken as part of the media strategy, which started unfolding step by step. Elaborate arrangements were put in place for faster dissemination of correct and authentic information of polling trends that had become equally imperative, given the continuing orchestrated anti-elections propaganda unleashed by Pakistan, terrorists, Hurriyat and their lackeys. The important question that haunted the media managers was 'who would hit the headlines first' the government through J&K Information Department or terrorists through their well established network? It would not only affect the trend of polling but also influence the entire electoral process. Since the elections were being held in phases, impact of good electors' response in one phase had the bearing on the remaining ones.

This situation had called for professional and imaginative handling by media managers to foil the designs of the enemy. They did perform well with rare coordination between the State government PR wing, Government of India controlled electronic media, administration and the security agencies. With local newspapers having shut down their offices, the dependence was largely on Doordarshan and All India Radio and partly on other private channels, which had not yet become 24 hours news channels with instant coverage. Special news bulletins on Kashmir polling were successfully arranged on the electronic media. National and international press were taken care of and their news needs were met by making the exercise as transparent as possible in view of the security situation.

To meet the deadline of news bulletins and to tell the millions of eagerly waiting people within and outside the State about the latest polling position, especially in the Valley, the Government requisitioned, for the first time, MI17 and 'Cheetah' helicopters and placed them at the disposal of Director Information for carrying local media persons as well as those from outside the State. Depending upon the number of desiring media persons, air sorties were arranged. One 'Cheetah' helicopter was exclusively chartered for Doordarshan crew, and they did the job well.

All India Radio too flashed series of spot reports and that too in the voicecast from local media persons from near and far off places. Be it Ganderbal or Kupwara, Baramulla or Tral, Pahalgam or Tangmarg Gulmarg, Doda or Poonch, Kargil or Leh the electronic media brought live encouraging scenes of enthusiastic voters. There was hardly any major town left uncovered by the media attention. This set the trend for subsequent polling. Almost every district was covered by road and air sorties of media parties representing local, national, international print and electronic media.

The results were rewarding. Most of the newspapers wrote positively about the return of democracy in J&K and commented well about the electoral process which is evident from following headlines–"Voting in Kashmir mostly peaceful (*Kuwait Times*, May 8, 1996); "Heavy turnout in Anantnag, Baramulla–Terrorists, rain fail to deter Kashmir voters (*Indian Express*, May 24, 1996); "Kashmir proves a point (*The Hindustan Times*, June 1, 1996); "A Significant Poll (*The Hindu*, June 1, 1996), "Kashmiris vote for peace (*The Tribune*, June 1, 1996); "Mandate for Democracy (*The Times of India*, June 4, 1996); "Way paved for J&K Assembly elections (*The Hindustan Times*, June 1, 1996); "Carry on Kashmir (*The Telegraph*, June 5, 1996); "End of Terrorism? (*The Statesman*, June 6, 1996); "Voters in the Valley did exercise a choice (*The Pioneer*, June 6, 1996); "A popular vote Results prove J&K polls were fair, says Ghazanfar Butt (*The Pioneer*, June 12, 1996); "A new start in Kashmir (*The Hindu*, June 16, 1996); "Polls in J&K: The other side of the story (*The Statesman*, June 19, 1996); "UK Minister lauds elections in J&K (*The Hindustan Times*, June 19, 1996); "Kashmir's vote and the political implications (*Frontline*, June 28, 1996); "Positive polls Interview with Yusuf Tarigami (*Frontline*, June 28, 1996); "Polls in J&K From fear to hope (*Indian Express*, June 19, 1996); "What a contrast! (*The Hindustan Times*, July 3, 1996).

This experience of media management was of a great help in preparing for September Assembly poll where even the National Conference, which had declined to participate in the Lok Sabha elections, jumped into the fray. Their joining the election was also significantly influenced by the successful conduct of May poll and the confidence generated among the people. Towards this elaborate coverage and subsequent good comments in the press and excellent media management also contributed significantly.

Musings

Between Phase-II and Phase-III of the elections in the State, political fortunes were changing at fast pace in New Delhi. Atal Behari Vajpayee who had been sworn in as the Prime Minister following completion of the Parliamentary elections in the rest of the country on 7th May, was unable to prove his majority in the Lok Sabha and announced the resignation of his government during his speech in the house on 28th May, paving the way for H.D. Deve Gowda to become the next Prime Minister and form the new government. The State administration and the security forces were put under constant pressure of another kind throughout the entire month of May by the Home Ministry and the Department of Jammu and Kashmir Affairs by constantly seeking all kinds of details about various activities not only on day-to-day basis but at times on hourly basis. To this was added a constant stream of references regarding the welfare of polling parties from the concerned parent departments as well as family members who would endlessly inquire about the welfare of their employees and relatives from whosoever could be contacted on telephone. It was only due to meticulous maintenance of records and monitoring of movements that almost a continuous track was kept of each polling party and each unit and sub-unit of the security forces. This effort was further helped by the excellent communication network that had been put in place by all wings of the security forces and which had functioned extremely efficiently during the entire period.

The policy of transparency followed by the State and the Central Governments also paid handsome dividends during the period prior to, as also during the elections as well as post election periods. A number of foreign delegates, human rights activists and Red Cross teams visited the Valley. From the beginning of 1994 to August 1996, as many as 384 ambassadors, diplomats, parliamentarians, 34 human rights activists and 149 other foreign visitors toured various parts of the Valley to have first hand knowledge about the ground realities. More particularly to assess the mood of the people and the human rights violations by the terrorists. These delegations and personalities visited jails, joint interrogation centers and spoke to some of the suspects, including the foreign mercenaries under custody. They also visited migrant camps in Jammu apart from meeting some of the secessionist leaders and having interaction with the government functionaries. One of the important milestones in the implementation of the transparency policy was the signing of Memorandum of Understandings between the Government of India and Geneva based International Committee of Red Cross (ICRC) following which ICRC teams were allowed to visit places of detention where the terrorists had been lodged. From December 1995, onwards the ICRC representatives visited all detention centers on more than one occasion in Jammu and Kashmir as well as outside the State to see for themselves the conditions in such places of detention. This was a major step forward in showing to the world that the government had nothing to hide and was open to the institutions and persons of impartial credentials to assess the conditions of the detenues.

The surrendered terrorists also played a positive role in the successful conduct of these elections. The process of surrender itself created a conducive atmosphere helping the return to normalcy. A number of them also helped the security forces in counter insurgency operations thus facilitating the task of the security forces as well as the State administration.

The security scenario immediately prior to the announcement of the Lok Sabha elections had contained the terrorists violence within the manageable limits and the public had become disenchanted with Pakistan backed machinations because of the continued violence in the Valley in the name of so-called jehad. The gaining of upper hand by the security forces and the firm handling of the Hazratbal incident in the last week of March 1996, further demonstrated the State Government's resolve to crush terrorism in all its forms. The announcement of Lok Sabha elections though initially received with some degree of skepticism and apprehensions by a section of the people reached a situation where the electoral process gained support from a major section of the public and proved to be a turning point towards the restoration of the democratic process in the State. Pakistan tried her best and continued sustained efforts to disrupt the onset of democratic process and to intimidate the people of the State particularly in Kashmir Valley and Doda district by engineering various acts of terrorism aimed at generating fear psychosis among the people. ISI specifically targeted its efforts to increase the level of infiltration and the proportion of foreign mercenaries, urging its agents to cause large scale sabotage and eliminate important political personalities as well as communalize the situation in important population centers of Jammu region and cause damage to the government buildings and communication infrastructure.

Announcement of Lok Sabha elections did not alter the pattern of violence perpetrated by the terrorists particularly in the killing and abduction of civilians, burning of school buildings and causing explosions of grenades and IEDs. The terrorists continued to hit soft targets and avoided direct confrontation with the security forces. The forces on their part maintained their target oriented operations which brought gratifying results. These operations were further intensified as elections approached. Increased vigil on the borders disrupted the terrorist line of supplies and communication, making it difficult for larger number of foreign mercenaries who were present across the border to infiltrate into the State. Even those who had managed to cross the LoC remained confined to their hideouts in jungles and high mountains due to the effective security operations undertaken by the forces. The cooperation of the people also helped in the success of counter terrorist operations. They were no longer welcomed by the public out of freewill. In some rural areas, however, they continued to get the food and shelter at the point of gun. A number of measures including the stepping up of operations by the security forces, publicity campaign in favour of the electoral process, making arrangements for the candidates and the political leaders to travel extensively amongst the people, dispelled apprehensions among the local population that the terrorists will be able to stall the initiation of the democratic process. The candidates in the Valley moved from village to village and held over six hundred public meetings. An environment was created where people articulated their political views expressing desire for revival of democratic process in loud and clear terms. Even the efforts of the Hurriyat Conference to sabotage the elections met with dismal failure, seriously undermining their oft repeated claims to be the "true representatives" of the people of the Valley. Thus even the combined efforts of rulers of Pakistan, ISI, the terrorist outfits and the APHC could not stop the successful implementation of the most important phase of the beginning of restoration of democratic rule in the State.

The Parliamentary elections could justifiably be termed as a watershed, a vote for peace and rejection of gun. A litmus test of the will be of people as well as the determination and capability of the administration and the security forces to break the impasse and move forward towards peace and normalcy. The peaceful conduct of these elections was also a major confidence building and morale boosting event for the public in general which had perceived this development as their capacity to defy the diktat of the terrorists and in furtherance of their own desire to have peace and tranquility. This led to rapid and visible further improvement in the overall environment, having signs of growing normalcy in the lives of the people and perceptible activisation in the political forces of the State. In the final analysis the successful conduct of these elections was the outcome of detailed planning of the measures required for properly conducting the exercise of such a vast magnitude which included catering for contingencies, excellent cooperation and willing support of various agencies and senior officers heading them who worked as a team without any ego hassles. Above all it was a manifestation of total commitment at individual levels as well as on collective basis for the furtherance of a national cause of great importance.

8 The Interregnum

The successful conduct of Parliamentary elections became a full dress rehearsal for preparing the necessary background and subsequent conduct of the general elections to the State Assembly. Whatever fear had existed in the minds of the government employees detailed on Parliamentary elections duty vanished almost completely as none of the employees brought from outside for the polling duties, or those of the State employees who had taken part in the polling process could be harmed by the terrorists. The security forces felt confident to make even better arrangements for the coming event which required all round effort of larger proportion. The efficacy of parameters and logistics of putting men and material, from the point of collection into the polling stations had been successfully tested. More importantly, the electors who had gone to the polling stations to elect their representatives for the Parliamentary seats, in which they had little direct stake felt secured and enthused to elect representatives for their own State Legislative Assembly.

Preparations for the Assembly elections commenced immediately after the completion of the Phase-III of the Parliamentary elections with a meeting of a large gathering in the Ministry of Home Affairs on June 4, 1996. It was an elaborate brainstorming session in which the mechanics of conduct of Parliamentary elections were gone into details, lessons learnt discussed in free and frank manner and a road map was prepared for the Assembly elections which were then expected to take place before the onset of winter the same year. Based on the deliberations of this meeting the State government conducted a detailed exercise and sent its recommendations on the immediate requirements envisaged during the forthcoming elections.

In the detailed analysis conducted by the State authorities it was anticipated that due to successful conduct of Parliamentary elections the likelihood of a surge of renewed activities by the terrorists could not be ruled out. Therefore, it called for extra vigil to be mounted for protecting those who had actively participated in the electoral process as well as candidates, political workers and their families. On this score there was no place for complacency as any harm even to a small number of this group could seriously jeopardize the bright prospects of the forthcoming event. It was also important to protect all vital installations, including the communication centers and essential facilities for which additions to static guards and mobile patrolling during the day as well as night needed to be intensified on a much bigger scale. All possible preventive measures were also to be undertaken against mischief mongers, particularly in the urban centers. Since Parliamentary elections had triggered a flurry of all round political activities, the security of political personalities, prospective candidates as well as political gatherings became a matter of very high priority for which planning and provision of resources was to be made on a much higher level. During the Parliamentary elections 110 candidates had contested for six seats, i.e almost 18 candidates per constituency. During these elections 136 Companies of CRPF were used for pre-election phase including the security of candidates. For polling duty the force deployment comprised over 550 Companies of central para military forces, which figure did not include the companies of the territorial army which were made available as the last minute reinforcement to the security grid from where same number of (CPMFs) Central para military forces could be deployed for polling duties. It was, therefore, anticipated that for actual conduct of Assembly polls, although the same level of force could be sufficient, however, the requirement during the peak elections phase including the security of the candidates, would be much higher. There were 87 Assembly constituencies and even on a conservative estimate of ten candidates per constituency the number of candidates could be in the range of 900 for whom adequate protection would be required including facilities like transportation and accommodation. This was the difficult part of the management problem. If the instructions of the Election Commission to provide equal level of security of each candidate, as was done during the Parliamentary elections, were to be followed, then only for 52 sensitive constituencies a force of 520 Companies would be needed. In addition security of equal number of ROs and AROs had to be catered for these sensitive constituencies and the same level of security planned for 156 election observers requiring additional force of 200 platoons for their security. Thus only in sensitive constituencies numbering fiftytwo, 728 platoons or 243 Companies of central para-military forces were needed.

For the less sensitive 35 constituencies, the number of candidates was expected to be in the range of 380. Adding to this figure 35 Returning Officers and 105 election observers, the number of protected persons was estimated to be in the range of 520. Even if one section was to be made available for security of each of them, at an average, the requirement of protection force itself would be in the range of 173 platoons or 58 Companies. Therefore, the total requirement of force for pre-election phase itself worked out to 301 Companies only to protect the individuals engaged with the election process. In addition, at least 50 more companies were required to provide area security for public meetings etc., throughout the State thereby raising the figure to 350 Companies for pre-polling duties, over and above the force which already on ground was engaged in area domination activities and anti-terrorist operations. Therefore, the total requirement of force for pre-election and election purposes was ideally in the range of 900 Companies of central para-military forces catering for 350 Companies for pre-poll election duties and 550 for the conduct of actual election.

Similarly the requirement for bullet proof cars and Gypsies was also many times more as compared to Parliamentary elections. This figure came to 728 bullet proof vehicles catering for the security requirements of 520 candidates, fiftytwo Returning Officers and 156 election observers in the sensitive constituencies. As compared to this requirement the State government had at its disposal only 170 bullet proof cars and 200 bullet proof. Gypsies which were just sufficient to cater for the existing protected persons, official visitors, special escorts and operational requirements, etc. Therefore, for the Assembly elections over seven hundred bullet proof vehicles were required to be procured and for this purpose alone an amount of over Rs. 36 crores was required. Apart from monetary requirements of this magnitude, fabrication capacity of bullet proof vehicles being limited both within and outside the State, the procurement of bullet proof vehicles became a critical component and required immediate decision and execution at various levels.

Similarly, very large number of non bullet proof vehicles for escorts and other duties was also needed. At the rate of two vehicles per candidate and officials of sensitive constituencies and one each for the rest, the total requirement of these vehicles worked out to be over 1900. With an average cost of Rs. 2 lacs per vehicle, the financial requirement for this was in the range of Rs. 40 crores. The money being available, the procurement of these vehicles was not to pose any major difficulty as these were readily available in the market over a period of couple of months which time was certainly available when these plans were being drawn up. However, the drivers for such a large additional fleet had to be catered for. Since this was a temporary requirement and the disposal of these vehicles after the elections had not yet been decided it was not possible for either the State government or the central para-military forces to plan for creation of such additional number of posts of drivers. Therefore, it was planned to pool the manpower resources of all the Central para military forces CPMFs and other organizations in terms of trained drivers and depute them to the State government on temporary basis. Even though with the change in the overall perception among the people and the government employees, in the aftermath of the Parliamentary elections, it was expected that the participation in the Assembly elections by the State government employees would be of much higher level, still contingency plans had to be prepared to get polling personnel from the Government of India as was done during the earlier elections, although the requirement could be much less this time.

Since most of the troops deployed for polling duties as well as polling personnel were required, for days together to stay in tents and sleep on the ground it could be very difficult to operate in the inclement weather conditions. This point was brought home very tellingly in the month of May when the whether had suddenly gone bad. It was, therefore, recommended by the State government that the election process should be completed by September 1996, after which the weather would start getting uncomfortably chilly in the Valley as well as mountainous region of Jammu. If the elections were carried beyond that date, weather conditions could make it very difficult for the troops and the polling personnel to operate, impede their mobility as well as effectiveness and also require huge extra administrative inputs.

Another reason for recommending early holding of Assembly elections, close on the heels of the Lok Sabha elections, was the presumption that it could deny Pakistan an opportunity to give fillip to its disinformation campaign and get time to reorganizing its terrorist network which had been kept under check during the Parliamentary elections. It would have also enabled the administration to continue the momentum of enthusiasm generated in the public as well as maintain the level of political activity thereby adding to the interest of the people in the revival of the duly elected government.

In view of the fact that multifarious preparations were required for the conduct of Assembly elections, it was not considered possible or feasible to complete the entire process before July 17, 1996, the date till which the current period of President's Rule had been extended in the State. Therefore, with the approval of the Parliament another extension of the President's

Rule was notified for a further period of six months beyond that date. High level political consultations were held at the State and the national capital with a view to mobilize the political opinion even further ensuring greater participation in the Assembly elections. For the first time since 1987, the Prime Minister came to Srinagar on July 6, 1996 followed by visits to Jammu and Ladakh a month later.

The day on which parliamentary elections were concluded, the issue of holding general elections to the Assembly started being discussed from many quarters. The National Conference members must have watched the parliamentary elections rather closely and critically. More importantly, they must have felt convinced by that time that the candidates who would be fielded by them would be safe while moving among the electorate and that the government in power had no desire to provide out of way help to the political groups floated by surrendered terrorists. Therefore, the National Conference lost no time in expressing it willingness to participate in the assembly elections. However, concerns were voiced by them as well as by other political parties that electoral rolls used for the Parliament elections did not carry names of many voters particularly in Kashmir Valley. There was hardly any time left to go through the elaborate process of intensive revision of electoral rolls or even summary revision. The Election Commission, therefore, decided to take recourse to the omnibus provision contained in Section 19 of the "J&K Representation of the People Act" which provides that any elector can approach the local ERO (DC of the district) or AEROs (local Tehsildar, Ward Officer in respect of Urban bodies) seeking inclusion of his name in the electoral rolls. The election machinery gave full publicity to this enabling provision of the Act and made a very large number of relevant application forms available to the political parties, organizations and individuals. As a result of this exercise, over a couple of lakh new names were added to the electoral rolls in the next few months.

By the first fortnight of July, the preparations within the State government were in full swing. A meeting of all the Deputy Commissioners was held on 8th to review arrangements for the

Assembly elections in which all the nuts and bolts of the electoral process and administration as well as security arrangements required were gone through in detail to ensure that nobody left the meeting with doubts in his mind. Broadly the issues discussed included the proposed election dates to be recommended, revision of electoral rolls, procurement of election material, printing of ballot papers, changes in the list of the polling stations, finalizing a list of Returning Officers and AROs. On the security side the prevailing security scenario was discussed in detail along with measures that were required to make it even more safe for the political activists and the general public, availability of forces for pre-poll and polling phases, establishment of campsites for central para-military forces and polling parties, as well as accommodation and security for the contesting candidates. Measures were also deliberated upon to ensure full participation of the government employees in the election process. This included finalization of package of incentives for men deployed on poll duties, progress of disbursement of incentive already announced to the employees who took part in the Parliamentary elections and regularization of daily wagers who took part in the earlier elections. It was felt that quick rewards as per the scheme announced to the government employees who had taken part in the Parliamentary elections would enthuse greater participation in the next round. This important meeting ended on a very optimistic note and each participant was confident of the successful conduct of the Assembly elections.

Based on the recommendations of the State government which had been sent to the Government of India by middle of June, earlier deliberations in the first week of June in the Ministry of Home Affairs and further discussions held within various department of the State government as well as Unified Headquarters and subsequently followed by meeting of the Deputy Commissioners on 8th July, a final round of discussions was held in the Ministry of Home Affairs towards the middle of July which, towards the end, was attended by the Union Home Secretary also. An overall review was undertaken of the security situation, availability of additional forces, requirement of other resources and most suitable election schedule. During these meetings it became evident that the level of forces available for the Assembly elections would be in the range of 220 Companies of central para-military forces for pre-election duties and 420 additional Companies could be spared for the conduct of election duties. The availability of this force was further circumscribed by the fact that as per the indications then available, elections to the State Assembly in Uttar Pradesh were expected to begin in the first week of October 1996. Therefore, in all probability the elections in Jammu and Kashmir and Uttar Pradesh could overlap for some period. A part of the additional forces that would be sent to Jammu and Kashmir would certainly be required for election duty in UP latest towards the last week of September. Keeping this stipulation in mind and also the desirability of conducting elections in the Valley first and in Doda district in the last phase for the same reasons which had obtained during the Parliamentary elections, it was felt that a four-phased poll spread over 23 to 25 days would be a viable proposition. If the polling could start and finish within the month of September that would be more advantageous from point of view of logistics as well as the availability of resources. Any schedule of elections before the beginning of September would be difficult to manage as the lead time for planning and preparations would be less than the required period, as also it would coincide with Shri Amarnathji Yatra taking place in the Kashmir Valley which itself required a major effort of the State administration and the security forces. If elections were to be held later than September then considerable difficulty would arise due to setting in of winter in large part of the State with possible clash of schedule with UP elections.

It was also agreed in these discussions that the pre-election forces would be made available to the State by the first week of August and the rest as early as possible depending upon the schedule of polls announced by the Election Commission.

The security of candidates which were expected to be in the range of eight to nine hundred and out of which over five hundred were likely to be in sensitive constituencies also came up for discussion. Due attention was also paid to the safety of Returning Officers, Election Observers, visiting dignitaries and political personalities including requirement of increased number of bullet proof vehicles. As procurement of such a large quantity of bullet proof vehicles was not possible within such a short period, even if the money for the same was made available, it was felt that the security to all the candidates even in sensitive constituencies and other protected persons could not be at a uniform scale and would have to be planned and provided for at a sliding level depending upon the assessed threat perception and availability of resources.

During the Parliamentary elections, the Ministry of Home Affairs had provided polling parties, from outside the State, at the scale of five persons per polling station. Since the elections were held only in two constituencies of the Valley on one day, over ten thousand polling persons had to be airlifted to the Valley and deinducted after the polls. This time not more than three persons per polling station would be required from outside the State and other two could be managed even from the Valley districts. Since the elections in the Valley were proposed to be held in three phases, the largest number of polling stations in a single phase was expected to be around 1100, keeping some margin for reserves, no more than 3600 polling persons would be required from outside the State during the Assembly elections. However, out of this number at least 1200 Urdu knowing personnel were required. The need for sleeping bags and bullet proof jackets for the central para- military forces and the polling parties also came under discussion and it was decided that since sufficient stocks were carried over from the Parliamentary elections with the CPMFs, there was no need to plan for any additional requirement in this regard.

Other issues which came under discussion and on which decisions were taken pertained to determination of additional financial resources to the State to meet various kinds of election expenditure including hire and POL charges for large number of vehicles to be requisitioned, making arrangements for accommodation of candidates, procurement of improved categories of arms and ammunitions for the central para-military forces, construction of pre-fabricated huts for the security forces and the candidates. A scheme of incentives was prepared by the State government for the employees who would take part in the polling process. The requirement of doctors, paramedical staff, medical equipment and drugs also came up for discussion and it was felt that the State government, in view of the changing conditions in the State, should work out a realistic plan of additional resources required from the Centre for this purpose after discussing these with the Union Ministry of Health and Family Welfare.

It was also decided to sanction additional posts of one thousand Special Police Officers for protection of candidates and five hundred Village Defence Committees for the Valley and one hundred additional Village Defence Committees for Doda district. The State government was asked to take immediate steps for recruitment and stationing of additional SPOs and VDCs as early as possible.

Preparing for Assembly Elections

The actual process for the conduct of Assembly Elections was set rolling on August 7, 1996, with the issuance of notification of the polling schedule by the Election Commission of India. The Notification mentioned request of the Ministry of Home Affairs, Government of India, to the Commission to take necessary steps for conducting the polls to the Jammu and Kashmir Legislative Assembly and that the Commission had decided to hold the elections to constitute the Legislative Assembly in the State in September 1996. It also made a reference to the amendments in the Electoral Laws which had come into force from August 1, 1996, which apart from other provisions enabled filing of nomination papers, etc., on different dates depending upon different phases of election process. As per the notification the elections were to be held in four phases with polling taking place in Phase-I on 7th September, Phase-II on 16th, Phase-III on 21st and the polling of Phase-IV was to be conducted on September

30, 1996. Different stages of each phase were to take place on different dates. For example for Phase-I polling notification was to be issued on 14th August with last date of filing nomination papers being 21st August. Scrutiny of nomination papers was to take place next day and the last date for withdrawal of candidature was fixed on 24th August and the date of polling on 7th September. Completion of polling process in all the four phases was to be ensured on the same day i.e. on October 8, 1996".

At the ground level elections in Phase-I were to be held in 26 constituencies of six districts – ten in Baramulla, five in Kupwara, two such in Leh, and Kargil, four in Rajouri and three in Poonch. In Phase-II the elections were planned for 34 Assembly constituencies with ten in Anantnag, six in Pulwama, five in Kathua and thirteen in Jammu. Phase-III involved three districts of Srinagar, Budgam and Udhampur with ten, five and six constituencies each, respectively, going to the polls, and in Phase-IV only Doda district was involved with six constituencies making a total of 87 Assembly constituencies. Over three regions of the State with forty-six constituencies in Kashmir Valley, thirty-seven in Jammu region and four in Ladakh, a total of 692 candidates filed their nomination papers. Out of these, 146 nominations were rejected or withdrawn leaving behind 546 contesting candidates in the fray with an average of five candidates per seat in the Valley and eight candidates per seat in the Jammu province.

Immediately on the announcement of elections by the Election Commission of India on August 7, 1996, the whole process of preparation of elections was put into high gear with the Union Home Minister himself visiting Srinagar on the very next day on 8th August. He was given a detailed briefing at the Unified Headquarters about the entire gamut of preparations and the outstanding issues needed to be sorted out. The Home Minister and his party also visited Baramulla and left for Delhi the next day after having an interaction with important political personalities as well as holding discussions with the force commanders and heads of intelligence agencies as also officers of the State administration. Before leaving for Delhi, the Home

Minister also paid a short visit, by helicopter, to Doda. The Home Minister paid yet another visit to Srinagar on 22nd August, to once again review the arrangements for the elections and left for Delhi the same day.

As already mentioned, the availability of forces ear- marked for the Assembly Elections was 220 Companies for the pre-election Phase with 450 Companies of central para-military forces detailed for polling duties. This comprised mainly of the CRPF and BSF but also included complements from ITBP, RPF, CISF, SSB and PAP as had happened during the Parliamentary elections. For movement, administration and maintenance of such a large body of troops as well as over three thousand of polling personnel coming from outside the State, large scale logistics had to be planned for and carried out effectively on time. One of the key components of the logistic arrangements was, once again, the requisition and keeping on road over three thousand vehicles of different kinds. This time around the whole process of marshalling of additional transport was a little easier than the Parliamentary elections as encouraged by the earlier experience, the transporters from Jammu region readily came forward for hiring of out their vehicles and over eighty percent of requirement was met from within the State with the rest coming from the neighbouring states of Punjab and Haryana. The availability of such a large component of transport from within the State not only made matters less difficult for the administrative machinery, it also ensured increased involvement of the people of the State in the electoral process. However, a day-to-day monitoring was carried out of the availability of transport throughout the month of August. For example on the first of the month, 135 vehicles could be requisitioned from Jammu and 20 more from outside the State. This figure was 108 and 13 respectively on 12th August. On 21st, 194 vehicles were marshalled from Jammu and 53 from outside the State. By 29th of the month the entire requirement of transport had been fully procured and most of it dispatched to the required stations.

The process of planning and monitoring for the supply of essential commodities and maintenance of essential services had also been set in motion and a high level review was carried out at New Delhi on 21st August. In this meeting the Food Corporation of India mentioned that they had built up buffer stock of foodgrains to meet two months requirement in advance keeping in view the possible traffic disruptions on national highway due to monsoon, terrorist activities, as also heavy movement of central para-military forces and Shri Amarnathji Yatra. Oil Companies had not yet topped up their entire tankage capacity which required increased efforts on their part and they were asked to do so positively by the end of August. In a departure from the method adopted during the Parliamentary elections when the patrol and diesel pumps in the Valley belonging to the State and Central organizations were allocated to various central agencies, central para military forces and the Deputy Commissioners, the CPMF representatives this time indicated that they would directly lift their stocks from the Oil Depots, and for further distribution to their units and sub-units they would make use of storage capacity already created by them in the shape of barrels and jerry cans. However, the Deputy Commissioners of different districts were authorized to make use of the storage capacity of the State and the Central Government organizations within their respective districts. The State Oil Coordinator was asked to ensure that all storage capacities were kept fully filled for use during the election period. For day-to-day requirement of all consumers in the State, stocks should be made available out of the daily dispatches directly made from Jammu and Jalandhar depots.

The contingency plan for medical arrangements drawn up by the State government in consultation with the Ministry of Health was also reviewed. Since the administration, unlike the Parliamentary elections, anticipated the functioning of the State health facilities at primary, secondary and tertiary levels to be normal during the election period, no requirement was felt to replicate the medical cover that had been made during the Parliamentary elections. However, it was decided to keep two Super Specialist teams in readiness in New Delhi to be airlifted at a very short notice. In case of requirement three Specialist

Teams and three medical teams were planned to be deputed to Srinagar for deployment in main district hospitals for the election period. Necessary airlifting arrangements for medical teams and equipment had been tied up. Similarly, stocks of essential drugs and other life saving medicines for the 14 district hospitals in the State and major hospitals in Jammu and Srinagar were approved and for this purpose an amount of Rs. 56 lacs was released by the Union Ministry of Health and Family Welfare. One hundred makeshift ambulances with necessary equipment and first aid kits were also made available to the CPMFs during the month of August itself. Right from 15 August onwards daily monitoring of essential supplies was made at the State capital by the Food, Supplies and Transport Department and daily report transmitted to Department of Jammu and Kashmir Affairs so that any intervention required at that level could be quickly made. By September 3, 1996, the available stocks with various agencies in the Valley included 29778 MTs rice, 7287 MTs of wheat and 329 MTs of sugar. The petroleum products were adequate in stock with 3522 KL of diesel, 1379 KL of Kerosene oil and 479 KL of petrol. The oil companies had still not been able to fully build up their reserve stocks, which was particularly due to the closure of the national highway for a week during the later part of August and, therefore, they were hard pressed to do the same at the earliest.

As planned, the movement of additional 220 Companies for the pre-poll duties had been completed by the first week of August thereafter the force level started building up according to the plan. The balance 450 Companies arrived in Jammu and subsequently moved to various locations depending upon their planned deployment during different phases of elections. For Phase-I major requirements of central para-military forces was in the districts of Baramulla and Kupwara in the Valley. Although the entire polling duty force was expected to reach their camps by August 31, 1996, this target could not be met not due to some inherent organizational and logistic difficulties but primarily because of closure of the national highway and rush of ongoing and returning pilgrims for Shri Amarnathji Yatra during the second fortnight of August.

The whole scenario was graphically described in one of the reports prepared by the CRPF, excerpts of which included:

"One of the main shortcomings noticed during the Parliamentary elections was the shortage of accommodation at campsites and lack of adequate water and deep trench latrines. The problem had been compounded by heavy rains. The situation was re-assessed and it was proposed to keep all the troops in built up accommodation rather than some of them staying under canvas. Extra troops were made available for assembly segments being manned by CRPF from within existing resources to set up these camps and to ensure that these camps got ready in all respects to receive the troops with all basic facilities. Two to three sections were sent for each campsite. Thus the number of campsites was increased to approximately 270. Instructions were issued by the Government of India to the State government to provide basic facilities at the transit camps and campsites. This was done by them and the troops were much more comfortable during the Assembly elections.

"The Assembly elections coincided with Shri Amarnath- ji Yatra and because of the massive publicity and an improvement in the situation perceived also by the successful conduct of Parliament elections, it was expected that one lakh yatris would visit Shri Amarnathji during the year. In actual fact the number went much beyond this figure. Twentyseven Companies of CRPF, which were available in the State as pre-poll force were deployed for escorting and security of the yatris as also for the security of Pahalgam town which is the base camp for movement of yatris to the holy cave. Amidst the Yatra, very heavy rain and snowfall started on August 21, 1996, and this disrupted the entire yatra as people could not move from wherever they were camping between Pahalgam and the cave. Because of the landslides on the National Highway, Yatris' movements from Jammu to Pahalgam also stopped on 24th August. Yatris stranded on the Pahalgam- Amarnath route also could not move for almost seventytwo hours because of snow, rains and heavy winds and arrangements for their evacuation had to be made on a priority. In all, over two hundred yatris died due to extreme cold and exhaution. Once the National Highway opened on 26th August, the first priority was to send back the stranded yatris at Pahalgam, who by now numbered about 80,000. It was obvious that alternate arrangements for moving 253 Companies from Jammu were to be made. It was decided to go in for emergency airlifting of troops from Udhampur and Pathankot by IAF planes. None of the forces had any base at Pathankot and the CRPF had to create one within twenty four hours under a Commandant who was to organize the airlifting of CRPF, ITBP & BSF from there. Three planes each were scheduled to take off from Udhampur and Pathankot everyday and make three sorties each. However, because of technical problems Udhampur Station could not carry out required number of sorties. All the troops were required to be in position by August 30, 1996, so as to receive the polling parties on the Ist, 2nd and 3rd of September. Although the troops started arriving by air there was a problem of providing transport and other logistic support to them as it was earlier planned to move them from Jammu by road with their transport and logistic support like POL, rations, water tanks, generators, bullet proof jackets, etc. Transport was the most critical item. It had to be pooled from local units and the State government also hired some local civilian transport. Whatever transport was made available was used for ferrying the troops to campsites and then coming back to take the troops arriving on the next day. About 1600 men returning from leave had also got stranded at Jammu. Making arrangements for their stay at Jammu added to the pressures being faced by the officers at Jammu. The route finally opened for traffic from Jammu to Srinagar on 28th August, but because of the bad road condition, heavy movement of transport of the airlifted units, as also movement of remaining troops which could not be airlifted, there were major road blocks all along the route. Although arrangements were made for staggering troop movement from Jammu and Udhampur, the condition of the road being bad it took twentyfour to thirtysix hours for the troops and the transport to reach Srinagar from Jammu. The earmarked transport for various Units was then re-distributed at Srinagar and sent to their respective campsites. With all out efforts made for transporting troops by air and by road, it just became possible to ensure that all troops were in position by August 31, 1996, barely one day behind schedule but still in time to receive the poll parties. The airlifting of troops and the arrival of poll parties had been so tied up that the troops for poll parties arriving on September 1, 1996, arrived in time in the Valley. This indeed was a difficult task for the security forces who had a very trying time moving from Jammu to the Valley under adverse conditions to meet a tight schedule."

Closure of the road in the last week of August adversely affected the movement plan of forces as well as logistic arrangements. When the road opened on 28th August, a system of daily monitoring of road traffic was installed and State Traffic Police was asked to allot priority to the election related traffic. The Traffic Control Room monitoring of August 31, 1996, was as follows – load carriers 512 vehicles, election material thirteen vehicles, police 15, armed forces 108, BSF 164, CRPF 264, and ITBP 15 vehicles.

As far as the availability of polling personnel was concerned, the Deputy Commissioners did not face much difficulty in enlisting the State employees for poll duties and calling them for three phases of training through the training camps organized at various places in the districts. However, it was apprehended that they might face threats from the terrorist organizations at the time of reporting for the polling duties. Therefore, the contingency plans already prepared were put in motion. Training personnel from outside the State were sent to the Valley, in the same manner as was done in respect of Parliamentary elections but in much smaller number of around 3600. In a large number of polling stations in the Valley, election duties ultimately were exclusively carried out by the State employees and the personnel brought from outside the State were kept in the reserve. The computer generated numbering of each polling party, now consisting of three members from outside the State as against five during the Parliamentary elections, their matching with the polling station numbers in different phases of the elections as also the unit/sub-unit of the central para-military forces with which they were attached right from the point of time of their arrival at the airport till return journey had followed the same pattern as was done during the Parliamentary elections. By September 1, 1996, the Special Coordinator was able to dispatch all polling parties to the far-flung areas of Baramulla and Kupwara districts as under:

Polling Party Number			Place to which sent
1	to	17	Gurez
18	to	82	Lolab
83	to	105	Machil
106	to	163	Karnah
164	to	263	Gulmarg
264	to	334	Langate
335	to	342	Kupwara.

Also by that time, most of the forces required for polling duties had reached their respective stations in spite of problems and disruptions in traffic. The large scale movement of troops, polling personnel, logistics as well as management of the security scenario including the important compliment of looking after the security of the contesting candidates and political personalities was effectively managed by instituting mechanism of coordination and regular monitoring which was done at the apex level by the Unified Headquarters, respective departments and agencies as well as the district control rooms established for the purpose. According to the deliberations of the Unified Headquarters on September 3, 1996, out of 114 Companies of CRPF that were required to arrive in the Valley, 106 had already reached and the rest were expected to come. By the same evening, the entire compliment of BSF and ITBP had arrived in the Valley. The troops of the Punjab Armed Police required for polling duty In Jammu and Kathua districts had not yet arrived but were expected to reach within next couple of days. Whereas the movement of other central para-military forces i.e. CISF and RPF, etc., was taking place as per plan., Tthe subsequent dispatch of these forces to their respective stations for conduct of the poll of the Phase-I was also taking place satisfactorily. Regarding dispatch of polling material in respect of Gurez, it was decided in the meeting that presiding officers with polling material should be airlifted on 4th September, by helicopter whereas the polling parties could move by road. The tour programme and security of Dr. Farooq Abdullah came up for special discussion during the deliberations of this meeting and Advisor (Security) specifically directed that security cover to Dr. Farooq Abdullah should be given top priority. Since he was in Kargil on that day, it was emphasized that he should be advised not to move to Srinagar during the night but halt at Drass and start for Srinagar only the next morning. The situation in districts, election arrangements as also the overall security scenario was reviewed in this meeting.

On the pattern followed during the Parliamentary Elections, a Core Group Advisor (Security), Additional Chief Secretary (Home), IG Operations CRPF and the zonal IG/Divisional Commissioner visited all the district headquarters as well as far-flung areas to oversee the election arrangements that were being made. With the experience of the earlier elections behind them, the entire security and administrative set up had planned and executed the elections arrangements in an even more effective manner and catered for all the contingencies that could arise.

Political activity is essential and constitutes the main ingredient of all electoral processes. However, due to prevailing conditions it became even more important during this Assembly Elections, particularly the security of the candidates, political personalities and other persons taking active part in the whole process. Adequate security was planned for and provided to the candidates particularly in the Valley and Doda districts. Since due to paucity of resources, all the candidates could not be given same security cover, they were divided into three categories and provided the following scale of security:

a. One bullet proof car, two armed gypsies, two PSOs and residential guard.
b. One BP vehicle, one armed escort, two PSOs and residential guard.
c. One non-bullet proof vehicle, one armed escort, two PSOs and residential guard.

For the remaining areas two PSOs were provided to each candidate and those falling in the higher security categories were given protection as per the assessed threat perception.

About five hundred public meetings were held during the electioneering of which nearly half were organized in the terrorist infested areas in the Valley and the Doda district. As expected, there were bigger gatherings as compared to the Parliamentary elections with some public meetings attracting an audience of over five thousand even in the Valley. The electioneering in the Valley passed off peacefully barring some minor incidents. The PSOs and escorts provided to the candidates had to open firing at about twenty places in return to the attacks by the terrorists. Security grid, road opening parties, escorts with candidates and political personalities and patrolling parties gave a good account of themselves in providing high quality security coverage to the candidates, election staff, polling material and polling stations, etc.

The highest concern for personal security was however, concentrated around Dr. Farooq Abdullah, because of his own personality, as well as his status as a former Chief Minister and also President of the National Conference, the most important political organization in the State with grassroots level organization spread across all the three regions. In fact the joining of National Conference in the electoral fray had added new enthusiasm and flavour to the whole electoral process for the Assembly Elections and in spite of non-participation and call for poll boycott by the APHC, the entire Valley seemed to be taking active interest and appeared to be waiting for the elections with a sense of keen anticipation.

Dr. Farooq Abdullah addressed his first public rally in seven years at Pattan in front of an impressive gathering and responsive audience. On the same day Mian Bashir, the most important Gujjar personality in the State with a large following in his community and a very senior Congress leader, joined the National Conference giving a fillip to the electoral prospects of the party in the Valley as well as Rajouri, Poonch and parts of Udhampur districts in Jammu province. Dr. Farooq Abdullah's style of political campaigning and movement from one place to another were a nightmare for the officers of the security establishment, particularly those directly responsible for ensuring his personal security right from his PSOs to DGP of the State. On more than one occasions, he disregarded very basic principles of security and moved during hours of darkness. Once when he was advised to spend night in Drass on 3rd September, and start for Srinagar next morning and even though arrangements for his stay had been made at Drass he didn't stop there and moved for Srinagar. The entire security establishment spent sleepless and anxious hours making whatever security arrangements they could and heaved a sigh of relief when he safely reached Srinagar. On another occasion, a few days later, he was to spend the night after campaigning, at Bandipura. However, after taking dinner around 9 p.m. he suddenly decided to head back for Srinagar even though he was advised by the local officers against such a move, particularly in view of the fact that in the entire three to four hours journey no road opening parties were in place. This again created considerable commotion and anxiety till he reached Srinagar well past night.

Participation in the election process by almost the entire political spectrum and the enthusiasm displayed by a large section of the population also had an impact on the local print media which, in spite of exhortation from the terrorist groups, refrained from going over board in criticizing the efforts that were being made for the restoration of democratic government in the State.

The APHC and the terrorist organizations made sustained efforts to disrupt and sabotage the electoral process. The APHC not only didn't join the election but also issued a call and campaigned actively for the boycott of the polls by the people of the Valley. The terrorists on their part, not being able to make a dent on the security grid and take on the security forces directly, resorted to striking soft targets. Some of the more condemnable attacks made by the terrorists included killing of six tourists from Rajasthan and Allhabad who had gone to the interiors of Srinagar city for sight seeing and purchasing local articles and were gunned down by the terrorists on 16th July.

Ten days later, 15 non-Muslims were killed at two different locations on the high mountains above Ramban where villagers had gone for grazing their cattle, and on 2nd September, two National Conference workers were killed in Bandipura and three were gunned down in Sopore area. Pakistan rulers, the ISI and the terrorist outfits appeared to be making a last bid effort to disrupt and stop the resolute march of the people of the State towards restoration of democratic government. The Independence Day celebrations on 15th August were a harbinger and indicator of the incidents that were likely to be unfolded. All over the Valley the Independence Day parades and other celebrations in the State, district headquarters and other administrative centers were conducted without even a single untoward incident for the first time in the last seven years. Notwithstanding the effort of anti-national elements and disruptive forces and overcoming security, organizational and logistic difficulties, all preparations had been completed for the Phase-I of the Assembly Elections by September 5, 1996. This had been made possible only by the untiring and combined efforts of the security forces and the State administration duly backed by the Central government and with unprecedented couragte, enthusiasm and participation of the people of the State.

9 Democracy Restored

As scheduled, Phase-I of the elections took place on September 7, 1996, with polling starting at 0700 hours. This phase covered twenty-six Assembly constituencies in six districts with ten in Baramulla, five in Kupwara, two each in Leh and Kargil, four in Rajouri and three in Poonch. The polling by and large went off peacefully in spite of sporadic efforts made by the terrorists to threaten the voters and disrupt the polling process. Some incidents were also reported of firing from across the border, particularly, towards the polling stations that were located near the LoC. At the end of the day, the polling across the board was fair to heavy and compared favourably with the percentage of votes polled during the parliamentary elections in the respective districts except Leh where according to first reports the electoral participation had been lower than the parliamentary elections.

During the intervening period between the first and the second phase the electioneering campaign picked up in the South Kashmir. In one of the public meetings being addressed by Dr. Farooq Abdullah on 12th September, the terrorists managed to throw a grenade towards the dais which missed the mark and exploded much beyond the intended target. This once again underlined the need for even greater vigil and efforts for tightening the security arrangements particularly in respect of important political leaders with specific emphasis on Dr. Farooq

Abdullah's security. Apart from this incident, no major event took place till the second phase for which polling was conducted on 16th September in 34 constituencies–ten in Anantnag district, six in Pulwama, five in Kathua and thirteen in Jammu district. Some attempts were made by the terrorists to disturb the smooth polling process in both districts of the Valley. In Anantnag, a grenade was lobbed near the Government Girls High School, Nai Basti, hours before the polling was to start to scare the voters. The grenade exploded without causing any loss. Another grenade was exploded near the General Post Office of Anantnag at 0630 hours without causing any damage. A time bomb kept on a tree in village Hardushtin went off at 0800 hours, there also no loss of life occured and polling in the nearby polling station remained unaffected. Three incidents of attempted violence took place in Pulwama district also. In Mandiroo village of Tral constituency a group of people pelted stones on the vehicles of a Congress candidate causing damage to it, but no harm was caused to the occupants. In village Peth-Dialgam a bomb exploded around 0820 hours some distance away from the polling booth without causing any loss of life or injury. In village Kapran in Shopian four gun shots were fired from distance by terrorists around 1200 hours but these did not hit any of the voters. There were a few interesting sidelights during the day's polling – about 120 years old Musa Begum, a resident of village Landu of Bani constituency, cast her vote; she was reportedly the oldest person who exercised her right to vote. Three blind persons of 64, 69 and 80 years of age respectively cast their vote at polling station No.81 in village Chack Navti in Hiranagar constituency of Kathua district. Another grand old person Haji Mir Mohammad of 116-year age voted at village Ghaluti of Mendhar in Poonch district during the repoll on that day. At the end of the polling process over 40% polling had been reported from Anantnag and over 50% from Pulwama district. Similarly, the provisional figure of Kathua district indicated over 60% votes cast with Jammu returning a figure of around 55%.

Between second and third phase, G.V. Krishanamurthy, one of the Election Commissioners, paid a visit to Srinagar to review the first two phases of the polling and also oversee the arrangements which had been put in place for the remaining two phases. The third phase of election took place on the 21st September, with ten constituencies of Srinagar district going to polls along with five from Budgam and six of the Udhampur districts. Whereas, polling in Udhampur district went off without any major incident the terrorists made a number of attempts and were able to disrupt polling at a few places in Srinagar as well as Budgam districts. During the day there were fourteen incidents of terrorist violence reported in Srinagar district and two in Budgam. In Srinagar a major incident took place at around 9.20 hours in Tulamulla High School in Ganderbal constituency where two polling stations had been set up. The terrorists fired a rifle grenade which exploded near a group of people who had gathered to cast their votes causing death of one civilian and injury to fourteen others. Four CRPF men on duty were also injured in this incident. Earlier at 0530 hours a grenade was exploded near the polling booth at Drugjan School in Sonawari constituency which caused injury to one civilian and five CRPF jawans. During the entire day two civilians died and fifteen were injured in terrorist violence in Srinagar district. The causalities amongst the security forces personnel included injuries to twelve CRPF and seven BSF jawans. In Budgam district two incidents were reported where terrorists made efforts to disrupt the polling process. One IED was exploded outside the polling station building of Girls Middle School Darambug in Chhattabal constituency at 1300 hours without causing loss or injury to any person. Another IED explosion took place at polling station in village Zulba in the same constituency in which three CRPF jawans sustained minor injuries, the polling was disrupted for one hour but resumed after shifting the booth to a nearby building. At the end of the day what could be termed as brisk polling, over 52% of votes were reportedly polled in Udhampur district with Gulabgarh registering highest percentage of 66 and Chenani constituency reporting lowest voting with 47%. Corresponding figures in respect of Budgam district were over 65% with Beerwah constituency showing voter turnout of over

70% and at the lower end Chadoora constituency reporting 62% polling. Following the pattern exhibited during the Parliamentary elections, the voter turnout in Srinagar district, particularly in the urban areas was low with provisional reporting of 29% polling in the entire district. Kangan constituency reported highest percentage of voting of 65% and Amirakadal, in Srinagar city had the lowest polling with 12%. There were three polling stations in Ganderbal constituency-one in Hazratbal, two in Iddgah and one in Batmaloo where more than 80% polling was registered. On the other hand no votes were reportedly cast in two polling stations of Zadibal constituency, one of Iddgah, two of Khanyar, five of Habbakadal and three of Amirakadal constituency. With the conclusion of polling in phase three of elections, 81 constituencies out of 87 had gone to polls in the State and only six constituencies in Doda district were left to be covered in the fourth phase.

The time between phase three and the last phase of the polling was utilized for deinduction of the polling parties and put in place arrangements for counting of votes which was to start immediately after the phase four of the polling was completed. It took place in Doda district on 30th September, covering six constituencies. Since most of the area in this district comprises mountainous terrain with very difficult communication facilities, at the end of the polling only sketchy reports were available indicating that around 50 to 60% voting had taken place and no major terrorist incidents of violence came to light. Also on the same day re-polling in 23 polling stations took place in the Valley. At these locations, the polling held earlier had been countermanded by the Election Commission due to different reasons. These included two polling stations each in Karnah and Sonawari constituencies and 12 polling stations in Baramulla constituencies. One polling station each of Gulmarg and Pattan constituencies of Baramulla district also had repoll conducted. This figure in respect of Pulwama district was two with one polling station each in Pampore and Bijbehara constituencies. Two polling stations of Tullamula in Ganderbal constituency also had repoll on the same day.

With the polling taking place in the six constituencies in Doda district with repoll in 23 polling stations in the Valley on 30th September, massive exercise of conducting Assembly Elections almost came to a close with only counting and installation of popular government left to take place. On the actual days of polling, the terrorists were not able to indulge in any significant acts of violence across the State except for one major incident in Srinagar district as already mentioned. The overall voter turnout in the State was around 54% and the percentage of invalid votes was nearly three percent. Both these figures compared very favourably with the normal national figure of voting pattern. There were hardly any complaints regarding any coercion by the security forces in spite of high propaganda by the Pakistani media, APHC and their henchmen. There were also other signs of normalcy reflected in these elections such as controversies and quarrels between the candidates and agents of different parties at a number of polling stations, and the fact that re-polling was ordered by the Election Commission in around thirty polling stations across the State reflected a healthy and buoyant democracy at work. The polling day scenario was, by and large, almost the repeat of the Parliamentary elections. Some of the polling stations had to be relocated almost at the last minute under orders of the local authorities due to different reasons. Firing was resorted to from across the border to intimidate the electors and the damage caused to the polling stations located near the LoC in the districts of Rajouri, Poonch, Baramulla, Kupwara and Kargil. Long queues of electors could be seen on the TV screens of almost all the TV channels. The event was observed with keen interest throughout the world, with many of the voters interviewed by the electronic media. The most common answer was that they wanted to constitute their own government and were looking forward to the return of peace and complete normalcy in their lives. Many of the youth expressed the hope that the newly elected government would provide jobs which they were keenly looking forward to.

Poll Results

The process of counting of votes started simultaneously in all the districts and the counting centers on Ist October, with major counting centers being in Sher-i-Kashmir International Convention Complex at Srinagar and MAM College in Jammu. By late evening the picture was emerging with clear contours of National Conference sweeping the polls in the Valley and Ladakh and had made considerable inroads in Jammu region, which would have significant political manifestations on the future political developments in the State. The entire counting process was completed by well past midnight. The National Conference had bagged forty out of fortysix seats in the Valley with two going to the Congress and one each to Janata Dal, CPI(M) and Awami Leagues and independent candidates. In Ladakh region National Conference had taken three out of four seats with Congress winning in the fourth constituency. The picture in Jammu region was more mixed. There National Conference once again emerged as the single largest party by winning fourteen out of the thirty-seven seats followed by eight of BJP, four each of Congress, Janata Dal and BSP. One seat was won by Congress(Tiwari), one by Panthers Party and one by independent candidate. The overall partywise position in the 87 Assembly constituencies of the State along with polling percentage were as follows:

Polling Information

Constituencies	87	
Electorate	4761095	
Polled votes	2567038	53.92%
Valid votes	2482922	96.72%
Invalid votes	83734	3.26%

Party wise Statement

	Party	Contes-tants	Seats won	Polled votes	% age
1	J & K National Conference	81	57	863612	34.78
2	Indian National Congress	84	7	496628	20.00
3	Janata Dal	76	5	269984	10.87
4	Bharatiya Janata Party	53	8	301238	12.13
5	J&K Panthers Party	45	1	55885	2.25
6	Communist Party of India (Marxist)	4	1	23774	0.96
7	Bahujan Samaj Party	29	4	159690	6.43
8	Communist Party of India	3	-	1391	0.06
9	All India Congress Committee (T)	9	1	17473	0.70
1	Independents & others	162	3	293247	11.81

The electorate of the Valley had been traditionally voting for the National Conference which always had a very strong grassroot cadre there and, therefore, its landslide victory in the Valley did not cause a very big surprise even though wining forty out of fortysix seats certainly was a spectacular achievement for any political organization. However, in Ladakh with two seats each in Muslim majority Kargil district and predominantly Buddhist population of Leh district the National Conference winning a seat outside Kargil district was something nobody had anticipated. Therefore, the success of the National Conference candidate from Nubra constituency of Leh district came as a pleasant bonus for the party. Similarly it made its presence felt in an impressive way even in the hitherto unrepresented areas of Jammu region. Particularly in Jammu district where National Conference had not so far won even a single seat, this time its candidates were declared successfully in four out of the thirteen constituencies. Thus the party had the single largest tally in all the three regions of the State separately. The National Conference had returned to power with a very impressive mandate from the people of the State across the board.

Wrap Up

Over twenty five lac electorate of the State had used their right of franchise in the Assembly Elections. Total number of candidates who contested the elections for 87 Assembly constituencies were 546 and the overall percentage of votes polled was 53.92% with district wise polling details as given below:

Statistical Details

Name of the District	Total Electorate	Total Votes Polled	Percent age of Votes Polled to Total Electorates	No. of Valid Votes	No. of Invalid votes	percent age of Invalid votes to Total Votes Polled.
Anantnag	507855	243923	43.71	230571	13352	3.81
Budgam	268504	177763	66.21	169558	8205	4.62
Kupwara	245818	97094	39.50	90313	6781	6.98
Baramulla	491835	265550	53.99	256987	8653	3.26
Pulwama	292702	157391	53.77	146146	11245	7.14
Srinagar	565452	141242	24.99	133716	7626	5.40
Kathua	286222	180344	63.00	177817	2527	1.40
Poonch	204136	141322	69.23	139608	1714	1.21
Rajouri	267756	150273	56.12	148436	1837	1.22
Udhampur	343388	196814	57.31	193876	2938	1.49
Kargil	71241	57262	80.38	56587	675	1.18
Leh	67156	39252	58.45	38704	548	1.40
Jammu	837248	468221	55.92	459784	8437	1.80
Doda	299297	190919	63.79	187262	3657	1.23

The other relevant statistics relating to these elections included:

Terrorist Attacks

S.No.	Incident	Nos.
1	No. of attacks on candidates while on move.	38
2	No. of attacks on candidates while in residence.	18
3	No. of attacks on polling booths.	20
4	Meetings held.	551
5	Attacks on such meetings	38

Terrorist Incidents During Elections

1	Total incidents up to September 30, 1996	75
2	Total effective incidents in which injury/killings	20
3	Civilians killed	15
4	Civilians injured	49
5	CRPF men killed	-
6	CRPF men injured	24
7	JKP men killed	1
8	JKP men injured	9
9	BSF men kiled	2
10	BSF men injured	21

De-Induction: The Special Coordinator had, in consultation with the Department of Jammu and Kashmir Affairs, finalized de-induction plan of the polling parties spread over three days from 22nd to 24th September. Each day five to six Boeing and Airbus aircrafts of the Indian Airlines carried the polling parties from Srinagar to Delhi in special chartered flights. As already mentioned the entire induction, transportation, administrative arrangements, security and de-induction of the polling personnel was as carefully planned and efficiently executed this time as was done during the Parliamentary elections. Four hundred and five employees were sent back on 9th September itself as they had become surplus after the first phase of polling. Fifty-seven of the polling party members returned after the second phase on 18th September including six due to sickness. Of the rest 924 men flew to Delhi in special flights on 22nd September, 1102 the next day and the rest 911 on September 24, 1996. With this the entire process of de-induction of 3399 polling personnel, stood completed. The entire gamut of induction and de-induction process during both the elections was very efficiently managed by the Special Coordinator, N.R. Gupta, in whose honour his colleagues organized a dinner on the evening of 24th September to felicitate him on successful conclusion of a very difficult and complex assignment.

Media: The media management also followed the pattern which had been established during the Parliamentary elections except this time around the local print media was very much present on the scene. Reporting, however, was more balanced and did not show much bias against the political process that had been initiated for restoration of the popular government. Daily briefing in the media centre established by the State Information Department continued to provide regular information about daily developments, including special media briefing sessions, during the polling and counting days. To facilitate the working of media persons as also to ensure wider coverage of elections, road transport and airlift facilities were arranged for them by the State Information Department. For instance, during the Phase-II when Anantnag and Pulwama districts of the Valley had gone to polls three media parties were provided with aircraft facilities and the fourth was given vehicles to see for themselves the process of polling in these two districts. One flight of Cheetah helicopter started in the morning from Srinagar and covered Shopian, Damhal Hanjipora, Kulgam and Kokernag before returning to Srinagar. The second was a MI 17 helicopter taking off from Srinagar in the morning and touching Pahalgam, Kulgam, Anantnag and Pulwama before returning to Srinagar. The third flight was also in a MI 17 helicopter, which took off and landed almost at the same time from Srinagar and covered Pulwama, Anantnag, Pahalgam and Kulgam. Fourth party of the media persons traveled by road, also starting from Srinagar and touching Pampore, Lethpora, Awantipora, Bijbehara, Khannabal and Anantnag before returning to Srinagar. The move of these parties was planned in a way to ensure their return to Srinagar before 1 p.m. so that video cassettes and other material could be sent through special messenger by the afternoon commercial flight.

In addition All India Radio and Doordarshan had made special and elaborate arrangements to extensively cover the events unfolding right from Phase-I of the elections till the swearing in ceremony of the popular government. The coverage of the State Assembly elections in the electronic as well as print media was extensive and widespread. Notwithstanding a barrage of anti-election campaign by the state controlled Pakistani print and electronic media, the coverage of elections within the State as in the rest of the country as well as abroad was extremely favourable. Of the whole process it was most gratifying to all those who had worked so hard for the success of these elections, within the ranks of the administration, security forces as well as across the political spectrum in this gigantic exercise in extremely difficult circumstances. The participation of voters was not in terms of hundreds and thousands but in tens of lacs. One of the most expressive descriptions of the whole electoral process was printed in the *Indian Express* in its issue of October 13, 1996, under the eye-catching heading "Peace Offensive".

The policy of transparency which had been followed by the Central and the State governments with very encouraging results was further given a fillip in the intervening period between the two elections facilitating visits by important foreign dignitaries to see for themselves the mood of the people and the election arrangements that were being made to reflect the collective will of the men and women of the State.

As part of this strategy, a number of foreign delegations, human rights activists and Red Cross teams visited the Valley. During the year as many as 116 diplomats visited the Valley, notable among them was Frank Elbe, German Ambassador, who arrived in the Valley on March 8, 1996. Apart from meeting the government functionaries he also met some of the separatist leaders.

A team of Heads of Missions which visited Srinagar on June 9, 1996, comprised David Gore-Booth, British High Commissioner, Frank Elbe, German Ambassador, Frank G.Wisner, US Ambassador, Arna Walther, Norweign Ambassador to India, Lan Hughes Ist Secretary British High Commission and Lt. Col. Stavan Sboto of the US Embassy.

Ambassadors of European Union visited the Valley during June 12-15, 1996. The team comprised Gaetane Zucconi, Ambassador of Italy; Phipippe Petit, Ambassador of France; Joop H.J. Jaurissan, Ambassador of Netherlands; Alvaro DE Castilla, Ambassador of Spain; and James Faavin Ambassador of

Ireland. On June 12, 1996, they met APHC leaders at Rajbagh where they were interviewed by media persons. On June 13, 1996, they met political leaders of Janata Dal, CPI, Congress-I, National Conference and Awami League with whom they discussed the prevailing situation and also interacted with State authorities incluing the Governor.

On June 16, 1996, Dr. Dargo Stambuk, the Ambassador of Croatia, arrived in Srinagar and met Government functionaries as also APHC leaders and a delegation from Handwara. German MPs delegation visited the Valley from July 4 to 7, 1996. The team comprised Bernd Hasrat MP, Mrs. Veera Langas Feld MP, Mrs. Gisala Schroter MP, Hohannes Salle MP, Mrs. Dr. Elbe Leponhard MP and Ms. Haike Gabriel of the German Embassy. They met APHC leaders like Syed Ali Shah Geelani, Umar Farooq and Prof. Abdul Ghani. The US Ambassador visited all the three regions of the State from July 29 to August 3, 1996. He met political leaders including those belonging to APHC to make an on spot assessment of the situation.

These visits helped the foreign dignitaries and journalists to see for themselves the conditions that were prevailing in the State, particularly in the Valley. Since no restrictions were placed on them in their interaction with any person or group of persons, they were able to have a balanced picture of the happenings and it helped in projection of the correct state of affairs before the international community.

Post Poll Security Requirements: During the middle of September the think tank established by the State government undertook a review of the post-poll security scenario in the State and made recommendations of the course of action required to be followed and the level of the security forces, particularly central para-military forces that were necessary to carry forward the threshold of peace and security that had been achieved during the year. It was felt that with the completion of the Assembly elections and installation of a democratic government, it would be the right time to take stock and review the overall scenario. While the head of the terrorism had been kept low, it had not yet been wiped out. Decrease in the terrorist activities had been largely due to the organized efforts of the security forces, the police and the civil administration and the general disenchantment amongst the people. With substantial number of trained terrorists still waiting across the LoC for opportunity to infiltrate, the level of violence after the elections was likely to continue and could even increase in case the guards were lowered.

The return of popular rule in itself could be deemed to be a defeat for perpetrators of violence and sabotage and greater accountability of the administration would make it to perform better which could further help in the return of the complete normalcy. However, if the terrorists were able to step up their activities, their primary aim would be to de-stabilize the newly formed government which would need full cooperation and support of the forces for at least a couple of years to ensure that it is fully entrenched and is able to consolidate its authority leading to decline and eventual elimination of terrorism; with consequential reduction in the extent and role of the security forces.

The successful completion of the elections, the study suggested, may not by itself mean a final blow to the terrorist outfits and their activities. On the other hand it was just likely that the level of militancy might go up and, if that happened, it would further the cause of Pakistan and ISI. In any case such a reaction coming out of their frustration could not be ruled out. The probable scenario would require substantial level of additional forces to pre-empt terrorism raising its head again. In Punjab also, this type of planning and retention was found necessary.

The popular government, having been installed, would need full cooperation from the security forces, CPMFs and the Police. The winter months should be utilized to mop-up the remaining elements of terrorism, aiming particularly at foreign mercenaries and upper ground workers. Surrenders of terrorists and the weapons would have to be induced in a big way, with the rehabilitation of the surrendered terrorists being one of the important priorities of the new government.

While ultimately it depended upon the sagacity and effectiveness of the new rulers as to how they handled the situation, the administration would have to carry out its task of giving them due support and advice based on professional norms and essential security considerations. From this point of view it seemed that during at least the following one year utmost vigil was to be maintained and no let up should be allowed in the level of pressure being exerted. To that extent it might be absolutely necessary to have appropriately enhanced level of security forces operating with increased qualitative involvement of the Police and public in general.

After the elections the number of highly protected persons would increase substantially and would include newly elected legislators as well as the Ministers of the new Government. Whereas enhanced level of security would be provided to these persons, the security to the contesting candidates, at least of 52 sensitive constituencies, those who contested Parliamentary and Assembly elections would continue even though reduced slightly. It was also anticipated that the level of counter-insurgency operations during the first three months of the newly elected government, coinciding with the closing of the passes, would be at the increased level. For this purpose more forces for law and order, as a back up to the local police, would be required. This requirement would be uniformly felt in the Valley as well as in Jammu region.

Presenting civil face of the government would be particularly relevant in the Valley where most of the counter-insurgency (CI) operations were being conducted by the security forces. It was proposed in the review that in certain identified towns, the security and CI duties be taken over by CRPF replacing BSF. This force of CRPF would work in close coordination with the State Police and to that extent it would appear that the State Police is back in force to look after the major population centers of the Valley. This concept was expected to create a psychological impact amongst the local population on the one hand and relieve 30 Companies of BSF to be used as a reserve for CI operations under the control of State government. It was proposed that the towns of Anantnag, Shopian, Pulwama, Budgam, Baramulla, Kupwara and Bandipora be taken over for security by the CRPF by deploying 30 Companies and the force of BSF thus relieved would be available with the State authorities for CI operations.

How much attention was actually paid to these recommendations of the security experts and what all measures were taken by the new administration would be a subject matter of a separate study all together.

Popular Government Takes Over: There was tremendous enthusiasm about the return of the popular government as was evident with enthusiastic participation of the local population in the public meetings and rallies which had preceded the elections all over the State. Their yearning for the democratic rule became even more pronounced in the form of long queues outside the polling stations even in the areas where terrorist activities had been more marked. Following the landslide victory of the National Conference, the public mood, particularly in the Valley, became even more jubilant and they were looking forward to installation of the new government with keen expectation. The administrative machinery, on its part, had commenced arrangements for this purpose by timely completion of necessary repairs and re-furnishing of the Secretariat, Assembly and Council complexes, Legislators' Hostels, etc., for deliberations of the legislators, official and residential accommodation of the ministers and the elected representatives of the people. Security arrangements had also been made in advance in SKICC Srinagar where the swearing in ceremony was expected to take place. The whole area had been sanitized and secured. The security arrangements were not only limited to the immediate confines of the SKICC but the perimeters were extended to a much wider circle to ensure that no untoward incident could be engineered by anti-national elements, even from the mountains and the lake surrounding the SKICC complex.

Dr. Farooq Abdullah, who had gone to Delhi before the counting of votes started, made a triumphant return to Srinagar on October 3, 1996. He was received by a huge crowd of political activists, his party workers and general public at the airport and driven to his residence in Gupkar Road in a large procession. Near his residence in a impromptu public meeting, he thanked the voters of the State for their overwhelming support to him and his party and also announced the appointment of new Chief Secretary and Principal Secretary to Chief Minister. On 9th October, the President issued a proclamation revoking President's Rule in the State and on the same day National Conference government headed by Dr. Farooq Abdullah was sworn in with a Cabinet of 27 ministers, including thirteen Cabinet Ministers, twelve Ministers of State and two Deputy Ministers. The swearing in ceremony took place in an impressive function held in SKICC on the banks of Dal Lake. It was undoubtedly an occasion of celebrations and happiness for the people of the State. The function became all the more memorable with the participation of the leaders of national stature from almost all the major political parties in the country.

Ashok Kumar, who had been serving as Chief Secretary of the State since December 1994, left for New Delhi to take up an assignment in the Defence Ministry the same afternoon. Lt.Gen. D.D. Saklani (Retd), Security Advisor to the Governor, also demitted his office and left for New Delhi by the afternoon flight. Except for one, no civilian officer was present at the airport to see him off.

10 The Sequel

The people of the State as well as the rest of the country had great expectations from the newly installed democratic government, particularly the one with such an overwhelming majority in the Assembly, and had expected that this would herald complete return of normalcy and peace in the State. They had hoped that with greater cooperation and participation of the population, remnants of terrorism would soon end. In his speech immediately after the swearing in ceremony, Chief Minister Dr. Farooq Abdullah promised this as well as the dawn of a new era of progress and prosperity in the State which had been torn asunder by the seven years of terrorism. During this period not only the economy of the State had suffered a serious setback, its structure had been gravely impaired but also people of the State-had gone through untold miseries and were left with bruised psyche.

The terrorism related statistics during 1997-98, did show some improvement in the overall situation although it was much less than what was expected with the installation of the popular government. Incidents of violence during 1997 and 1998 were 3420 and 2974, respectively, which were lowest in any year since 1990, although the number of civilians killed during this period being 1105 and 977 respectively, remained fairly high. Similarly, during 1997, 1075 terrorists were killed and 186 security personnel lost their lives, with corresponding figures during the next year being 977 and 234, respectively. These were certainly not very low statistics as compared to the earlier numbers.

With the installation of the popular government and the graph of the terrorist activities steadily going downwards, the ISI increased its exertions to give a fillip to the stagnant level of terrorism in the State to discredit the popular government as well as stoke the flames of insurgency. This was attempted in all terrorism infected areas. Due to thinning of security forces just after the elections were over, certain gaps had taken place in the security cover. Also the successful conduct of elections had given all round sense of euphoria with consequent general relaxation in every sphere leading to complacency. Another important factor in this regard was the reduced level of coordination between the civil administration and the security forces. Due to these reasons the activities of the disruptive and the anti-national elements started picking up once again. That the course of events took a different turn than expected appears to be largely due to wrong moves and, probably, the lack of proper comprehension of the existing and emerging situation by the people in responsible positions. The security related operations as well as preventive measures no longer remained well coordinated, and all out efforts against the terrorists and their supporters became the sole responsibility of the security forces, more so of the army. This was contrary to the expected principles of dealing with any insurgency situations where the effective drive against the disruptive elements has to be a joint and coordinated effort. The coordination mechanism at the district level particularly became ineffective.

The synergy of anti-terrorism efforts of various organizations was achieved at the apex level by the Unified Headquarters, which came into being in the first fortnight of May 1993. This concept had been worked out after careful considerations of the security requirements as well as keeping in mind the capabilities, sensitivities and peculiarities of different forces and organizations. In the next three and half years the UHQ became a focal point of pooling of information and expertise working as a think tank as well as spearheading the counter insurgency operations in the State, particularly in the Valley. Thus an extremely effective system was evolved, and constantly improved upon, for coordinating and channelizing the resources of the constituents by allocation of proper task and distribution of specific duties. Rolling back the tide of terrorism and successful conduct of elections were the most important objectives successfully attained and efficiently carried out through this mechanism.

With the formation of the popular government, the UHQ was practically wound up with the Director General of the State Police being asked to chair its meetings. It either showed lack of understanding about the concept behind the formation of the UHQ in the first place or the absence of appreciation about the sensitivity of the security forces hierarchy, or both. Within two months, the State Government realized its folly and, decided that there would be two UHQs at the divisional levels and the Chief Minister would chair the UHQ meetings and in his absence the two Corps Commanders would be the nodal points for coordination in respect of Kashmir and Jammu regions. The pendulum had fully swung in the opposite direction. Purely in theoretical framework, there can be nothing better than the Chief Minister himself chairing the UHQ meetings, but the person of a Chief Minister is so much involved and busy with the business of running the affairs of the State, that too a troubled state like Jammu and Kashmir, that it is almost impossible to achieve functional efficiency of the UHQ under his stewardship. The UHQ, it must be understood, was not a policymaking or an advisory body; it is a group, which had to involve itself directly with the CI operations and strategy and tactics related thereto on a continuing basis. It must meet at least once a week and when circumstances so demand--such contingencies are not uncommon or far in between--gathering even on a daily basis. This cannot possibly be done at the level of the Chief Minister. Even otherwise it is not a good strategy to involve the head of the government in supervising the functioning of UHQ. The Chief Minister should issue guidelines and lay down parameters within which the UHQ should operate. He may occasionally review its functioning whenever such need arises. The UHQ should ideally be headed by a person of such position and eminence that heads of all forces and organizations in the State, connected with CI operations, should have no hesitation in taking instructions, seeking guidance and advice from him. Two UHQs have been functioning under the respective Corps Commanders. This has created its own dynamics and problems of less than adequate participation of some key-functionaries outside the army. Without going into a detailed analysis of the concept and requirements of an apex level coordination mechanism, it can be said without any fear of contradiction that after October 1996, the level of coordination of forces and resources has considerably come down as compared to the earlier three and half year's functioning of the UHQ.

The statistical details of terrorist related violence and counter action by the security forces during 1990-2001 given below would amply support what has been mentioned above.

Terrorist Incidents

S.no.	Year	Incidents of violence	Civilians Killed	S.F. Personnel Killed	Terrorists Killed
1	1990	4158	1012	154	550
2	1991	3765	947	168	844
3	1992	4817	1167	177	819
4	1993	5247	1136	195	1310
5	1994	5829	1189	198	1596
6	1995	5938	1355	234	1332
7	1996	5014	1530	185	1209
8	1997	3420	1105	186	1075
9	1998	2974	977	234	977
10	1999	3122	941	357	1052
11	2000	3153	945	397	1520
12	2001	4593	1090	546	2020
	Total	52030	13394	3031	14304

Weapons recovered

S.No.	Year	AK Rifles	Pistols/ Revolvers	UMGs	Sniper Rifles	Rocket Launchers
1	1990	1240	751	77	0	108
2	1991	2320	849	130	0	29
3	1992	3504	756	164	9	62
4	1993	2209	921	142	54	36
5	1994	2196	940	127	41	31
6	1995	2055	965	67	38	36
7	1996	2150	1052	84	49	43
8	1997	1725	1024	64	60	81
9	1998	1520	584	80	34	257
10	1999	1244	385	33	13	186
11	2000	1405	482	21	16	59
12	2001	1656	370	10	12	39
	Total	23224	9079	999	326	967

Explosive material recovered

S. No.	Year	Grenades/ HG	IEDs	Explosive	Elec. Detonators	Detonators	AP Mines	AT Mines
1	1990	2502	0	231	97	2634	723	27
2	1991	1784	18	274	544	2350	123	13
3	1992	2391	86	285	508	3085	212	14
4	1993	4363	136	2950	604	2381	570	22
5	1994	2603	126	1342	196	2572	989	17
6	1995	2870	811	1484	130	4728	529	105
7	1996	3949	245	2381	174	5138	517	35
8	1997	5124	1020 +13 boxes	6448	172	19442	373	35
9	1998	8130	514	2922	NA	NA	404	70
10	1999	6000	466	2182	NA	NA	261	44
11	2000	4807	718	1798	481	3303	292	86
12	2001	4152	450	2446	433	1919	106	11
	total	48675	4590 + 13 boxes	24743	3339	38552	5099	479

It is particularly noteworthy that the number of terrorists killed and the loss of life in respect of security forces stood at all time high during the years 2000 and 2001. The figure of terrorist casualties of 1520 during the year 2000 has to be seen in the background of the fact that during the first five months of the year the security forces had held their hand due to the unilateral declaration of non-initiation of combat operations by the Prime Minister, otherwise this figure would have been in the range of 1700-1800.

Two important development in relation to the situation in J&K took place during the period 1999-2001. These were Kargil ingression by Pakistani forces and a series of peace initiatives taken by Government of India lasting for one year from July 2000, onwards.

During the first week of May 1999, Pakistan unleashed a storm of unprecedented magnitude in the little known Kargil area of Jammu and Kashmir. Even though India has been inured to, and conditioned by, the last one decade of Pakistan-inspired proxy-war in the State, these belligerent incursions across the Line of Control came as a rude shock, taking both the government and the security forces completely by surprise. It took India over two months to clear this transgression. Operations involved considerable concentration of troops with over one thousand soldiers killed and wounded and strenuous diplomatic effort as well as enormous costs.

Pakistani Army regulars along with ***Lashkar-e-Toiba*** and ***Hizb-ul-Mujahideen*** **men** were responsible for crossing the LoC and occupying important heights as well as areas of tactical importance, right from the Mushkoh Valley in Drass area to Chorbat La in Batalik and to Turtuk in the north. Though the exact timing of this ingress and occupation, and the preparation of defences in respect of each of the positions occupied, is yet to be reliably determined, it is safe to assume that this was done during the autumn of 1998 and spring of 1999. Ironically, at the time of Lahore-Bus-Diplomacy, and the meeting between the Indian Prime Minister and his Pakistani counterpart, in February 1999, considerable effort and resources of the Pakistan

Army had already been expended towards creating trouble across the LoC in the Kargil sector. The confrontation between the Indian army and Pakistani forces, which commenced in early May 1999, continued for two and a half months and even threatened to develop into a much wider conflagration at certain points, before the situation was defused in the second fortnight of July. During this period, the Indian army, under ***Operation Vijay,*** used air power for the first time since 1971, although on a restricted scale and under considerable constraints.

There has also been criticism as well as analysis of the failure of the army and the intelligence agencies to detect the occupation of Indian territory by Pakistan, and the handling of the Kargil operations, in all its manifestations, by the Government. Some defence analysts and strategic thinkers maintain that the Indian response to the challenge posed by Pakistan was, once again, muted and lacking in the sting that such an adventure should have attracted.

It would also be worth mentioning that the year- long peace initiatives from July 2000 onwards which started with great promise and throughout the year raised lot of expectations within as well as outside the State regarding some peaceful means becoming available to end the violence in Jammu and Kashmir. On the culmination of Kargil crisis, Pakistan not only suffered a military setback, though in a limited measure, its diplomatic loss of face in the world community was particularly significant. India's continued diplomatic initiatives, certain behind the scene activities as well as rising aspirations of the local population for restoration of normalcy created its own dynamics stimulating an urge for peace. Subsequently, at a press conference in Srinagar on July 24, 2000, Abdul Majid Dar, the Hizb-ul-Mujahideen commander in the Valley, announced a unilateral ceasefire for three months. This was followed by a high profile media meeting between the Union Home Secretary and a few terrorist representatives in Srinagar about ten days later. However, intense pressure from the ISI and the entire Pakistani establishment headed by military dictator General Parvez Musharraf made Hizb-ul-Mujahideen's Syed Salahuddin announce the withdrawal of ceasefire on 8th August, from Islamabad.

Even though the Hizb cease-fire had failed to yield any results, it had whetted the people's appetite for peace. The residents of Srinagar could not forget the fortnight of near tranquility that they had experienced, and the sense of jubilation that had spread across the length and breadth of the State during that period. This popular mood and a strong urge for peace created a positive momentum. Early in October 2000, Abdul Ghani Lone, a senior functionary of the APHC and chief of the Peoples' Conference, organized a convention in Srinagar, in which, approximately 3000 delegates from across the Valley participated. The first political convention organized by Lone in the last decade, it signaled his intention to participate in the future peace process. The dissension within the Hizb on the scope of its earlier peace initiative, as also between terrorists of Kashmiri and Pakistani origin, was another factor having a bearing on the dynamics of the peace process.

On November 19, 2000, Prime Minister Atal Behari Vajpayee announced the Non Initiation of Combat Operations (NICO – referred to as cease-fire hereafter) by the security forces against terrorists during the holy month of Ramadan commencing from November 27. It was a bold and statesmen-like initiative which brought about a qualitative change in the terrorism-affected State.

Pakistan's immediate response, on the day after the PM's announcement, emphasized that a declaration of ceasefire should be followed by de-escalation and dialogue, meaning thereby tripartite parleys. On December 2, Pakistan declared that its Army would observe 'maximum restraint' on the Line of Control in order to strengthen and stabilize the ceasefire. But, these postures by Pakistan were merely cosmetic in nature as its actions failed to reflect any sincere attempt to take the peace agenda forward.

The Indian Prime Minister announced an extension of one month Ramadan ceasefire on 20th December, and the extension was welcomed by all important political parties across the nation as also, by the people of J&K. In spite of certain initial reservations, the State Chief Minister Dr. Farooq Abdullah, also expressed his support to the ceasefire extension. The period of non-initiation of combat operations was further extended by another month making it operative up to ending February 2001. On February 22, 2001, the Prime Minister announced a three months extension to the ceasefire beyond 26th February, but also added that the Indian security forces had clear instructions to act decisively against Pakistan based terrorists outfits. He said that the government was ready to enter into dialogue with any group in the State that abjure violence. However, reaction from the jehadi outfits as well as APHC remained negative, apparently on instructions from across the border.

Whatever may have been the other positive or negative features of the non-initiation of the combat operations, the biggest advantage was a sense of relief and the mood of expectation that prevailed amongst the people of the State, particularly in the Valley. They had not failed to note that the Government of India displayed genuine concern at the highest executive level for the safety and well being of the public. However, some analysts felt that the impact of six months of NICO had not been favourable on the security situation in the State as the security forces practically ceased operations against the terrorists and by and large maintained a defensive postures, reacting only during an attack or under an imminent threat of attack. This resulted in comparatively lower casualty rate amongst the terrorists and higher ratio of security forces/terrorists killed. Even the civilian casualties did not decrease significantly.

The political impasse that had been a major point of criticism against the peace initiative was sought to be broken with the announcement, on April 5, 2001, of the appointment of K.C. Pant, Deputy Chairperson of the Planning Commission, as the Chief Interlocutor of the Union government on the Kashmir issue. The official announcement inter alia mentioned, "The Government invites people of good-will, who desire the restoration of peace and normalcy in the State to come forward and participate in the dialogue. The doors are also not closed for Kashmiri organizations which are currently engaged in militancy in the State but are desirous of peace." However, the Pant initiative failed to make any headway in changing the ground situation in the State or bringing the separatist elements any closer to the negotiating table.

Amidst considerable expectations in both countries, accompanied by an unprecedented media hype, the summit meeting between Indian Prime Minister and the Pakistani Military dictator, who had only few days ago donned the mantle of his country's president by summarily dismissing the real incumbent, took place at Agra during the middle of July 2001. However, the great euphoria generated during the Vajpayee-Musharraf summit wilted into disappointment after making a very promising beginning and starting on optimistic note from both the sides. With the Agra summit not reaching any fruitful results, the peace initiative which had been started exactly an year ago came to an end, in July 2001.

Two months later, the dynamics of whole gamut of Pak sponsored terrorism and the security environment in South Asia underwent significant change with climactic events of destruction of the World Trade Centre in New York and attack on the Pentagon in Washington by Islamic terrorists. This resulted in a two-month long air and ground operations by United States and its allies in Afghanistan breaking the stranglehold of Taliban rule there, as also forced General Musharraf to take a U-turn in denouncing all acts of terrorism anywhere in the world. In his two important telecasts to the nation, on September 17, 2001, and January 12, 2002 the General publicly aligned Pakistan with the American invasion of Afghanistan, destruction of the terrorist network that had been set up with Pak help by the Taliban and Osama bin Laden, as also made a public resolve of rooting out of terrorism from his country.

However, insofar as India was concerned Pakistan's efforts to foment trouble not only in J&K but also in other parts of the country continued unabated albeit in an even more covert manner. Abortive terrorist attempt to strike at the Indian Parliament, when it was in session on December 13, 2001, was the most glaring example of her continuing endeavour. The Indian response was swift in the form of deployment of its troops along the LoC and international border and for some time it appeared that the Indian state, for the first time in the last 12 years, was seriously contemplating to take matters in its own hands and precipitate efforts to remove threat to its security and national integration. However, soon enough the whole exercise turned into a stalemate with Pakistan also deploying its forces in the forward positions and once again effectively using its new found cozy relationship with America and its allies as a self-styled frontline state helping an anti-terrorism western alliance to bring intense diplomatic pressure on India to back-off from taking any precipitative military action.

By the time the dust settled on the huge forward movement of the Indian Defence Forces, the elections to the State Assembly were almost round the corner. The J&K Legislative Assembly had been elected in October 1996, and its term of six years was to expire on October 17, 2002, and therefore, the elections to the State Assembly had to be completed in all respects before that day. By the middle of the year serious preparations had begun to ensure successful conduct of the Assembly elections. This was also another opportunity for the Central government to determine the choice and the collective will of the people of the State as also to fulfill their aspirations, taking into consideration their actual and perceived grievances. Track two efforts registered a step-up and there were reports in the media of considerable enhanced behind the scene efforts by the intelligence agencies to encourage and persuade separatist elements and at least some of the terrorist outfits to join the electoral fray. The Central government also announced the formation of a Kashmir Committee, headed by Ram Jethmalani, the former Law Minister and an eminent lawyer to initiate dialogue with the broad spectrum of the opinion leaders in the State. The Prime Minister appointed Arun Jaitly, Union Law Minister, to start negotiations with separatist elements. Whereas due to paucity of time the initiative of constituting Kashmir Committee and nomination of Arun Jaitly as Prime Minister's point man did not make any impact in respect of the electoral participation by the separatist elements, the other efforts did seem to have met with some success. By the beginning of the summer it had started becoming evident that some terrorist outfits as well as a part of the APHC could be willing to take part in the elections provided some of their conditions, including the assurance that the elections would be free and fair and would be held under Governor's Rule and not under the National Conference government, were met by the Centre.

Obviously alarmed by this turn of events the ISI moved in quickly and during the month of May, Lone was gunned down in broad day light in the midst of huge public meeting which was organized by APHC. With Lone's assassination the efforts to involve separatist elements in the forthcoming elections received a serious setback. Abdul Ghani Lone was not only a founder member of the APHC as well as president of his political outfit – People's Conference, but had been a minister in the State and elected legislator more than once. He was always regarded as a erudite politician and an able legislator as well as an effective administrator. It was widely believed in political and administrative circles that with Lone and his associates joining the elections, it would stimulate similar action by a good number of outfits and individuals. However, even after this setback, behind the scene efforts to persuade separatist elements continued but the chances of their taking part in the elections appeared very remote, even though till very near the announcement of elections, the Government of India kept propping hints that it would not be averse to holding elections under Governor's Rule if that would make an appreciable and positive impact on the separatist elements joining the electoral process. The Prime Minister himself on the occasion of his Independence Day address on August 15, 2002, gave an assurance, from the ramparts of the Red Fort, that the elections to the Jammu and Kashmir Assembly would be absolutely free and fair. The Election Commission of India had also set in motion various steps to ensure the conduct of the elections in a free, fair and a transparent manner.

Following the assassination of Abdul Ghani Lone, the hardliners in APHC and the pro-Pak terrorist outfits stepped up their anti election activities, particularly targeting the political activists mostly of National Conference and those who were actively advocating the recourse to negotiations and political resolution for the ongoing problem. On the other hand the moderate elements in the APHC and even those outside it, like Shabir Shah, started pleading for postponement of elections beyond October 2002, and imposition of Governor's Rule for a short period with the hope that this would give enough time for negotiations with the Government of India to reach some understanding enabling them to participate in the electoral process. In the midst of these developments *Greater Kashmir* – a Srinagar based daily – in its issue of June 30, 2002, came out with an interesting statement from Ghulam Mohammad Bhat, Ameera-e-Jama'at of JEI saying, "We have made it clear that we would not participate in the forthcoming Assembly Elections but at the same time we would not launch poll boycott campaign — even Election Commission recently said it is against forcing people to vote and also preventing their participating in the elections is against law and the Jama'at does not believe in unlawful activities. Ours is a democratic set up and does not believe in forcing things. There is no compulsion in religion." The ambivalent and differing stands taken by various overground separatist leaders, the detention of Syed Ali Shah Geelani and Yaseen Malik, two hardliner APHC leaders, and the pressure put by the American diplomats on the APHC to join elections resulted in blunting the edge of the poll boycott efforts by the APHC, although the terrorist outfits tried to offset this by intensifying their activity to undermine the polling process.

On the political front certain important developments had started taking place by the month of June. An important landmark in this direction was the change of guards in the most visible and dominant political organization in the State, the National Conference. Omar Abdullah, Lok Sabha MP from Srinagar constituency and Union Minister of State for External Affairs and son of Dr. Farooq Abdullah, took over as President of the National Conference from his father on June 19, 2002. It was then widely believed that he would also take over as Chief Minister, from his father before the formal notification of the State elections and that Farooq Abdullah would likely move to the Centre either as the next Vice President of India or to an important cabinet position. However, this speculation did not come through and Omar Abdullah continued only as the president of the party and his father as the Chief Minister of the State. All the same the change of guards to the younger generation, had lot of significance on the political scene of the State as the party leadership passed to the new generation with a manifestly modern and progressive approach to manage the affairs of the party and the government. It also meant the National Conference leadership passing to the third generation from Sheikh Mohammad Abdullah to Dr. Farooq Abdullah and then to Omar Abdullah.

In Jammu region a demand for trifurcation of the State, including separate statehood for Jammu region and Union Territory status for Ladakh region was raised by the VHP on 23rd June. Six days later the RSS passed a resolution in its meeting at Kurukshetra demanding separate state for Jammu and Union Territory status for Ladakh. This generated a set of political dynamics with confusion being sown in the ranks of BJP State unit, creation of a separate outfit called Jammu State Morcha in Hindu dominated areas of Jammu region and several National Conference leaders along with elements in the State Bahujan Samaj Party demanding a Chenab Hill Development council, a separate autonomous unit for the Muslim majority areas within Jammu region. This move was to have a distinct political impact on the electoral fortunes of a good number of candidates in Jammu region, a couple of months later.

The elections to the State Assembly were announced by the Election Commission of India on August 2, 2002, and with this announcement it also imposed the Model Code of Conduct in the State administration. Almost on the pattern of 1996 Assembly Elections, the election was to be held in four phases over a period of twentytwo days. With the polling in Phase-I taking place on 16th September, and the last date of polling being October 8, 2002. To ensure that the time period between the last date of filing of nomination and the date of poll in each phase was same, different notifications were to be issued for each phase. With the date of notification for elections in Phase-I being 22nd August, last date of filing of nominations for this phase was fixed on 29th August, scrutiny on 31st and last date of withdrawal of candidature was to be September 2, 2002. The polling for Phase-I covering districts of Kupwara, Baramulla, Leh, Kargil, Rajouri and Poonch was to take place on 16th September. Elections in Phase-II were to be held on 24th September for the districts of Srinagar, Budgam and Jammu. In Phase-III on 1st October, the polling was to take place in Pulwama, Anantnag, Udhampur and Kathua districts and the last phase of poll was to take place for district Doda only on the 8th October. The counting for all the Assembly constituencies was scheduled to commence on 10th October, and the date before which the election was to be completed was determined as October 12, 2002.

With the announcement of schedule of elections, the polling process in the State had been set in motion. This also heralded shifting of political activities in the State across the board into high gear. The feverish activities associated with any State Assembly elections were witnessed in Jammu and Kashmir also, though with the mandatory security precautions in the Valley and the mountainous areas of Jammu region where the terrorists were intensifying their efforts to thwart the election process. With the rising election fever the terrorist violence also registered an upswing. Between 1st August and September 10, 2002, there were 405 terrorist related incidents in which 22 political activists were killed. The civilian casualties were 26, and 62 security forces personnel lost their lives. The main targets of terrorist attacks were the National Conference ministers and activists followed by the Congress, CPM and the PDP leaders and workers.

In spite of the security arrangements made for the safety of the candidates, the terrorists managed to kill an independent candidate from Kupwara constituency, Sheikh Ghulam Rasool. Since he did not belong to a political party his death did not countermand the poll in the constituency. Sakina Yattoo, Minister of State for Tourism, escaped four attempts on her life during the electioneering period in her Noorabad constituency of

Anantnag district though a number of her PSOs and security guards were injured and killed in the attempts on her life. However, the most important casualty of the terrorist violence was Mushtaq Ahmad Lone, Minister of State for Law and Parliamentary Affairs, who was earlier the MOS in charge of Home Department of the State Government, a National Conference candidates from Lolab constituency in Kupwara district. He fell to the terrorists' bullet while addressing a public meeting in his constituency on 11 September. Two days later the *Times of India* in its lead editorial mentioned, "—With the first phase of elections drawing to a close, the extremist groups have joined the battle of the ballot in the only way they can: by terrorizing those willing to give politics and peace a chance.— As is universally the case, extremists in Kashmir too dread the prospect of free and fair polls because that threatens to address the alienation that sustains terrorism. Consequently, they will do all they can to disrupt the elections. The idea obviously is to create an environment of pervasive fear which will deter citizens from coming out in large numbers to vote or otherwise participate in the process.—"

In spite of these setbacks and sustained efforts by the terrorists, the political process even in the terrorist infested areas continued unabated. In the words of a political analyst, "Kashmir Valley seems to be fully immersed in the election gush. People are thronging the public rallies of different political parties in large number. Although the terrorists have issued threats to public not to attend the political meetings, it has no impact on the political meetings." Mushtaq Lone's killing, however, also resulted in postponement of the election in Lolab constituency from Phase-I to Phase-IV on 8th October, as he was the candidate of National Conference, a recognized political party by the Election Commission.

One of the important developments during the election period and certainly spurred by terrorist killing of Abdul Ghani Lone during May 2002, was a mood of defiance in the People's Conference, including that of slain leader's younger son Sajjad Lone who took over the reigns of the party. Three members of

People's Conference quitted the party, it is largely believed, with the support of Sajjad Lone to take part in the elections as independent candidates. This development added a new dimension in the election process in Kupwara district and ultimately ensured a very high turnout and a keen contest in the three constituencies of Handwara, Kupwara and Lolab.

As mentioned earlier, the trifurcation demand created a rift between the BJP State Unit as it had to toe the line of the party high command which had openly come out against the principle of trifurcation of the State and the RSS backed newly created Jammu State Morcha. In spite of best efforts of local BJP leaders, there was hardly any meeting ground between the two outfits which resulted in almost vertical split in the traditional BJP support belt in rural and urban areas of Jammu district and parts of Udhampur and Kathua districts. In the last week of August when the nomination papers were being filed for Phase-I of the election which included Leh district also, Ladakh Union Territory Front, LUTF, was floated in Leh district. In a series of dramatic political developments leading to the formation of LUTF, district units of all political parties merged into the new organization and all sitting members of the State and the Central Legislatures resigned and joined LUTF. The front reiterated its demand for Union Territory status to Ladakh region. Apart from various political organizations all sections of the local population, including both Buddhists and Muslims, extended their support to LUTF which put up one candidate each, unanimously supported by all sections of district for Leh and Nubra Constituencies. All other candidates who had till then filed nomination papers withdrew in favour of the LUTF candidates thus ensuring election of Nawang Rigzin from Leh constituency and Pintoo Narboo from Nubra constituency.

The fast pace of political activities generated by the election also witnessed the electoral poaching being indulged by various parties trying to woo and attract important members from the ranks of political adversaries. It resulted in swapping sides by three sitting MLAs, R.S. Sharma, a Congress MLA from Nowshera constituency of Rajouri District, joining National Conference and so did Ch. Piara Singh the BJP MLA from Gandhinagar constituency of Jammu city. However, the National Conference also lost one of its MLAs, Mohammad Shafi Bhat from Amira Kadal constituency to Congress. Whereas, Ch. Piara Singh did not contest the elections, R.S. Sharma lost his seat from Nowshera and Shafi Bhat was returned from Amira Kadal constituency on the mandate of the new party that he had joined.

The most graphic description of the mood of the people of the Valley and their expectations from the Assembly elections were mirrored in local vernacular daily from Srinagar, *Uquab*, which mentioned, "As poll dates in Kashmir draw nearer, local newspapers are flooded with reports of daily killings of political leaders and workers at the hands of militants, unidentified gunmen and so on. However, these killings have failed to instill fear and derail the overall enthusiasm for the polls, both among people and candidates. The tempo of election rallies, poster campaigns and other poll-related activity is increasing. The reason is that death or killings in Kashmir—is now a spent tool in the hands of perpetrators. The people of Kashmir, who have witnessed 13 years of continuous turmoil, seem to be craving for a change. Not that they are unaware of the pending resolution to the Kashmir issue or have forgotten the sacrifices in form of death and destruction of past over a decade, they simply want someone to meet their basic necessities. Employment, potable water, good roads, irrigation facilities, electricity – this is the list of their demands and carry the most weight when it comes to voting. This is something the "gunmen" have not understood. The gun is a spent force here now. A bird can fly high only on a full stomach. Humans are no exceptions."

As per schedule, elections in the six districts, two each from Valley, Jammu region and Ladakh region took place on September 16, 2002, with good overall voter turn- out of 47.9%. During the day the highest poll percentage was recorded in Zanskar constituency of Kargil district with over 78% electoral exercising their right of franchise and lowest being in Sopore with 7.8% turnout.

Phase-II of the polling covered the important districts of Srinagar, Budgam and Jammu. As expected the voter turnout in Srinagar district was very low, around 11 percent because of very lukewarm participation by the electorate in mainly the urban constituencies of the district. However, rural constituency of Kangan registered over 50% polling, in Ganderbal from where Omar Abdullah was contesting the traditional family stronghold, earlier represented by his grandfather as also his father, the polling percentage was over thirtyfive. In Budgam district the overall polling figure exceeded 45% with Jammu district registering a figure of 57% plus.

Phase-III and Phase-IV of the polling took place as scheduled on Ist October and 8th October, respectively. Also on Ist October, repolling, which had earlier been ordered by Election Commission was conducted in two polling stations of Budgam Assembly constituency, one polling station of Gandhinagar in Jammu and three polling stations each of Surankote and Mendhar constituencies of Poonch district. Similarly on 8th October, four polling stations in Pahalgam constituency of Anantnag district, one polling station of Kathua constituency and one polling station of Surankote constituency in Poonch district witnessed repoll. The next day repolling took place in three polling stations of Doda Assembly constituency and one polling station of Kishtwar Assembly constituency of the same district.

Of the eighty-seven assembly constituencies which went to the poll, eighty fell in general category and seven were reserved seats for scheduled castes. Total number of candidates who filed nomination papers were 856 out of which sixtyfive nomination papers were rejected at the scrutiny stage and eightytwo were later withdrawn leaving in the field 709 contesting candidates of which twentynine were women. The lowest number of candidates were one each in two constituencies of Leh and Nubra with Kathua constituency registering highest number of twentytwo candidates. Thus the average candidates per constituency came to eight. The overall percentage of the polling in the State, as per the figures released by the Chief Electoral Officer came to 43.28. The participation of male voters at 47.81% was 10% more than the women electorate which touched the figure of 37.87%. There were total of 7085 polling stations which, from security point of view were divided in three categories – hyper sensitive polling stations requiring the highest level of security cover were 3045, followed by 2612 polling station declared as sensitive and only 1428 polling stations categorized as normal. Average number of electorate per polling station worked out to a figure of 865 with largest number of voters in a polling station being 1800 and minimum number as low as eleven.

To oversee peaceful polling process in the State over 400 additional companies of para-military forces were deployed, beefing up the existing security deployment. The Election Commission also deputed sixtythree Observers with highest number of eight designated to Jammu district and lowest number of three each sent to the districts of Budgam, Leh, Kargil and Poonch.

Since electronic voting machines were used all over the State, for the first time in the Assembly elections, the counting process which used to take at least two days and a night earlier, was over within seven-eight hours on the day of the counting on 10th October, and by the late afternoon that day all the poll results had come. The National Conference had emerged as the single largest party with twentyeight seats – almost reduced to a shadow of its performance of winning fiftyseven seats in the 1996 Assembly elections, followed by Congress with twenty seats, with PDP making spectacular maiden entry into the legislature with sixteen seats. The other winners included four candidates of Panther's Party, two of the CPI(M), one each of the BJP and BSP. The independents won a large number of seats –fourteen- which included two candidates from Leh district and one of Jammu State Morcha. A number of independent candidates were rebels from the National Conference and the Congress. Two of the candidates of People's Conference who had contested elections as independents won their seats. Partywise performance of the candidates was as follows:

Name of the Party	BSP	BJP	CPI	CPI (M)	INC	NCP	JKNC	JKNPP	JKPDP	JKAL	IND & Others
Number of Candidates	33	58	5	7	78	11	87	34	58	9	331
Elected	1	1	0	2	20	0	28	4	16	1	14

The National Conference which obviously was the biggest loser reduced its tally in sharp contrast to the performance in 1996 polls in all the three regions. It was able to get 18 seats in the Valley against 40 in 1996. In Jammu region its tally came down from fourteen to nine and in Ladakh region from three to one. The electoral set- back to the National Conference hurt the party more painfully due to Omar Abdullah losing his election in Ganderbal constituency and not less than twelve National Conference ministers also losing their respective constituencies – more notable amongst them being Dr. Mustafa Kamal, brother of Dr. Farooq Abdullah, Mohammad Shafi Uri, Ajat Shatru Singh, son of Dr. Karan Singh, Surjit Singh Slathia and Choudhary Ramzan. Even the Speaker of the Assembly, Abdul Ahad Vakil, lost the electoral battle and so did Khalid Najib Suhrawardi MOS Home. Apart from Omar Abdullah, President of the National Conference, other two state party presidents who contested the elections viz Daya Krishan Kotwal of BJP and Sheikh Abdul Rehman of BSP also lost their elections. The president of the Pradesh Congress Committee, Ghulam Nabi Azad, and the PDP President Mufti Mohammad Sayeed did not take part in the elections. The prominent amongst the winners were PDP Vice President Mehbooba Mufti, former minister and Member Parliament from Congress-I Mangat Ram Sharma.

Political observers and analysts would continue to comment upon and analyze the results of these assembly elections for a long time. Admittedly, the reason for National Conference debacle was the traditional factor of anti-incumbency and absence of good governance paving the way for remarkable performance of the PDP in the Valley and quite considerable improved tally by the Congress in Jammu region. The entire media was full of post electoral assessment and expert comments. However, the representative sample was reflected in the editorial of *The Times of India* dated 11th October, which mentioned, "—That the polls were the fairest in the two decades became evident soon enough, a truth now being reinforced by the results—the saddest outcome without doubt is the defeat of young Omar Abdullah acknowledged across the political spectrum as man of some political talent and vision. Yet, democracy places one key factor above all and that is performance, here, the National Conference in particular its former Chief Minister failed entirely. The National Conference's string of drawbacks – it was thought to be uncaring and self indulgent, were further compounded by its alliance in the Centre with overtly nationalized BJP". In a similar vein the editorial in *India Today* opined, "Though there is no clear majority, the vote is clearly for a change in a region raven with corruption and terrorist violence. The vote is also an affirmation of faith in democracy.'

It was also generally accepted that next to the people of the State who voted in large number under terrorist threats and actual violence, the credit for making these elections credible, free and transparent goes to the Election Commission. Right from the assurance of the Chief Election Commissioner a few months before the polling schedule was announced till the completion of the counting, the Election Commission took a series of steps to ensure this and sent a message across to all the major players in the electoral process- political parties, the contesting candidates, the electorate, the State administration as well as the security forces- that it meant to see through exactly what it had been promising. Towards this end the Election Commission undertook a number of measures which included polling through the electronic voting machines which, by its very mechanism, drastically reduced the complaints of rigging as had been proved in earlier elections in other parts of the country. The Election Commission also decided that at least two of the persons manning each polling booth will be from outside the State and which should include preferably the Presiding Officer, one out of the two should be Urdu knowing. Going a step further the presence of the local police in the immediate vicinity of the polling booth was replaced by the CRPF so that no one could complaint of the local police getting influenced and in turn pressurizing the voters and the polling staff. That it meant business was, further demonstrated by the Election Commission when it ordered immediate transfer of officials against whom allegations of adopting partisan attitude were made. These included two Deputy Commissioners and two Deputy Superintendents of police. Similarly a significant number of polling staff of a constituency was changed on receiving adverse reports by the Commission. The Election Commission also introduced an element of greater transparency by allowing foreign diplomats to witness the conduct of elections in the State. A record number of over four hundred media persons from rest of the country as also abroad descended on the State to cover these elections. Twentyseven foreign diplomats also visited the State during this period. It included members of the diplomatic community mostly belonging to the Western countries with the highest numbering five from Britain, two from the United States of America, one from European Commission. No diplomat from the third world countries visited the State during the elections.

Due to the fractured mandate that had been given by the people of the State, no party by itself, was in a position to form the government. With the outgoing Chief Minister Dr. Abdullah and the National Conference President Omar making statements that they would prefer the role of a constructive opposition rather than cobble the majority and stake a claim to form the next government, the next big players in the field remained only Congress with twenty seats and PDP with sixteen seats in the new legislature. In a House of eighty seven, they need support of at least forty- four members. It was very difficult for any of these two parties to stake claim by itself to form the government unless the two came together. Their initial efforts to form a coalition and attract splinter groups to cross the number of fortyfour did not succeed even though the Governor of the State had extended the time of the formation of government from 17th to 21st October. With the refusal of Dr. Farooq Abdullah to continue as the caretaker Chief Minister of the State beyond the expiry of the Assembly on 17th October, the Governor under Section 92 of the J&K Constitution imposed Governor's Rule from 18th October. In his first press conference the same day he expressed the hope that the Governor's Rule would be for a very short period and that in that expectation, he was not appointing Advisors. Following this a series of discussions took place between Congress and PDP in Srinagar and Delhi on 26th October, in which it was decided that the Congress and the PDP would, with the support of four members of Panthers' Party, two of the CPI(M) and a requisite number of independents would stake a claim to form the government on the basis of a Common Minimum Programme agreed by the two main constituents of the coalition. It was also decided that during the six-year term of the Assembly the Chief Ministership would be shared for three years each between PDP and the Congress with Mufti Mohammad Sayeed taking over as Chief Minister for the first three years term. The Chief Minister and eight members of his Cabinet were sworn on November 2, 2002, thereby bringing the process of Assembly Elections in the State to a logical conclusion.

Notes:

1. India Today, October 21, 2002. 233.

11 Reflections

The elections in 1996, particularly the Parliamentary elections in the month of May, was a remarkable joint effort by the agencies of the Central and the State governments to successfully attempt the exercise of franchise by the people of the State after stemming the tide of terrorism through sustained efforts of seven years. It was also a massive administrative and logistic exercise involving transportation of over five hundred companies of central para-military forces as well as polling personnel from outside the state exceeding ten thousand and arranging their arrival in the State and move them from one place to another under constant threat of terrorist attacks, without suffering even a single casualty for almost a month of their stay in the State. This was made possible by a number of factors and affirmative actions taken at different levels. The most important being an effective and credible security set up to deal with the terrorist violence that had spread across the State from 1989 onwards.

The first major step in this direction was taken by the then Governor G.C. Saxena, practically from the day he joined in the second half of 1990, and it involved rebuilding the intelligence gathering mechanism in the State while trying to keep the terrorist violence within manageable limits. After General K.V. Krishna Rao (Retd) took over reigns of the State administration as Governor in March 1993, his topmost priority as stated by him in his inaugural address was to work ceaselessly for the restoration of the democratic rule in the State. The elections in the State became the mainstay as the administration focussed its attention. He initially envisaged that he would be getting this done within a period of six months to one year but it took more time to bring the terrorist violence under reasonable control where the process of elections could be started. Being a former Chief of the Army Staff, General Rao realized that the efforts of the security forces and the intelligence agencies needed a much more coordinated and cohesive action than what had existed at the time of his joining and started working towards this end right from very beginning of his tenure. The breakthrough in this respect came in the beginning of May 1993, with the formation of Unified Headquarters. It really required all the persuasive skills of the Governor, the weight of his office, his influence over the then Army Chief and the senior army commanders being their former chief as well as his personal equation with the Prime Minister P.V. Narasimha Rao to make the commanders of the army and other para- military forces as also heads of intelligence organizations to agree to work under the umbrella of the Unified Headquarters, headed by Security Advisor to Governor. The Unified Headquarters was basically a forum for planning, evolving strategies and review and coordinated and collective action at the State level, while not interfering with the functioning and the command structures of each of the organizations which retained individual capacity to operate within their own spheres of activities as also with their own administrative hierarchy intact. Even though establishing a Unified Headquarters fell short of the initial concept of General Rao and his Security Advisors to formulate a Unified Command, which had been envisaged to actually take over the command, control and direction of all the security related resources available within the State, still the Unified Headquarters was an appreciable improvement where practically no system of centralized coordination mechanism had existed earlier other than the personality of the Security Advisor and the office of the Governor himself.

To any informed observer and analyst of the happenings in the sub-continent over the last five decades, Pakistan is at best an enigma; its creation itself devoid of reasons and logic. Consider the fact that the end result of a nation created on the basis of a religion left millions of Muslims in India and today India has larger Muslim population than Pakistan; that a nation was divided into two parts separated by more than 1000 kms.; that none of the four provinces of present Pakistan was expressively keen for its creation almost till mid 1940s; that the official language of Pakistan, Urdu, is not the spoken dialect of any of its province as well as the erstwhile East-Pakistan; that right from the beginning the province of Punjab has ruled over the other regions and provinces. The list is endless. Added to these is the fact that in spite of the kind of ruthless and degrading treatment that has been meted out to POK and the Northern Areas, there have not been serious problems in those areas in the last 50 years. In spite of her smaller size, weaker economic base, internal dichotomy and smaller armed forces, Pakistan has not only managed to do well for herself but also created constant difficulties for India right from 1947. She initiated three wars against India and came out, in totality, a net gainer. Let facts register. Pakistan's affairs, so far, have been well managed; better certainly than India at least in the field of Defence and Foreign Affairs.

India has had to deal with Pakistan as a difficult neighbour and a source of constant trouble; mostly irritant though at times downrightly dangerous. It would be a useful exercise, in fact an essential endeavour, to take an overview of the developments, particularly over the last ten years, to analyze and try to understand the broad contours of policy formulations and dynamics of pursuit of national objectives, both in respect of Pakistan as well as our own.

Support from the Central Government, particularly from the Ministry of Home Affairs, was crucial, first in effectively dealing with the terrorism and then in the planning and conduct of Parliamentary elections. This backup came in the form of additional forces, financial resources as well as coordination with other central ministries. The support from the Home Ministry and the Department of Jammu and Kashmir Affairs was crucial to the successful conduct of the elections. The efforts of the concerned officers from Union Home Secretary downwards were particularly praiseworthy. Planning and collecting a huge number of polling personnel as also making available over 3500 vehicles from outside the State during Parliamentary elections were remarkable achievements by any standard. On the flip side was the constant nagging and proclivities to advise and interfere in even day-to-day security related affairs in the State as well as a constant desire to monitor and get informed on such a regular basis that at times it made the senior officers working in the field difficult to carry on effectively their activities. Things reached such a stage during the beginning of 1996 that Additional Chief Secretary (Home) of the State sent copies of a letter written in 1810 by Duke of Wellington to Lord Bred Ford, the then Secretary of State for War for Great Britain, which read as follows:

"My Lord,

If I attempt to answer the mass of futile correspondence that surrounds me, I should be debarred from all serious business of campaigning.

I must remind your Lordship – for the last time – that so long as I retain an independent position, I shall see that no officer under my command is debarred by attending to the futile driveling of mere quill driving in your Lordship's office – from attending to his first duty – which is, and always has been so to train and lead the private men under his command that they may, without question, beat any force opposed to them in the field.

I am, My Lord

Yours Obedient Servant

Wellington."

Copies of this letter were sent to all concerned officers of the Home Ministry except the Union Home Secretary. It, however, found its way to Home Secretary's desk and he didn't take it too kindly. But this gentle reminder did partly serve its purpose with visible reduction in the pointless reminders and telephone calls from New Delhi.

The active interest and support from the Election Commission of India in successfully re-establishing the electoral process in the State was another force multiplier in the efforts of the State administration towards this end. The additional efforts and the support from the Election Commission became all the more evident during the period one year prior to the Parliamentary elections resulting in a number of measures, both administrative as well as legislative, undertaken by the Commission to facilitate the conduct of elections. The Chief Election Commissioner as well as other Election Commissioners made a number of visits to the Sate to assess for themselves the developing situation, the security and the administrative arrangements that were being made by various agencies. Leaving aside the occasional outbursts of T.N. Sheshan, the Chief Election Commissioner who was famous for losing his temper, these visits did provide useful feedback, guidance as well as inspiration to all concerned officers who were working tirelessly to see through the successful conduct of elections.

The concept of creating a Central Para-Military Forces coordinator in the State in the form of IG CRPF in the State, selecting a competent and dedicated officer to man this post was another crucial step in ensuring the success of the whole effort. The support that he received from his higher ups and the organization that he created in the field, with coordination mechanism right down to the district level as well as his own effective command and team effort were some of the major ingredients of the success of his endeavour.

People's participation in anti-terrorist efforts went to contribute a lot towards this end. Apart from constant and increased flow of intelligence, the participation of the civilians in anti-terrorism operations came in the form of surrendered terrorists and the Village Defence Groups.

The Surrender Policy announced by the State government which took effect from August 15, 1995 gave a marked impetus to terrorists giving up arms. The policy was aimed at providing meaningful opportunity to the strayed youth for getting into the mainstream of national life. It was also aimed at the rehabilitation, encouraging them to live a normal life and contribute their mite towards the progress and prosperity of the State as well as the nation.

It was envisaged that the surrenderees would be given an option to go to the rehabilitation centers. A monthly stipend of Rs. 1,500/- and monetary incentives for surrendering weapons were announced. In the rehabilitation centers the surrenderees were to be imparted vocational training in selected trades so that they could take up self-employment with liberal aid from the State government. The policy also envisaged recruitment of surrenderees as Special Police Officers and sponsoring them for employment in army, paramilitary forces and public or even the private sector.

The announcement of Surrender Policy gave positive results and from August 15 to December 31, 1995 as many as 435 terrorists surrendered. During 1996 (up to ending August) 427 terrorists had surrendered. The year- wise number of militants surrendered was as follows:

Year	Terrorists surrendered
1991	612
1992	444
1993	98
1994	32
1995	601
1996(up to 31.8.1996)	427

During this period, a large number of weapons had also been surrendered which included:

AK Rifles	474
Pistol/Revolvers	116
Grenades	341
UMGs	13
Rocket launchers	7
Wireless sets	21
Explosives	72 kgs.

The Surrender Policy was not meant to be an end in itself but was envisaged to be a means to stimulate return of an appreciable number of terrorist ranks to the normal life. It did achieve its purpose during the first two years and tapered off later on due to less enthusiastic follow-up of the rehabilitation efforts by the State and the Central agencies for the surrendered terrorists. A section of former terrorists also helped the security forces in the counter-insurgency operations. Their contribution in stemming the tide of terrorism, particularly in relation to the foreign mercenaries, was of no mean proportions and has not received appreciation within and outside the State. Although they came under adverse criticism for certain acts which would be hard to defend in any civilized society, it should not be a reason to totally ignore the positive aspects of the contribution of some of the former terrorists who joined the mainstream and had genuinely turned around for restoration of the peace and normalcy in the State. In all counter-insurgency operations it is always necessary to ensure that instruments used to achieve the desired end are handled properly and with due care and caution. In certain cases this was not done and that created a momentum of anger in the affected section of the population as well as gave rise to adverse publicity in the media. However, the fact remains that these elements did make a difference first in creating a proper climate in favour of starting the electorcal process and then in the successful conduct of Parliamentary as well as Assembly elections in 1996.

The active participation of the local population in the security of their villages, along the borders in Jammu region, as well as important installations in the vicinity, was successfully tried during the conflict with Pakistan in 1965 and 1971. These Village Defence Groups (VDGs) supplemented efforts of the security forces and helped in checking trans-border movement, etc., during this period. For this purpose, the State Police had issued over 2,500 rifles along with ammunition to selected villagers, most of them ex-servicemen, who were proficient in handling of the weapons and were prepared to work voluntarily for the defence and security of their homes and hearths.

In the prevailing security scenario, the Kashmir Valley, Rajouri-Poonch area, the district of Doda as well as certain hill regions of Kathua and Udhampur districts of Jammu region were affected by terrorist activities. In addition to this, frequent trans-border movement had been taking place in the plain areas of Kathua and Jammu Districts, especially between river Ravi in the east and Munnawar Tawi in the west. There were also incidents of acts of sabotage in this border belt, especially targeting the infrastructural facilities. A need, therefore, was felt to revive the Village Defence Groups, both on the borders of Jammu and Kathua districts, as was done in 1965 and 1971, as also in Doda district and the depth areas of Kathua and Udhampur districts. It was with this intent, that the Village Defence Groups Scheme was put in operation in October 1995.

The aim of the Village Defence Group Scheme was to organize a small group of volunteer-armed civilians, in the identified villages along the borders as well as in depth areas of Jammu region. This was done with a view to ensure safety and security of such villages, infrastructural installations in and around them and to check the trans-border movement. For this purpose 660 such groups were organized in Doda, Udhampur, Jammu and Kathua districts initially. Each group consisted of 10 to 15 volunteers who were armed with rifles, average five numbers per group, provided by the government as also their own licensed weapons. District magistrates were authorized to issue gun licences to such volunteers. Every group was headed by a designated SPO (Special Police Officer) who was a retired officer/JCO from Army/Para-military Forces or Police. That SPO was issued a semi-automatic weapon and paid an honorarium of rupees 1500 per month. In the next phase, the scheme was expanded in Doda area and also extended to Rajouri and Poonch districts. Simultaneously a modest beginning was also made in selected villages of the Valley.

The village Lambardar, Chowkidar and the Panchayat members were instructed to assist the SPO and his volunteers to carry on their duties. Night and day patrolling was to be carried on in a systematic manner. At the local level the SPO and the VDGs were to work under the supervision of the Tehsildar and the

SHO concerned. The Deputy Commissioners were also made responsible for dove-tailing the VDGs with the security forces both on the border as well as in depth areas in consultation with the local security commanders thus ensuring optimum utilization of manpower and the weapons. The selection of villages where VDGs were constituted was made after carefully taking into consideration the threat of terrorists, location of the security forces in the nearby vicinity as well as capacity and the willingness of the villagers to organize themselves for this purpose. In the beginning six hundred and sixty VDGs were sanctioned and organized with one hundred and sixty in Kathua district, three hundred and fifty in Jammu district, fifty in Udhampur district and one hundred in Doda district. By the time the Parliamentary elections were conducted this figure rose to one thousand. The contribution of the VDGs in ensuring the safety and security of the villagers and the areas around their respective locations, as well as in improving the overall security scenario and instilling a perception of safety has been considerable. Their effectiveness in counter-insurgency efforts is clear from the number of VDG members that have been targeted and eliminated over the years.

Both during the Parliamentary elections as well as Assembly polls, there were motivated allegations of security forces exceeding their brief and using coercion to make people go to the polling stations. Partly these originated as the disinformation campaign launched by Pakistan, her agents and sympathizers to discredit the Indian efforts for restoration of democracy. In certain cases the allegations against the security forces were used as a survival defence mechanism by some people who felt threatened that their voluntary participation might result into harm to them and their families by the terrorists who had actively threatened all those of dire consequences who took part in the election process. In some cases the village elders had themselves gone to the nearest security forces camps, a few days before the elections and identified the individuals actively involved in anti-election campaign and requested that they should be made to first cast their vote so that later they should not be in position to accuse others of doing the same and create any mischief in collaboration with the terrosits. As it happens in any endeavour of such magnitude there could have been some cases where the over enthusiasm of the local unit or sub-unit commanders had transgressed the confines of the security related duties but these were by any reckoning negligible in number. No recognized political party or contesting candidate either in the Parliamentary elections or in the Assembly polls made allegations against the security forces for using any coercion or influence with the voters in favour or against a particular candidate or political party. The system of casting a vote and the secrecy involved in the process is such that even a person who is forced to go to the polling booth can very well refrain from marking his choice or do in such a manner so as to make the ballot paper invalid. A very small percentage of invalid votes almost at par with the national average was the ultimate rejoinder to the dis-information campaign of coercion being used by the security forces.

An analysis of the successful candidates in Parliamentary as well as Assembly elections would point towards similar conclusion. The successful candidates during the Assembly elections came from different political parties. Similarly the electoral performance of the National Conference in the Assembly polls was equally impressive in all the three regions of the State, and in the absence of any allegations of coercion or bias in Jammu and Ladakh region the conclusion in respect of the Valley could not be more obvious.

District administration, at the cutting edge level, played very important role in the success of the State administration. For the conduct of elections, role of the district administration, particularly of the Deputy Commissioners and Senior Superintendents of Police, was crucial. The effective functioning of these two key districts officers, working of the district administration as a well oiled machine and an efficient team, as well as coordination with the security forces at ground level were critical components in the difficult counter-insurgency operations and election related measures. As the elections neared the functioning, the role of the Deputy Commissioners became increasingly important. Fortunately, the selection of the Deputy Commissioners, more so of the terrorism affected areas, especially in the Valley was done with considerable care. Of the six districts in the Valley five were manned by officers of outstanding capabilities, considerable drive and capacity to lead their teams from the front. It was a fearless and dedicated lot enthused with the spirit of achieving the results and treating their duties as a cause of national importance. One out of this group, unfortunately lacked the requisite spirit and capacity to deliver goods. It was obviously a case of wrong selection and the choice had been made against the advice of senior functionaries of the State administration. However, in this case also the momentum of activity generated in other parts of the Valley did see through the successful conduct of various activities prior to and during elections. These Deputy Commissioners not only acquainted themselves admirably in pushing through developmental schemes in their respective districts but also became focal points for redressal of grievances of the local population, for both development related issues as well as their complaints in respect of security forces matters. They also functioned as integral part of the anti-terrorism drive of the State and worked in very close coordination with the security forces. Of course all kind of support in terms of financial resources, men and material was provided to them in ample measure and they received due consideration and cooperation from senior commanders of the forces who generally were much older in age and also, in most cases, very senior in rank and experience. Bharat Vyas in Srinagar, Sandeep Nayak in Budgam, Arun Kumar in Baramulla, Brij Sharma in Kupwara and Yameen Qureshi in Pulwama became household names in the respective districts and were equally popular with the public and the security forces for their bold initiative, upright and just personal conduct as well as leadership qualities. Their good work also exploded the myth, a general wrong perception, that in a particular district the administrative head should preferably be from the same community which lives there in majority. Of these five officers four were non-Muslims in the districts almost exclusively inhabited by Muslims and there was not even a single occasion where a complaint surfaced from the local population hinting towards the religious bias of the Deputy Commissioners. Of the lot, managing Srinagar district was particularly much tougher assignment, because of its inherent turbulent political atmosphere and the focus of media attention apart from being the centre of all kinds of activities as a State capital. Thus a difficult assignment was very well carried out by Bharat Vyas. The role of the district administration in ensuring peaceful and effective conduct of Parliamentary elections can hardly be overemphasized.

Management of security apparatus and the conduct of elections involved a large number of Central and the State organizations and departments as well as different wings of security forces with their involvement extending from manning of the international border and LoC to management of the security grid and providing security cover to the electoral process. To plan, organize and conduct the individual and collective efforts of such a large and diverse group of establishments, with no central or unified control required a highly efficient team work. It goes to the credit of the heads of these organizations that they were able to achieve this in a spirit of camaraderie and collective participation. There were a number of occasions when differences and disagreements surfaced and even heated arguments took place but all issues were ultimately resolved in an amicable manner after thorough discussions in the Unified Headquarters, in smaller group discussions or even at informal meetings over a meal or a cup of tea. Working under pressure and for an identified higher cause creates its own group dynamics which facilitates creation of informal systems and channels enhancing capacities of individual organizations as well as increasing the effectiveness of the collective effort. It was either a happy coincidence or may be a divine intervention that none of the functionaries, heading the respective organizations at the State level had any ego problems between themselves or with the Security Advisor to the Governor who, by virtue of his position, was heading this group. Each one in his collective as well as individual capacity strived to achieve the desired goal. Two small incidents would amply illustrate this point. After the schedule for Parliamentary elections was announced towards the end of March 1996, it became evident that the efforts of the CRPF to acquire large quantities of sleeping bags, bullet proof jackets and tents for large deployment in the State for the entire central para military forces was not going to materialize from the open market and that the only way to get the requisite items was to take it on loan or purchase from the stocks of the army. When written requests did not produce the desired results the Addl. DG of the CRPF made an appointment with the concerned General in the Army Headquarters and went over to his office for the crucial meeting. The General, obviously, having been briefed about the requirement of the CRPF told his visitors almost point blank on arrival that he was sorry to convey that the army was just not in position to part with these items as these were needed in its own scheme of things. Even after this near blunt refusal it required tremendous amount of persuasion and pleadings by the Addl. DG to finally get from the army all the requirements that had been indented for.

On a different occasion but in the same sequence, when the force level of the CPMF for election duties was finally determined and it was found to be short of the required level, the only alternative was to request the army to take over additional responsibilities in the security grid so that the requisite number of central para-military forces units, thus spared, could be made use of for the election duties. Only GOC-in-C Northern Command could take this decision as the officers below him had expressed their inability to extend their areas of deployment. General Saklani, Security Advisor, along with Additional Chief Secretary (Home) flew to Udhampur to meet the Army Commander. The Army Commander had been junior to the Advisor when the latter was in service and the ACS Home had done the National Defence College Course with the Army Commander, so this small group met in an informal and cordial atmosphere. However, the request regarding army taking over additional areas of responsibility was not agreed to by the Army Commander and he had his own reasons for not doing so. All the arguments and persuasions by the visitors failed to get the requisite response. As it appeared that the meeting was heading towards a fruitless termination, General Saklani suddenly got up from his chair and stood before the Army Commander with folded hands and said, "Forget about the official requirement from the Security Advisor to the Army Commander but take it as a personal request from Saklani to Surinder, please do something about it. I need the CPMFs units really badly." Taken aback by this sudden gesture, the Army Commander too stood up and promised that he would try to see what could possibly be done within the resources available to him. A few days later General Saklani did get most of his requirement of additional troops. One to one requests and personal pleadings at such high levels could be made only when the person concerned was totally immersed in the job at hand and treated his official duties as his own work and was completely committed to see the final and positive outcome of the endeavour that had been initiated. The crowning glory of the collective effort of the whole team was a reaction on May 24, 1996, when almost 50,000 central para-military forces and 10,000 polling personnel were moving in over 5,000 vehicles in six different directions, practically all over the Valley, performing series of tasks from depositing polling material to striking camps, moving to various locations, returning some polling parties to airfields and taking the rest of them to the new locations –carrying out the entire gamut of activity successfully without any mishap and in a professional manner.

All the senior functionaries of different organizations connected with security and election related work performed their task admirably well with professional competence in their individual capacities as well as members of a very functional and efficient group. Their collective efforts resulted into keeping the security situation well under control and conduct of successful Parliamentary elections in May 1996. This was the most important task performed by the administration which ultimately paved the way for the Assembly elections and restoration of democratic government five months later. Notwithstanding the much larger number of the contesting candidates in the Assembly elections, the real beginning and the more difficult assignment was the conduct of Parliamentary elections. In more than one ways the

Assembly elections were almost a repeat exercise of the Parliamentary elections, requiring even less effort as by that time the employees of the State government and its various departments had turned around to perform election duties and assist in the formation of democratic government. A major reason for the change in the mood of the government employees was also due to the fact that the State had been able to unmistakably bring home the point that it was capable of and determined to carry out the task it had set before it in an efficient and effective manner.

The experience of conducting elections in J&K in 1996 after a long interregnum forced by abnormal ground conditions, which had resulted into a near total collapse of the local administration's authority over its own machinery, absolute lack of people's faith in the government as provider of security to the masses, an all pervasive fear of the wielders of the gun in exercising the most potent weapon of democracy–the ballot, extreme political cynicism and wide open watch by the international interests of what was always a local event in the past has many great lessons in store for the posterity interested in the art of public administration, craft of politics and science of human behaviour. Right from the word "go", if one thing was never in doubt, it was the firm determination of the governments at the Centre and in the State and the clarity of purpose in the local administration that the elections had to be conducted no matter the problems, the perils and the uncertainties which lay ahead. Ultimately it was resolve of a mighty democratic nation and in fact the Truth *(Satyam)* that prevailed *(Jayate).* Various international, national and local observers described the event of twin elections in their own words, ranging from mild appreciation to great euphoria, but which had a clear positive tone in common. Shri T.N. Seshan, the then Chief Election Commissioner, in one of his personal communications described it thus –

> **"... The odds were heavy and the quantum of work was truly phenomenal. And yet everything was done with thoroughness, precision and impartiality to have enabled the Country to re-appreciate the values of democracy..."**

The 1996 elections, by all standards, were an end in themselves. However, they also firmed up the ground for further consolidation of democratic process for future. Subsequent bye-elections, general elections to the parliament in 1998, and again in 1999, were held without any serious difficulty. The most important gain of the exercise done in the years preceding 1996 elections was creation of a new drill, unique to J&K in many ways which remarkably withstood the test of time. The biggest gain of the exercise was holding of yet another credible general election to the State Legislative Assembly in September 2002 when the people wielded the power of the ballot with confidence to bring in a peaceful mighty political revolution by removing admittedly the strongest and the biggest political party of the State from power and installing a government led by a political party which was not even known in 1996. This augurs well for restrengthening of the roots of democracy in the State and one can hope that the more vexed political issues will get similarly resolved in a peaceful and democratic manner thereby bringing back peace and serenity to the renowned happy valley of Kashmir and the whole State of Jammu and Kashmir.

Annexure I

Year	Name of the Party	Seats Contested	Seats Won
1957	National Conference	72	68 (including 43 Uncontested-37 in valley and 6 in Jammu)
	Praja Parishad	21	5
	H.M.	6	1
	P.S.P.	8	-
	Independents	21	1
1962	National Conference	71	70 (including 34 uncontested-33 in valley and I in Jammu)
	Praja Parishad	24	3
	H.M.	10	1
	D.N.C.	20	-
	P.S.P.	2	-
	Independents	39	2

Contd.

Contd.

1967	National Conference	38	8
	Indian National Congress	53	39 (including 22 uncontested-21 in valley and 1 in Jammu)
	D.N.C.	20	-
	Jan Singh	29	3
	Independents	43	3
1972	Congress	69	58 (including 5 Uncontested
	Jan Sangh	32	3
	Jamait-I-Islami	22	5
	Congress (o)	9	-
	Socialist Party	4	-
	Swatantra Party	4	-
	C.P.I.	1	-
	Independents	196	9
1977	Congress	63	11
	National Conference	75	47
	Janata Party	72	15
	Jamait-I-Islami	19	1
	C.P.I.	6	-
	Independents	179	2
1983	National Conference	76	47
	Congress	73	26
	Peoples Conference	37	1
	Panthers Party/Ind	28	1
	BJP	28	-
	LD	7	-
	Jamit-I-Islami	27	-
	Janata Party	7	-
	CPM	1	-
	CPI	1	-
	Independents	227	1

Contd.

1987	Congress	31	26
	National Conference	45	40
	Muslim United Front	44	4
	Bharatiya Janata Party	29	2
	Janata Party	11	-
	Lok Dal	11	-
	CPI	7	-
	CPM	3	-
	Congress (S)	2	-
	Panthers Party	23	-
	Bahujan Samaj Party	22	-
	Independents	278	4
1966	National Conference	81	57
	Congress	84	7
	Janata Dal	76	5
	BJP	53	8
	Panthers Party	45	1
	CPM	4	1
	BSP	29	4
	Congress (T)	9	1
	Independents	163	3
2002	National Conference	85	28
	Congress	78	20
	PDP	59	16
	BJP	58	1
	Panthers Party	36	4
	CPM	7	2
	BSP	33	1
	Independents & Others	237	15

Annexure II

A. School/ Bridges/Govt.Buildings Damaged Up to Sept. 15, 1996

Year	Schools	Bridges	Govt. Buildings
1990	138	45	718
1991	29	35	161
1992	45	21	185
1993	71	47	305
1994	119	46	172
1995	133	16	127
1996 (Up to Sept. 15)	57	2	41
Total:	592	212	1709

B. Number of Religious Places Burnt/Damaged Due to Militancy for the Period From January 1990 to Sept. 15, 1996.

Year	Temples	Mosques	Gurdwaras	Shrines
1990	5	4	-	-
1991	4	12	-	-
1992	70	1	-	-
1993	5	4	2	-
1994	9	6	-	-
1995	31	2	-	3
1996 (Up to Sept. 15)	2	2	-	-
Total:	126	32	2	3

Annexure - III

Schedule of Assembly Elections 1996

Stages	Phase - I	Phase - II	Phase - III	Phase - IV
Notification	14.8.96 (Wednesday)	23.8.96 (Friday)	27.8.96 (Tuesday)	6.9.96 (Friday)
Last date for filing nominations	21.8.96 (Wednesday)	30.8.96 (Friday)	3.9.96 (Tuesday)	13.9.96 (Friday)
Scrutiny of nominations	22.8.96 (Thursday)	31.8.96 (Saturday)	4.9.96 (Wednesday)	14.9.96 (Saturday)
Withdrawal of candidatures	24.8.96 (Saturday)	2.9.96 (Monday)	6.9.96 (Friday)	16.9.96 (Monday)
Dates of poll	7.9.96 (Saturday)	16.9.96 (Monday)	21.9.96 (Saturday)	30.9.96 (Monday)
Completion of poll	8.10.96 (Tuesday)	8.10.96 (Tuesday)	8.10.96 (Tuesday)	8.10.96 (Tuesday)

Annexure - IV

Programme of Assembly Elections - 2002

S.NO.	Activity	Phase - I	Phase - II	Phase - III	Phase - IV
1	Date of Announcement of Schedule of Elections	2.8.2002	2.8.2002	2.8.2002	2.8.2002
2	Date of Issue of Notification for Elections	22.8.2002	29.8.2002	6.9.2002	13.9.2002
3	Last date for filing Nominations	29.8.2002	5.9.2002	13.9.2002	20.9.2002
4	Scrutiny of Nominations	31.8.2002	6.9.2002	14.9.2002	21.9.2002
5	Last date of withdrawal of candidatures	2.9.2002	9.9.2002	16.9.2002	23.9.2002
6	Date of Poll	16.9.2002	24.9.2002	1.10.2002	8.10.2002
7	Commencement of counting	10.10.2002	10.10.2002	10.10.2002	10.10.2002
8	Date before which elections shall be completed	12.10.2002	12.10.2002	12.10.2002	12.10.2002

Annexure V

Assembly Elections - 2002

Highlights:

- Announcement on 2nd August, 2002
- Elections in four Phases.
    - Phase I: 16th Sept. 2002 Kupwara, Baramulla, Leh, Kargil, Rajouri, Poonch.
    - Phase II 24th Sept. 2002 Srinagar, Budgam, Jammu.
    - Phase III 1st Oct. 2002 Pulwama, Anantnag, Udhampur, Kathua.
    - Phase IV 8th Oct. 2002 Doda
- Hours of Poll: 7.00 a.m. to 4.00 p.m.
- Counting for all the 87 Assembly Segments simultaneously from 8.00 a.m. on 10th October, 2002.
- Repoll:

  I[st] October, 2002: 2 polling stations of 27-Budgam Assembly Constituency.

  1 polling station of 71-Gandhinagar Assembly Constituency.

  3 polling stations each of 85 Surankote

	and 86 Mendhar Assembly Constituency.
8th October, 2002:	4 polling stations of 46-Pahalgam Assembly Constituency.
	1 polling station of 65-Kathua Assembly Constituency.
	1 polling station of 85-Surankote Assembly Constituency.
9th October, 2002:	3 polling stations of Doda Assembly Constituency.
	1 polling station of Kistwar Assembly Constituency.

Index